double take

double take

ONE FABULOUS RECIPE, TWO FINISHED DISHES

Feeding Vegetarians and Omnivores Together

A. J. Rathbun
and Jeremy Holt

THE HARVARD COMMON PRESS • BOSTON, MASSACHUSETTS

The Harvard Common Press
535 Albany Street
Boston, Massachusetts 02118
www.harvardcommonpress.com

Printed in the United States of America
Printed on acid-free paper

Library of Congress Cataloging-in-Publication Data
Rathbun, A. J. (Arthur John), 1969-
Double take : one fabulous recipe, two finished dishes, feeding
vegetarians and omnivores together / A.J. Rathbun and Jeremy Holt.
   p. cm.
   Includes index.
ISBN 978-1-55832-423-7 (hardcover : alk. paper) —
ISBN 978-1-55832-424-4 (pbk. : alk. paper)
   1. Cookery. 2. Vegetarian cookery. I. Holt, Jeremy, 1972- II. Title.
TX714.R375 2010
641.5—dc22

                         2009022187

Special bulk-order discounts are available on this and other Harvard
Common Press books. Companies and organizations may purchase
books for premiums or resale, or may arrange a custom edition,
by contacting the Marketing Director at the address above.

Cover recipe: Osso Buco, page 154
Back cover recipe: Shrimp and Grits, page 140

BOOK & COVER DESIGN BY DEBORAH KERNER
COVER PHOTOGRAPHS BY HEATH ROBBINS
FOOD STYLING BY TRAVIS GRANDON
PROP STYLING BY BETH WICKWIRE

10 9 8 7 6 5 4 3 2 1

For Megan *and* Beatrix

and for Natalie

and Sookie *and* Rory,

our favorite dining companions

contents

acknowledgments

To put together a full *Double Take* table takes a lot of chefs and servers and assistance at every level, and while we can't (at this moment at least, though we can hope to at some point) sit everyone who helped down and serve them a big veg-meat feast, we do want to give a hearty "Thanks!" to those who helped during the process, with some extra servings of gratitude for a few specific folks. These extra portions start with a giant thank-you to Valerie Cimino, whose vision for this book helped shape it and keep it tasteful from the opening bites. A huge thanks also to all the fine and friendly folks at The Harvard Common Press for their help in bringing *Double Take* into the world, and for giving it such fine and scrumptious form. You've all been a great bunch of folks to work with, and we can't wait until the next time we get to sit down with you around the big office lunch table to discuss all things related to cooking and drinking and writing.

A big double helping of thanks has to go to Michael Bourret as well, for not only being there whenever the e-mails or calls come humming his way (really, take a break, pally), but for also turning the burners down to simmer whenever the pot seems like it might boil over. Michael, you rule, and the next time you're in Seattle, Jeremy promises to cook a whole pig, and A.J. promises to cook a whole head of broccoli.

We could never have put together such a community-building cookbook without the help of our own local pals, and so a big thanks goes to anyone in the greater

Seattle area who tasted or tested or just listened to us talk over our *Double Take* ideas, with special shout-outs to Eric, Rebecca, Meg, Mark and Leslie (as well as able assistants Ron and Ame), Holly, Kaiser, Coen, and Al. Thanks for keeping those stoves and stovetops lit and cooking.

Also, a big thanks to some other favorites who are always ready to pitch in (even when it's just a needed pat on the back) and give their support, including Andrea S. (thanks for the early readings), Brad K. (thanks for the video-ing madness, and thanks to Cash and Christi, too), Lisa Ekus and the Lisa Ekus crew, man-about-town Brad P., and of course our amazing families, the fantabulous Holt, Noller, Redmond-Wyatt, Rathbun, Fuller, and James contingents.

Before we start eating our next meal, though, a final thanks to all of those who have served us delicious meals along our various ways, both at home and out and about, both meaty and veggie. Without all the inspiration you provide, we couldn't have written this book. And we'd be awfully hungry besides.

introduction

Sitting down to eat a home-cooked meal with family or friends is one of the most enjoyable experiences possible: good talk, laughter, and a respite from the pressures of daily life, surrounded by delicious dishes that all can enjoy. But with today's diversity of diets and lifestyles, these communal dinners are often becoming, sadly, moments of division instead of sharing—with vegetarian diners having one meal and meat-eaters another, or, in really sad cases, these differing dietary types not sitting down together at all—because of a lack of common meals.

This problem occurs at both big family get-togethers and gatherings of friends, where people become unsure of what menu to serve when there's a vegetarian married to a meat-eater, or when they have guests coming that fall into both dietary camps. It also happens more and more at regular, everyday family meals. Isn't dinner supposed to be fun, whether it's a party or just a Wednesday night? Shouldn't serving a meal where everyone eats at the same table, and enjoys delicious food, be a display of that communal nature that meals are supposed to have? These dietary dilemmas are enough to make people give up and order pizza. This is a shame, because the options for making creative and tasty meals that can entice vegetarians and meat-eaters alike are more plentiful than ever. In stores, the amount and variety of produce and spices have expanded, as have both vegetarian meat substitutes and meat options. And today, we need these communal moments over the table more than ever, as people are becoming busier with jobs that take up lots of time and little electronic devices beeping and blinking and tethering us to them. Today, sitting down to a good meal with friends or family is an oasis in a hectic world—unless putting together that meal makes the day more hectic, of course.

This book was created to bring the communal feeling back to the table. It's designed to teach folks how to make meals for both vegetarians and meat-eaters—at the same time. Instead of serving separate dishes for each side at the table, it brings people together. Instead of causing you, the cook, to tear out your hair wondering how to make different dishes for separate culinary needs, it helps you put together one meal that meets all tastes and bridges that once-divided table.

It's fitting that a book designed to bring vegetarians and meat-eaters together is written by two such folk. We realized, as a vegetarian and a meat-eater who have remained close friends and culinary companions in spite of, and in some ways because of, our different culinary lifestyles, that it was more fun and easier, and would bring more people to the table, to make menus suitable for both vegetarians and meat-eaters, instead of trying to make two completely separate menus. Together, we could combine our backgrounds and interests: A.J. is a vegetarian who enjoys updating his old down-home, meat-packed favorites with modern meat substitutes, while Jeremy is a classically trained omnivorous home cook who gets a rush from culinary experiments that show his vegetarian pals how their options can be endless with a fresh take on classic recipes. So we started creating meals that featured the same dishes—with results that could be served to our vegetarian friends and our meat-eating pals alike. This way, we started bringing people together over food again, a situation that we believe is ideal.

We endorse cooking for groups of all sizes, which is why you'll see recipes for four, for six, and for more. And we know that sometimes your group will consist solely of vegetarians or that you'll be serving a dish and want to make it all meat-based. Because of that, each recipe tells you how you can make that dish all meat, or all vegetarian. This gives you a little flexibility when you're planning your menus, which we think makes cooking even more enjoyable. Another enjoyable idea—especially when cooking for larger groups when you have a lot of ingredients to think about—is cooking with a pal, or that special someone. A little division of labor doesn't have to be divisive—on the contrary, it's a kick, and awfully helpful, especially when you have two skillets and can get more cooking done at the same time.

Taking time to eat slowly, talk and laugh, and make memorable moments around a table that's brimming with delicious dishes is what it's all about. The table has always been a gathering place, and *Double Take* lets you gather your friends and family around your table and serve them a meal they can all enjoy. So, what are you waiting for? Turn the pages to learn how to use this book and how to stock your kitchen, and then pick out a few recipes to try. You'll be serving tasty dishes to those closest to you—no matter what their eating preferences—in no time.

double take

how to use this book

Double Take is a book in which all of the recipes (except for some in the Satisfying Sides chapter) are for one master dish, but you end up with servings for both meat-eaters and vegetarians, a concept that we realize may seem a little confusing at first glance. But don't be put off—it's actually very easy. Each recipe starts by using ingredients that both meat-eaters and vegetarians would eat, and continues on like any normal recipe, until it gets to the part where a meat ingredient is added. At that point, the recipe splits into two parts—one that uses meat and one that doesn't. This means that, for example, for The Best Biscuits and Sausage Gravy (page 126), you make a pot of gravy with flour and butter and milk and seasonings, and then separate it into two pots, one of which has sausage added and one of which has vegetarian sausage added. Both your meat-eating and vegetarian friends can eat together at your monthly Sunday brunch, and enjoy the same dish. It also means that you can whip up a bucketful of chicken noodle soup on a chilly November day (cold and flu season, after all) for both of your children, even when one's a vegetarian and one's a chicken lover. Just cook the carrots, onion, and celery in one pot, then split off half the veggies into a second pot. Chicken and chicken stock then go into the second pot, and vegetable stock and vegetarian chicken go into the first, and noodles go into both of them.

Since our recipes split off at some point into meat and vegetarian versions of the same dish, we suggest always reading through them completely before you begin cooking so you're sure of what extra pans or bowls you might need, and also so you're ready to break it out into two parts as necessary. (We go over the necessary equipment for this double-dish making in Cookware Basics, starting on the next page.) This isn't to say that the recipes are complex, though. We've worked hard to provide clear and concise directions that are easy to follow, but it is a different approach from other books, so it's always good to be prepared.

Also, unlike books that break out their recipes by main ingredient (chicken or vegetarian chicken, for example), we've broken out the recipes in *Double Take* by more thematic and situational groupings. For example, the recipes in the chapter called A Brunch Bunch are meant to help out when you're having folks over in the morning hours. The Entertaining Entrées chapter comes to the rescue when you want to have a few friends over for an interesting meal that's a cut above the everyday. Then there are those times when you just want to have a hearty and healthy salad, or to warm up a bit, or to get back to those basic dishes that make you warm up both through their ingredients and through the nostalgia they bring. For these occasions, take a look at the Soups, Salads, and Sandwiches and the Comfort Entrées chapters. Because not all occasions where you'll be serving vegetarians and meat-eaters revolve around regular dinner hours, and because we love a good party, the Sundry Snacks chapter offers recipes for any occasion or time of day. And because many main dishes need a sidekick, the Satisfying Sides chapter provides lots of choices for scrumptious sides that will enhance your enjoyment of the main course.

Much the way the recipes themselves are designed to help you easily cook for meat-eaters and vegetarians at the same time, the chapters are designed to help you plan menus easily. Want to get a little upscale and try something Continental? Skip to the Entertaining Entrées chapter. Having a party where you know folks with varying dietary restrictions are attending? Flip to Sundry Snacks and start searching out those perfect nibbles. The idea is to have fun and make great food—a philosophy we heartily endorse.

Stocking Your Kitchen

As any home cook knows, without a well-stocked kitchen, your meals will too often end up coming from the delivery menu—which isn't nearly as entertaining or healthy as homemade food. It's important to pick out the right kitchen equipment to prepare that food, especially for our recipes, where you will be often using two saucepans, two sauté pans, and so forth. Having the right items in your cabinets (or hanging from the ceiling, or in blocks, or in drawers) makes it possible to put together the meals you want with a minimum of fuss.

This doesn't mean that you need to take out a second mortgage to equip your kitchen, though. Start with a few of the more frequently used items and work to fill in the remaining equipment gaps over time, and you'll be whipping out *Double Take*-style meals in no time. To help get you started on this stocking process, and to make the shopping list a little more focused, we've broken out our suggestions for essentials and helpful extras into various categories, starting with cookware and bakeware, then sharpening up the necessary cutlery, opening the drawer on helpful and handy gadgets, and finally plugging in a few appliances that will prove to be useful electric kitchen helpers. Once you've stocked your kitchen with these tools, you'll be ready to make meals that both vegetarians and meat-eaters will smile about (a scrumptious situation that's so much nicer than dialing up a mediocre meal).

Cookware Basics

This is most likely the part of the book that will create the most handwringing and teeth gnashing among readers, but we'll be as gentle as possible. While we are firm believers in hardware simplicity, certain aspects of timing and technique in this book will be greatly aided by having some extra pieces of basic cookware around. Our recipes tend to be split into two cooking containers (and often containers that are identical, or close to it). It's good to remember, when thinking about pans, that you shouldn't cook for a vegetarian in a pan that's been used for meat, unless the pan has been thoroughly washed between uses. As with most things in life, you tend to get what you pay for, so keep your pocketbook in mind when heading to the cookware store, but also realize that high-quality (and hence more expensive) cookware tends to be more durable and less disposable. That said, here's a short list of items that will make preparing the recipes in this book a relative snap.

Stockpots: You'll need at least one, but really two if you want to make a vegetable stock and a meaty stock at the same time. And two will come in handy for making the soup recipes in this book, as well as some of our other recipes. Choose stockpots with a capacity of at least 12 quarts.

Dutch ovens: They should have high, straight sides, a heavy bottom, and an ovenproof lid. Ideally you should have two of these, each with a capacity of 4 to 8 quarts. Enameled cast-iron is a perfect medium for this category, and while far more expensive than cast-aluminum or aluminum-copper amalgam pots, a well-cared-for enameled cast-iron stockpot will last a lifetime. Le Creuset is by far the biggest player in this market, but seriously old-school (since 1896) cast-iron cookware maker Lodge has recently come out with an enameled cast-iron line—and the company's regular cast-iron line is nice, too, and very reasonably priced. Another French manufacturer, Staub, makes fine enameled cast-iron cookware as well.

Skillets/sauté pans: It's a no-brainer that you'll need these pans, and if you do any cooking at all, you should already have at least one in the house. For our purposes, you should have at least two, and they should be 10 to 12 inches in diameter and have low-ish sides. You may wonder whether you should choose pans with an uncoated or a nonstick finish. Nonstick coating offers the obvious advantage of keeping foods from sticking to the pan, but care should be taken not to gouge or harm the nonstick coating; otherwise your food might begin to have unsightly and unsavory black specks in it. Nonstick pans also tend not to be ovenproof at all temperatures, and several of our recipes call for you to transfer skillets from stovetop to oven, so take that into consideration.

Necessary miscellany: Other valuable items for your kitchen include pie tins, baking sheets, loaf pans and/or terrine molds, a colander, and baking dishes of assorted sizes—two rectangular 8½ x 11-inch casserole dishes will come in handy often (though if you already have some that are of a slightly different size, you don't need to run out and buy more).

Nice-essary miscellany: We like to use pizza stones and peels for home-made pizza, though you could certainly use baking sheets instead. We also suggest owning a hand-crank pasta roller for preparing homemade fresh pasta.

Slice, Dice, Mince, and Chop— A Word About Cutlery

We've all seen the pros on TV plowing through piles of onions, carrots, and other foodstuffs with steely blades in their hands, dispatching mounds of food into neat piles. But just because we don't get paid to do it on the telly doesn't mean we shouldn't take a page out of the pro playbook and have a few nice knives in our home kitchens. Most people have had the unenviable chore of trying to prepare a meal with dull cutlery, but wouldn't you prefer to know the elation of effortlessly slicing through a ripe tomato without fear of the bloodshed commonly experienced when using poorly constructed or maintained knives? Since the joy of high-quality knives is only experienced if you own a few (and only a few are absolutely necessary—two if you're a die-hard herbivore, three if you're an omnivore), here are a few recommendations on the "must-haves."

The absolutely most important knife in the kitchen is the appropriately moni-kered "chef's knife." You will use it to do just about everything: slice, dice, mince, chop, and peel large items. The blade ideally should be 6 to 14 inches long (depending on the size of the person using it) and "full-tang," which means that the metal of the blade extends all the way through the handle, giving it balance and strength. A good chef's knife should cost around $50 on the low end of the spectrum and up to whatever amount common sense or your pocketbook dictates. As mentioned earlier, this knife is the single most important piece of equipment in the kitchen, so it is really worth it to spend a little money here. A well-maintained, high-quality knife will last at least half a lifetime—Jeremy has had the same set of R.H. Forschner knives for 17 years and counting. In addition to the R.H. Forschner brand, Wüsthof and J.A. Henckels are very popular and reliable brands. There are also some Asian knife makers emerging in the American market that make quality products, like Shun.

The second most important knife in the kitchen is a good paring knife. This knife will be used for peeling, slicing, and mincing ingredients too small for a chef's knife. The blade should be 3 to 4½ inches long. A good paring knife should cost at least $20.

The third most important knife to have is a boning knife, which is a very narrow knife with a curved blade. As its name implies, its primary job is removing bones from meat, or meat from bones, depending on how you look at it. The blade should be 5 to 8 inches long, and a good knife will likely cost at least $40.

In addition to these knives, you should purchase a sharpening steel. This is generally a long piece of metal or ceramic attached to a handle, and it is used to sharpen knives dulled by use. The sharpness of a knife is created by thousands of microscopic serrated teeth on the edge; when the knife is used, these teeth become misaligned. When the steel is properly put to use, it realigns these teeth, and the knife cuts more efficiently. However, depending on how much use your knives are getting, these teeth will eventually be totally ground down and the knife will require a true sharpening, either by taking it to a sharpening service or by acquiring an appropriate whetstone and doing the job yourself. As with knives, the quality and durability of a sharpening steel will generally go hand in hand with its cost—we recommend spending at least $25.

Get Your Gadget On

The gadget galaxy is large already and seems to be ever-expanding—what are all these things that look like aliens with tentacles this way and that, a blade sticking out one side, and a twisty thing that looks sort of like a bad haircut? And what are those holes for, anyway? The gadget galaxy is large enough that there have

Know Your Sauce Basics

I'm pretty sure my marriage is consistently re-mortared by my ability to make sauces. It is a sheer joy to see my lovely and otherwise tidy wife, Megan, sticking her face into a plate or bowl to lap up the last bit of sauce that no spoon could ever take purchase of. Sauces are science mixed with art and a little luck—I can impart the science, but the rest is up to you. Here are the three most common sauce types/techniques.

Pan sauce:

Brown stuff in pan (a.k.a. *fond*) + deglazing liquid + cold thickening agent

Example:

After removing your pork chops and tofu slabs from their pans, add 1 cup of white wine (deglazing liquid) and reduce over high heat until only a few tablespoons are left. Be sure to scrape all the brown goodness off of the bottom of the pan in the process. When the wine has reduced, remove from the heat and whisk in 2 tablespoons cold butter (thickening agent). Serve over your pork chops and tofu slabs.

Gravy:

Fat + thickening agent + diluting liquid

Example:

Heat 3 tablespoons butter (fat) and 2 tablespoons flour (thickening agent) over medium heat, stirring constantly for 3 minutes. Add 1 pint half-and-half or stock of your choice (diluting liquids) and whisk over medium heat for 5 minutes. Serve over biscuits, toast, or just about anything. Everyone loves gravy. The recipe for Fricassee Acadienne (page 182) also uses this method.

Emulsion:

Water-based protein + emulsifier + fat

Example:

Whisk together the juice of ½ lemon and 1 egg yolk (water-based protein). Add 1 tablespoon Dijon mustard (emulsifier) and whisk. Slowly drizzle in ½ cup olive oil (fat), whisking like mad all the while. Caesar salad dressing is a classic example of this technique.

been books written about it, and many gadget-seeking souls have been lost when wandering its aisles (okay, maybe that's a bit much, but those aisles can be daunting). The sad part is that many of these wonders aren't actually wonderful, and shortly after you buy them, they end up huddled and dusty in the back corner of a drawer until you trot them out for a garage sale, forgetting what you bought them for in the first place. However, there's a happy part, too, because not all gadgets are like this— many are super-helpful and make meal prep and construction much easier, and we'd even say that some of these gadgets are essential.

The first gadget we'd like to mention isn't even that "gadget-y" (but we'd be remiss if we didn't mention it right away), and that's a good, reliable set of measuring devices. While we understand that taste is a varied thing, and that different folks like different flavors and degrees of flavor in their food, it's a good idea to at least start with the exact measurements found in the recipes. And to get to these measurements, you'll need a set of measuring spoons and some measuring cups in almost all circumstances. It's a good idea to invest in ones made of stainless steel, to keep things clean and consistent.

The next item on our gadget list is one close to our cheesy hearts, and that's a good cheese grater. We use cheese in lots of recipes, so that grater's going to come in handy again and again. You can find box graters almost everywhere—look for one with larger grating holes on one side (for soft cheeses, such as cheddar) and smaller holes on the other side (for hard cheeses, such as Parmesan). Also, focus on getting one that's sturdy and that sits well on the counter. There are also very good hand-held cheese graters; if going this route, just be sure to get two, so you'll be prepared for both kinds of cheese, and shop for ones that fit well in your hand—you don't want to get blisters during the grating process. On a related note, advanced students may want to procure a Microplane grater, which turns Parmesan cheese into savory snowflakes that dance across your pasta dishes, zests your lemons for use in gremolata (page 156), and turns whole nutmeg into a subtle yet ethereal delight when added to any cream sauce, like Béchamel (page 168).

There are a number of helpful items that fall into the utensil category, but three are particularly essential: whisks, peelers, and stirring spoons. There are several whisk styles to choose from, but going with a standard balloon-style model will serve you well when making roux and sauces and combining ingredients of all kinds (though A.J. also has a love for the ball whisk for beating eggs).

A peeler seems so standard you might be wondering why we even mention it, but it's that very standardness that makes it worth mentioning. You'll end up using your peeler a lot (unless you have mad knife skills), so it's worth getting one that's hearty and sharp, with a metal or sturdy plastic body as well as good metal blades.

Stirring spoons are not sharp in the least, but still a key item, because you're going to find that many recipes in this book involve some (here and there you could even change "some" to "a lot of") stirring. We like a good set of wooden spoons, but metal ones can work, too. You'll probably want to have a few slotted and a few not-slotted spoons, but you will need at least two, so you can have a meat stirrer and vegetarian stirrer when making the recipes in this book.

While some consider them to be only relatives of gadgets, a good set of mixing bowls is something you're also going to need. Ideally you'll want two of each size (or thereabouts), because you'll be mixing separate batches of meaty ingredients and non-meaty ingredients in the same recipes. You might want to get a set that has two small, two medium-size, and two large bowls (six in all), but at least get two large ones, made of either metal, glass, or sturdy plastic.

Because we're spicy fellas, we also know that a good garlic press can come in handy. You can definitely mince the garlic yourself, but having a press takes a little prep time out of the equation. We swear by the Zyliss model, but there are many good ones available. In this spicy vein, you might want to pick up a spice grinder, so that you can easily add fresh spices to your dishes (this can take the taste from pretty dandy to sensational quickly). If you're in a zesty frame of mind, you should know that Jeremy couldn't live in his scurvy-free world without his handheld lemon/lime squeezer.

Electric Kitchen Helpers

While perhaps not as essential as a set of good skillets, there are a number of small kitchen appliances that can be incredible aids when you're putting together your *Double Take* culinary masterpieces. These plugged-in powerhouses can help with preparation as well as provide extra cooking prowess—or at least extra cooking space. Of course, there are lots of choices out there, but we suggest starting with a few select electric helpers.

Whether you're using it to chop veggies, rapidly grate a lot of cheese, or combine the ingredients to make Corny Corn Pudding (page 192), a reliable food processor chops prep time down to a more manageable size. We think you should plug in one with a good amount of oomph—one that's in the 700-watt range. Also, pick one that has a capacity of 7 to 12 cups, has a pulse setting as well as a full-on power mode, and comes with a multi-purpose blade and slicing and shredding disks (there are also many other attachments that can be helpful, but these are the most used). A.J. has a KitchenAid food processor that he swears by, and Jeremy has both small and large Cuisinart food processors, but there are good models from other brands as well.

Somewhat related to the food processor, you might want to get a blender, too, for smoothing out soups and sauces or even chopping the ingredients for salsas (not to mention making yourself a nice icy blended drink to go with your meal). Find one whose jar holds at least 27 ounces—though one that holds 48 ounces is even better—and is made of glass, not plastic. You'll want a blender with multiple speed settings and a pulse feature, a tight top seal to avoid spillage, and stainless-steel blades. A model with non-slip rubber feet and a pouring lip isn't a bad idea either.

Going the extra appliance mile can be enjoyable, but don't appliance yourself out of counter and closet space (it can be a dangerous addiction). If you do have the space, other useful appliances worth owning include a rice cooker (look for "fuzzy logic" models like those made by Zojirushi, which make cooking perfect rice a breeze), a hand mixer, and, last but not least—especially if you plan on doing a lot of baking—a stand mixer.

Meat Alternatives 101

Whether you're a full-on vegetarian or a meat-eater with vegetarian friends, or you fall somewhere along the spectrum between those categories, the explosion of meat alternatives in the past decade or so has to have put a smile on your face. Not because vegetables aren't good by themselves, mind you, and not because vegetarians have wild cravings for meat (though maybe some do), but because these alternatives expand the range of cooking options for more people.

Of course, some of these "alternatives," and the building blocks for most of them, have been around and have been used by cooks of the home and professional variety for thousands of years. With that in mind, let's go over a few of these classic vegetarian staples first, and then hit on some of the newer products and what they bring to the table. One caveat, though: This isn't meant to be an exhaustive list, or even a complete one, as there are new versions and varieties of meat alternatives coming out all the time. But this will at least start to set the table.

Tofu

The granddaddy of vegetarian protein sources (and used often in meat dishes as well, especially in Asian cultures), tofu is bean curd made with coagulated soymilk that's been pressed into blocks. According to the most widely accepted theory, tofu has been around since around 164 BC, starting in China and then moving throughout Asia and eventually the world. The beauty of tofu is twofold. First, it doesn't tend to have a lot of flavor on its own (unless it's altered in some way), which makes it ideal for using in all kinds of dishes, but it does have a lovely silky texture. Second, it's very healthful, high in iron and protein and with no saturated fat or cholesterol. There are three kinds of fresh tofu: silken/soft, Asian firm (often labeled as firm), and Western firm (often labeled as extra-firm). Different brands have different levels of firmness, though, so try out different kinds to see which works best for you. There are also many varieties of prepared tofu available, including baked varieties;

seasoned, marinated, and otherwise flavored kinds; fermented tofu; and frozen tofu (which, when thawed, has a different texture from fresh). You can also bake your own (page 48), which is easy and fun.

Tempeh

A tofu cousin originating in Indonesia, tempeh is also made from soybeans, but a fermentation process binds the soybeans into cake form. This fermentation process also ramps up the healthy factor to an even higher level, giving tempeh more protein than tofu, as well as higher vitamin content and more fiber. The fermentation process also gives tempeh a much firmer texture than regular fresh tofu, which means it's a little less flexible, but also that it has a sturdy mouthfeel, as well as an often smoky and nutty taste. This texture and flavor combination makes tempeh a hit in sandwiches and breakfast fare, as well as other dishes. Tempeh is very versatile: It can be fried until it's crispy and golden brown for stir-fries; thinly sliced, pan-fried, and used as a substitute for bacon or vegetarian bacon in a BLT; grilled and eaten steak-style; or just cut up uncooked and tossed into a salad. It adds a lot of texture to dishes and can take on other flavors easily. In the grocery store you might see pre-flavored varieties of tempeh (such as Lightlife Organic Smoky Tempeh Strips), which can be fun to work with, but which will take a little of the flavor control out of your hands. You will also encounter tempeh in which the soybeans used to make it have been combined with other grains to add flavor or a particular health benefit (such as tempeh made with flax seeds or brown rice). Again, it's fun to experiment with these options, but just be aware of what other flavors they are bringing to the table.

Seitan

Seitan is not a misspelling of the head of Hades, as some oh-so-funny meat-eaters might have you believe. Instead, it's just another name for gluten, specifically wheat gluten, which is created by washing wheat flour dough in water to remove the starch. This results in a sort of messy product that's then processed further until it achieves a good chewy and firm texture. Often seitan is flavored, sometimes with mushrooms, spices, or even barbecue sauce, and it can even be shaped into ribs or chunks to more easily sub in for meat in vegetarian dishes. Its almost stringy texture works very well when used in this way, and makes seitan one of the more versatile ingredients to use in vegetarian versions of dishes that call for heartier meats. It also soaks up liquid fairly well, allowing it to be nicely seasoned with stock or sauces. The chewy texture of seitan sets it apart from tofu's silkiness and tempeh's more crumbly quality.

Modern Meat Alternatives

As mentioned above, there's been an explosion of meat alternatives recently, with many new brands, products, and styles. Often, these products are soy based, but some use textured vegetable protein and other sources, including a variety of different vegetables and grains. While many of the products are directly imitating certain types of meat (vegetarian burgers for hamburgers, for example), they can also often be used differently from their original intention (cutting up those veggie burgers to use in the chili on page 120 is a good start). It's fun to play around with this wide range of products, but in many of our recipes we've found that a particular product works the best. For example, our Meat-and-Not-Meat Loaf (page 138) calls for vegetarian ground beef, but we've found that Morningstar Farms' Meal Starter vegetarian crumbles don't work well here, because they don't stick together well enough. We suggest that you use Yves Meatless or Lightlife's Gimme Lean ground beef substitute instead. On the flip side, the Morningstar Farms crumbles work dandily in Beefy Bierocks (page 124). While there are new meat-alternative brands popping up every day, following are a few of the main ones to watch for when browsing the supermarket.

A word about textured vegetable protein (TVP): We do not call for TVP specifically in any of the recipes in this book, but it is a building block of some of the modern meat alternatives, so it's good to know a bit about it. TVP comes from defatted soy flour (usually obtained during the making of soybean oil). It's a high-protein, low-fat substance, which makes it good for your health, and it can be highly textured without a distinctive flavor of its own, which makes it a versatile addition to some dishes. (This versatility is also why it's used as a base ingredient for many manufactured meat alternatives.) If you'd like to buy TVP on its own, you'll find it comes in granules, flakes, and chunks, all needing rehydration before being used in recipes.

FIELD ROAST

Field Roast Meat Grain Co. makes products that are a bit different from some meat alternatives in that they are not advertised as correlating to a particular meat product (no "vegetarian beef" here). Instead, their "vegan meat" products are a whole other animal (excuse the pun) made mostly from grains, with other vegetables and flavorings added for certain products. The Field Roast line was developed in Seattle in the late 1990s and follows along in the seitan tradition, with a more Western flavor palate. You can get Field Roast in slices (for sandwiches) in various flavors, and the company also makes grain sausages in flavors like smoked apple-sage, Italian, and Mexican chipotle; flavored cutlets, such as hazelnut-herb, coconut, chipotle-corn, and porcini-Dijon; tofu cheese; and vegetarian pâté. But our favorite is probably still the original Field Roast lentil-sage loaf, which is key to making Osso Buco (page 154).

LIGHTLIFE

Lightlife's slogan is "veggie goodness for you and the planet," and the company's focus is on foods that are all-around flavorful and good for your health. Lightlife's range of products is wide, and it covers items as varied as flavored and unflavored tempeh (which is what the company started with), deli slices, imitation hot dogs and sausages, Smart Stuffers "chicken-style fillets" in flavors such as Chick'n Parmesan and Chick'n Cordon Melt, Gimme Lean and Smart Ground fat-and-cholesterol-free ground beef substitutes, and much more. Many of the company's products are made from soy, but they also use wheat gluten and vegetable protein. You'll probably find Lightlife products all around your local store, both in the refrigerated section and the frozen-food aisle.

MORNINGSTAR FARMS

One of the first vegetarian meat companies, Morningstar Farms has a large range of products, from vegetarian burgers and imitation chicken patties to broccoli-cheddar Veggie Bites snacks and Meal Starters vegetarian steak strips (and the company is continually testing new products). Much like the other makers of meat alternatives, Morningstar Farms' products are often soy-based, but also feature textured vegetable protein (which itself is made of soy protein and wheat gluten), wheat gluten, vegetables, and spices. Be sure, however, if serving a vegan, to double-check whether a Morningstar product contains eggs, as some do. All of the company's products are frozen, and Morningstar has perhaps the widest distribution of any vegetarian food company, with products in stores across the United States. We like their breakfast items best, though, especially the vegetarian sausage patties, which are key for The Best Biscuits and Sausage Gravy (page 126).

YVES VEGGIE CUISINE

Yves was founded in 1985 and boasts a wide assortment of products for health-conscious consumers looking for meatless foods that are low-fat, cholesterol- and preservative-free, convenient to prepare, and, best of all, tasty. The company's products, great for snacking and quick meals, include vegetarian hot dogs, sausages, burgers, deli slices, breakfast patties, and packaged vegetarian entrées such as meatless chili, lasagna, penne, and macaroni and soy cheese. Yves also has a good line called Ground Rounds, ground-meat substitutes that work well in all your favorite meat-based recipes. The Ground Rounds include original flavor (a replacement for ground beef), seasoned taco meat, Asian-style ground meat substitute, and ground turkey substitute. You can find Yves products in the refrigerated section near the vegetables in many supermarkets.

QUORN

A line of all-natural, meatless, frozen-food products that made a splash when first released in the United States in 2002, Quorn products are also soy-free. Quorn's expanding range of offerings currently includes vegetarian versions of chicken cutlets, chicken wings, chicken nuggets, ground meat, meatballs, roast turkey, and more. The company's Naked Chik'n Cutlets are an excellent substitute for boneless, skinless chicken breasts. All Quorn products contain mycoprotein, a high-protein fungus (so, a cousin to mushrooms) that contains nine important amino acids. Mycoprotein is low in fat and calories, high in fiber, cholesterol-free, and easily digested. It gives Quorn products their distinctive texture, which simulates the texture of meat products in vegetarian versions of meat-based dishes.

sundry snacks

saying "I love entertaining" is one thing, but actually

becoming a legendary host or hostess, one who is talked about in song and story, one whose events, both big and small, make folks' hearts skip a beat when they see the invites—that's a position to aspire to. But to reach those rarefied rollicking heights, you'll need to deliver the goods—good drinks and snacks, that is. Whether you're having a handful of pals over to watch the big game on Sunday, inviting friends and their kids for a madcap game of tag in the backyard, hosting a couple of couples for movies and munchies, or throwing a saucy soiree for a larger group, be sure you serve up snacks that all attendees can enjoy, no matter what types of foods they've decided to eat.

The following chapter will become your perfect party assistant, once you've dived into the recipes within it. These merrymaking menu hits are not only pretty easy to prepare but also take away any worry you might have about everyone at your house, both vegetarians and meat-eaters, having delightful nibbles (and you sure don't want to be sweating the snacks when getting ready for revelry, because you need to have fun, too). Whether you want to throw a home-on-the-range hoedown with Barbecue Skewers, host a white-tie affair on the lawn with Pâté Your Way, or add a little oomph to your sporting showdown event with Sweet Meatballs and Munchy Cheddar Bites, this chapter's recipes will ensure your fête is fantastic.

Creative Crudités

Serves 5 to
6 vegetarians and
5 to 6 meat-eaters

1 cup ranch dressing

1½ teaspoons chili
powder

½ teaspoon freshly
ground black pepper

2 dashes of Tabasco or
other Louisiana-style
hot sauce

2 cups cauliflower florets

2 cups baby carrots

2 cups green beans, cut
into 3-inch pieces

1 yellow bell pepper,
seeded and cut into
strips

1 red bell pepper, seeded
and cut into strips

4 ounces thinly sliced
prosciutto

The too-often sad standby of the party buffet (whether you're a meat-eater or vegetarian—no group escapes this trap), crudités should be a host's or hostess's dream, as they aren't hard to prepare, provide a nice base for any spread, and are easy to make for groups encompassing a wide variety of diets. Unfortunately, crudités frequently take the form of a bag of old carrots dropped solo into a bowl. With a little planning and a variety of veggies (the main event here is raw veggies, as the word *crudités* does trace back to "raw"), an eye on freshness, and a few key additions (some spicy dip and, for meat-eaters, some slices of the Italian dream meat, prosciutto), your crudités can become the star of your soiree instead of an afterthought.

1. In a small bowl, combine the ranch dressing, chili powder, pepper, and hot sauce, stirring well with a fork or whisk until everything is well mixed. Divide the dip equally between two smaller bowls and place the bowls in the middle of two medium-size serving platters.

2. Keeping each type of veggie together (this helps the colors to stand out), place half of the veggies around the bowl of dip on one of the platters, in the following order: first the cauliflower, then the carrots, green beans, yellow pepper, and red pepper (so that you have the red pepper next to the white cauliflower).

3. Repeat this with the second platter, using the remaining vegetables, but add the prosciutto to the arrangement, between the two kinds of peppers (if you want our suggestion, that is). You can roll the prosciutto slices into "cigars," if you like. Serve with little plates and a spoon for each of the dips.

Note: We have alluded to this before, but just to emphasize: Fresh veggies are what make any crudités platter work.

 MAKE IT ALL VEGETARIAN: Simply omit the prosciutto, add in a few more of the vegetables of your choice, and divide the veggies equally between the two platters (arranging them in the order listed in step 2).

 MAKE IT MORE MEAT: Increase the amount of prosciutto to 8 ounces and divide it equally between both platters.

Bacon-Wrapped Shrimp or Mushrooms

Makes 24 pieces • 12 for vegetarians and 12 for meat-eaters

A classic (if slightly messy) party snack, this simple-yet-tasty combo leaves a bit of a problem for the vegetarians in the house, as there isn't a reliable vegetarian shrimp available (at least that we've discovered). Inserting sturdy and well-textured portobello mushroom pieces does the trick, though, thanks to their good toothsomeness and how well they match up with the vegetarian bacon.

¼ cup olive oil

2 tablespoons freshly squeezed lemon juice

1 teaspoon freshly ground black pepper

12 large shrimp, peeled and deveined

3 portobello mushrooms, stemmed and cut into 12 shrimp-size pieces

6 bacon slices

6 vegetarian bacon slices

4 lemons, each cut into 6 wedges, for garnish

1. In a medium-size bowl, whisk together the oil, lemon juice, and pepper until combined. Pour half of the marinade into another medium-size bowl.

2. Put the shrimp in one bowl and the portobello pieces in the other bowl. Stir briefly (using separate spoons). Cover and refrigerate for 1 to 2 hours.

3. Preheat the broiler.

4. Cut each slice of bacon in half widthwise to make two short slices. Wrap each short slice of bacon around one of the shrimp, securing with a toothpick. Place the shrimp in a single layer on a baking sheet.

5. Cut each slice of vegetarian bacon in half widthwise. Wrap each half slice around one of the mushroom pieces, securing with a toothpick. Place the mushrooms in a single layer on a separate baking sheet.

6. Put the baking sheet with the shrimp in the oven, close to the broiler. Cook for 4 to 5 minutes, turning the shrimp over (using tongs for safety) halfway through the cooking time.

7. Move the baking sheet with the shrimp down to a lower oven rack. Place the baking sheet with the mushrooms on the top rack, close to the broiler. Cook for 4 to 5 minutes, turning the 'shrooms (again, use tongs for safety) halfway through the cooking time.

8. Remove the two baking sheets from the oven. Arrange the bacon-wrapped shrimp on one platter and the bacon-wrapped mushrooms on another. Divide up the lemon wedges evenly between the platters. Serve immediately, with a squeeze of lemon juice.

MAKE IT ALL VEGETARIAN: Use 6 mushrooms and 12 vegetarian bacon slices, and omit the shrimp and bacon. Use just one bowl in step 2, and serve everything on one platter.

MAKE IT ALL MEAT: Use 24 shrimp and 12 bacon slices, and omit the mushrooms and vegetarian bacon. Use just one bowl in step 2, and serve everything on one platter.

Barbecue Skewers

Makes 16 skewers • 8 for vegetarians and 8 for meat-eaters

8 ounces beef flank or sirloin steak

8 ounces vegetarian beef strips

1 cup barbecue sauce (see Note)

3½ teaspoons freshly squeezed lemon juice

3 garlic cloves, crushed

¾ teaspoon red pepper flakes

¾ teaspoon freshly ground black pepper

½ teaspoon salt

We're not saying that you must wear a 20-gallon hat and yodel around an open fire when serving these beefy treats to your posse, or that you need a cooler full of cold American-style lager along with a bottle of bourbon, or even that you should say things like "get along, little dogies" or "that's fine as cream gravy" during the evening. But if you don't at least sing a verse of "Home on the Range," we can't be held responsible for any cowboy curses that descend upon you.

1. Build a hot fire in a charcoal grill or preheat a gas grill to medium-high.

2. Slice the steak diagonally into 1-inch wide strips. Thread the steak strips onto 8 skewers (if using wooden ones, soak them in water first to prevent burning during cooking), using multiple strips as needed. The threaded strips should look like a series of s's. Set the skewers aside on a plate.

3. Thread the vegetarian beef strips onto 8 other skewers, using the same technique as in step 2. If the vegetarian strips aren't long enough to make s's, just skewer them in smaller pieces.

4. Whisk together the barbecue sauce, lemon juice, garlic, red pepper flakes, black pepper, and salt in a bowl. Reserve ¼ cup of the mixture. With a barbecue or pastry brush, coat the vegetarian skewers with half of the sauce. Coat the steak skewers with the remaining sauce.

5. Place the steak skewers 6 to 7 inches over the fire on one-half of the grill, and cover the grill. After 3 minutes, turn them over, and place the vegetarian skewers on the other half of the grill. Cook for 3 more minutes. Check to be sure that all of the steak and vegetarian skewers have reached their desired doneness. Place the skewers on two serving platters (one for the vegetarian skewers and one for the steak skewers) and serve with the reserved sauce on the side.

Note: If you're adept at making your own barbecue sauce and have time to whip up a batch, then by all means do so. But if you go for store-bought, be sure to pick one that you've already tasted and know to be reliably good.

 MAKE IT ALL VEGETARIAN: Double the amount of vegetarian beef strips to 1 pound, and omit the steak. Check the skewers for doneness after 3 minutes of cooking time.

 MAKE IT ALL MEAT: Double the amount of steak to 1 pound, and omit the vegetarian beef strips. Cook the skewers for 3 minutes on one side, turn them over, and check for doneness after another 3 minutes of cooking time.

Club Sandwich Crunchers

Makes 16 mini
sandwiches · 8 for
vegetarians and
8 for meat-eaters

4 vegetarian bacon slices

4 bacon slices

**12 slices hearty white
bread, toasted**

¾ cup mayonnaise

**4 large romaine lettuce
leaves, cut in half**

**1 large tomato, cut into
8 slices**

**2 slices vegetarian
smoked turkey**

2 slices smoked turkey

The history of the club sandwich is not entirely clear. It could be that the sandwich comes from the Saratoga Club, which was once owned by a gentleman named Richard Canfield, in the late 1800s. Or it could be that a nameless man, home hungry one night when his butler was out, concocted a late-night nibbler out of what he could find in the kitchen, and then, so pleased with the results, took the recipe back to his club, where its fame spread. It's best not to get too bogged down in the details here, or else by the time you've decided which history you want to go with, all the sandwiches will be gone. And then you'll be the sadder for it. So make a snap decision, tell your story well, and always keep a Club Sandwich Cruncher in one hand.

1. Cook the vegetarian bacon according to package directions. Cook the meaty bacon until crisp.

2. Spread one side of each bread slice with the mayonnaise. Place 4 of the bread slices, mayo side up, on a cutting board.

3. Place one piece of romaine on top of each of the 4 pieces of bread. Top each piece of romaine with a tomato slice.

4. For the vegetarian sandwiches: Top 2 of the sandwich halves with a slice of vegetarian smoked turkey. Next, place a second slice of bread, mayo side up, on top of the vegetarian smoked turkey, then add another piece of romaine, another tomato slice, and 2 slices of vegetarian bacon (the bacon can be broken into small pieces to fit as needed). Add a final piece of bread, mayo side down, to each sandwich.

5. For the meat sandwiches: On each of the remaining 2 sandwich halves, place 1 slice of smoked turkey; a second slice of bread, mayo side up; 1 piece of romaine; 1 tomato slice; and 2 slices of bacon. Add a final piece of bread, mayo side down, to each sandwich.

6. This part's a smidge tricky, but we have faith in you. Place four toothpicks in a diamond pattern on one of the vegetarian sandwiches, with one toothpick near the top (about ¼ inch from the top), one near the bottom, and one near each of the two sides. Push the toothpicks all the way through the sandwich. Then, carefully cut the sandwich diagonally, from one corner to the other, then from the third corner to the fourth. You should end up with four triangles, and each should have a toothpick in it. Repeat this step for the remaining three sandwiches. Serve immediately.

Variations: This is the standard recipe, but there are some substitutions out there that no one should frown about. For example, substitute slices of cooked chicken breast for the turkey (in fact, the first published recipe for this sandwich—published in the *Good Housekeeping Everyday Cookbook* in 1903—says to use either chicken or turkey), or use ham instead of bacon. One other variation that we wouldn't dismiss is adding slices of Swiss or cheddar cheese (unless, of course, you're serving vegans). Because a little cheese is almost always good for any meal.

 MAKE IT ALL VEGETARIAN: Omit the bacon and turkey, and use 8 slices vegetarian bacon and 4 slices vegetarian smoked turkey.

 MAKE IT ALL MEAT: Omit the vegetarian bacon and vegetarian smoked turkey, and use 8 bacon slices and 4 slices smoked turkey.

Crostini Toscana

Makes 20 crostini • 10 for vegetarians and 10 for meat-eaters

Crostini are a cousin of bruschetta, but different enough (thinner, crispier, with more spreadable toppings) that they need to be recognized in their own right. This version is the classic from Tuscany, using chicken livers for those who eat meat and mushrooms for those who don't.

¼ cup (½ stick) unsalted butter

1 medium-size carrot, finely chopped

½ medium-size red onion, finely chopped

1 celery stalk, finely chopped

½ teaspoon salt

½ teaspoon freshly ground black pepper

4 ounces chicken livers, soaked and drained twice in cold water, then patted dry

4 ounces mushrooms of your choice, coarsely chopped

4 sprigs fresh thyme, leaves only

½ cup dry white wine

1. In each of two medium-size sauté pans over medium heat, melt 1 tablespoon of the butter. Divide the carrot, onion, and celery evenly between the two pans and sauté for 6 to 8 minutes. A little browning here is okay, but don't let the mixture get too brown. Season with the salt and pepper.

2. Raise the heat to high, and add another 1 tablespoon butter to each pan. Add the chicken livers to one pan and the mushrooms to the other. Sauté both for 2 to 3 minutes each, stirring frequently. Divide the thyme leaves evenly between the pans and sauté for 1 minute more. Add ¼ cup wine to each pan for deglazing, and cook, stirring to scrape up any browned bits, until the mixtures are almost dry.

3. Place 1 teaspoon of the Vin Santo, 1 tablespoon of the olive oil, and the contents of the mushroom pan in a food processor. Adjust the seasoning with salt and pepper as desired and pulse until everything is in a fine mince. Spoon the mixture into a bowl and refrigerate until it reaches room temperature.

4. In the meantime, wipe out the food processor and repeat the process with the remaining 1½ teaspoons Vin Santo, the remaining 1 tablespoon olive oil, and the contents of the pan with the chicken livers. Adjust the seasoning with salt and pepper as desired and pulse briefly. Some people like a smoother pâté, while others like it rougher and more rustic—it will taste great either way. Pulse until the mixture has reached the desired consistency. Refrigerate until the mixture reaches room temperature.

2½ teaspoons Vin Santo
(see Note)

2 tablespoons olive oil

1 baguette, sliced into
20 rounds and lightly
toasted

2 tablespoons nonpareil
capers, rinsed and
patted dry, for garnish

1 tablespoon chopped
fresh flat-leaf parsley,
for garnish

5. Slather the baguette rounds with a tablespoon or two of either mixture. Garnish all with a sprinkling of capers and a dash of parsley and serve.

Note: Vin Santo is an Italian sweet dessert wine. You can find it at most wine shops. If you have difficulty locating it, you can sub in Marsala or sherry.

 MAKE IT ALL VEGETARIAN: Double the amount of mushrooms to 8 ounces, and omit the chicken livers. You can cook everything in one sauté pan and combine everything in the food processor at the same time in step 3.

 MAKE IT ALL MEAT: Double the amount of chicken livers to 8 ounces, and omit the mushrooms. You can cook everything in one sauté pan and combine everything in the food processor at the same time in step 3.

End-All Antipasto

2 cups pepperoncini
(see Note), drained

12 ounces Italian fontina
cheese, thinly sliced

12 ounces whole-milk
mozzarella cheese,
cut into ¼-inch-thick
slices

2 cups marinated
mushrooms

4 ounces thinly sliced
prosciutto

1 cup sliced marinated
red peppers

6 sprigs fresh basil, for
garnish

2½ teaspoons olive oil
(optional)

Don't get us wrong, we don't mean anything apocalyptic by the title of this recipe. On the contrary—we never want the party to stop. The "end-all" here refers to the fact that once you have the setup of this antipasto down, you won't ever have to worry about your Italian-style spreads again. Like many good things in life, when thinking antipasto, you want to have balance. Five or six first-class ingredients get you where you want to be without being overwhelming, if you have a nice variety within that list. Serve this with crusty Italian bread.

1. Start your antipasto-ing with a medium-size platter—round works best (you'll need two). Using that old friend, your imagination, visualize one platter divided into five pizza-esque slices. Place half of the pepperoncini onto one imaginary slice.

2. Place half of the fontina on one side of the pepperoncini (keeping it in its own "slice"), and half of the mozzarella on the other side of the pepperoncini. Then spread 1 cup of the mushrooms on the other side of the fontina, and place the prosciutto between the mushrooms and the mozzarella, filling up the platter.

3. Repeat steps 1 and 2 with the second platter, substituting the sliced red peppers for the prosciutto.

4. Place 3 sprigs of basil onto each platter, then drizzle 1¼ teaspoons of the olive oil, if you are using it (we always do), over each platter. Serve immediately.

Note: Pepperoncini are slightly spicy, light green Italian or Greek peppers that are available pickled in jars in most grocery and gourmet stores.

 MAKE IT ALL VEGETARIAN: Omit the prosciutto, and increase the amount of red peppers to 2 cups, substituting red peppers for the prosciutto in step 2.

 MAKE IT MORE MEAT: Omit the red peppers, and add a second variety of *salume* (cured Italian meat), such as mortadella or salami.

Jammed Tom Toms

Makes 20 tom toms · 10 for vegetarians and 10 for meat-eaters

20 good-size cherry tomatoes

1 tablespoon unsalted butter

¼ cup finely chopped yellow onion

¾ cup bread crumbs

1 tablespoon minced fresh thyme

½ teaspoon freshly ground black pepper

½ teaspoon salt

½ cup grated Parmesan cheese (2 ounces)

¼ cup lump crabmeat, picked over for shells

No, this isn't a mutant dessert-appetizer combo created on a moonlit night by a mad doctor who had a thing about jelly and the vegetable patch. And no, you don't have to play a handheld drum and sit around a fire mumbling with a lot of dancing men when you eat these (though if that's the kind of party you throw, go right ahead). Jammed Tom Toms are tomatoes stuffed to bursting with all sorts of goodness, and guests of all dietary persuasions will enjoy them.

1. Preheat the oven to 400°F.

2. With a sharp knife, carefully slice the tops off the tomatoes. Then, with a sharp-ish small spoon, carefully scoop the seeds and pulp out of the tomatoes (you don't want to break the skin).

3. Put 2½ teaspoons of the butter into a large sauté pan over medium heat. Once the butter begins bubbling, add the onion. Sauté until the onion is softened and golden brown, 5 to 7 minutes.

4. Remove the pan from the stovetop, and add the bread crumbs, thyme, pepper, and salt. Stir well to combine, then add the cheese to the mixture and stir a bit more.

5. Divide the mixture equally between two bowls. Add the crab to one bowl, and mix lightly—you don't want to break up the crab too much.

6. Grease two medium-size baking dishes with the remaining ½ teaspoon butter. Using a small spoon, carefully fill 10 of the tomatoes with the vegetarian mixture, placing them in the first baking dish. Spoon the crab mixture into the remaining 10 tomatoes, and place them in the second baking dish. Place both dishes in the oven, and bake for 10 to 15 minutes, until the tops are slightly brown. Serve warm or at room temperature.

 MAKE IT ALL VEGETARIAN: Omit the crab, and increase the cheese to ¾ cup. You can use only one bowl when mixing things together.

 MAKE IT ALL MEAT: Increase the amount of crab to ½ cup, and mix everything together in one bowl.

Meaty and Meatless Mini Sandwiches

Makes 36 mini sandwiches • 18 for vegetarians and 18 for meat-eaters

8 ounces watercress, stems trimmed

1 cup cream cheese

½ cup mayonnaise

½ teaspoon salt

½ teaspoon freshly ground black pepper

½ cup chopped smoked ham

12 slices potato bread

2 cups sliced button mushrooms

When Shakespeare wrote, in *Antony and Cleopatra*, "When I was green in judgment," he may not have been referring to a time when either he or the leads in the play were whipping up these tasty and easy-to-prepare small sandwiches for a bit of last-minute merrymaking. But, then again, maybe he was thinking about the delicious watercress and cream cheese filling. It makes a good story when you serve these and people start to ask about them (which they will, and quick), so we suggest you go with William S.

1. Place the watercress, cream cheese, mayonnaise, salt, and pepper in a food processor, and pulse 5 to 6 times, so that everything is completely mixed together. Divide the watercress mixture equally between two bowls. Add the ham to one bowl and stir to combine.

2. Spread 6 of the bread slices on a cutting board or clean counter. Place the mushrooms on the bread slices, making sure each slice gets an equal amount of mushrooms.

3. Spread the vegetarian watercress mixture on 3 of the remaining bread slices. Place each of these slices, watercress side down, onto 3 of the mushroom-topped slices.

4. Spread the watercress-ham mixture on the remaining 3 bread slices, and place each of these, spread side down, onto the remaining 3 mushroom-topped slices.

5. Here's where you get to use your imagination (sorta like Shakespeare). Looking at one of the sandwiches, mentally trace two parallel lines down it vertically, creating 3 equal-size pieces. Next (again, in your mind), trace another line horizontally through the middle of the sandwich so that it is divided into 6 rectangles. Place a toothpick in the middle of each of these imaginary rectangles. Using a chef's knife or sharp bread knife, cut along those imaginary lines. Repeat this process for the remaining 5 sandwiches. Arrange the sandwiches on two small platters (one with the meaty sandwiches and the other with the meatless sandwiches) and serve.

 MAKE IT ALL VEGETARIAN: Omit the ham, and combine the ingredients in step 1 in one bowl.

 MAKE IT ALL MEAT: Increase the ham to 1 cup, and in step 1 combine everything in one bowl.

Mixed Grill

It's rare that the word *mixer* is used nowadays, which is a shame. Serve these enjoyable nibbles—a variety of grilled veggies and meats, lightly seasoned with salt, pepper, and olive oil (an ideal simplicity)—at your next party and call it, in throwback fashion, a "Mixed Grill Mixer." Your pals are sure to start salivating in anticipation.

6 portobello mushrooms, stems removed and cut into 1-inch-thick slices

6 zucchini, ends trimmed and cut lengthwise into 1-inch-thick slices

1 large yellow onion, cut into 1/2-inch-thick slices

2 yellow bell peppers, seeded and cut into 1/2-inch-thick slices

2 red bell peppers, seeded and cut into 1/2-inch-thick slices

3 tablespoons olive oil

1 tablespoon freshly ground black pepper

1 tablespoon salt

1 pound boneless, skinless chicken breasts, cut into 1-inch-thick strips

1 pound Italian sausage, cut into 1-inch-thick slices

1. Build a hot fire in a charcoal grill or preheat a gas grill to medium-high.

2. Put the mushrooms and zucchini in one bowl, and the onion and bell peppers in a second bowl. To each bowl, add 2 1/4 teaspoons of the olive oil, 3/4 teaspoon of the pepper, and 3/4 teaspoon of the salt, and toss with a spoon to coat the vegetables.

3. Put the chicken and sausage in a third bowl, and add the remaining 4 1/2 teaspoons oil, 1 1/2 teaspoons pepper, and 1 1/2 teaspoons salt to the bowl. Toss with a spoon to coat the meat with the oil and spices.

4. Using tongs, place the chicken and sausage on one side of the grill and cook for 5 minutes, turning halfway through the cooking time. Put the onion and bell peppers in a grill basket, and place the basket on the other side of the grill. Cook everything for 1 minute, turning the onion and peppers once with a different set of tongs from those used on the meat.

5. Place the zucchini and mushrooms right on the grill grate, on the side of the grill with the grill basket. Grill everything for 2 more minutes, then toss the veggies in the grill basket and turn the meat, zucchini, and mushrooms (using your meat tongs for the meat and separate tongs for the veggies). Continue to cook for another 3 minutes.

6. Arrange the veggies on one platter and the meat on another. Serve with napkins, toothpicks, little forks, bibs, or some combination of the above.

Notes: This a lot of food to have on the grill at once, so, depending on your grill size, you may have to cook in batches, making sure you have some meat and some veggies coming off at the same time (so no one goes hungry). If you want to vary the flavor of your marinade, you could add a little lemon juice, paprika, honey, or vinegar-based hot sauce to each of the bowls in steps 2 and 3.

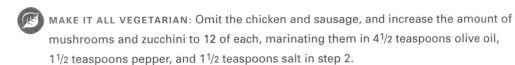 **MAKE IT ALL VEGETARIAN:** Omit the chicken and sausage, and increase the amount of mushrooms and zucchini to 12 of each, marinating them in 4$\frac{1}{2}$ teaspoons olive oil, 1$\frac{1}{2}$ teaspoons pepper, and 1$\frac{1}{2}$ teaspoons salt in step 2.

MAKE IT ALL MEAT: Omit the mushrooms and zucchini, and increase the amount of chicken and sausage to 2 pounds of each. Marinate the chicken and sausage in 3 tablespoons olive oil, 1 tablespoon pepper, and 1 tablespoon salt in step 3.

Munchy Cheddar Bites

Makes 30 bites • 15 for vegetarians and 15 for meat-eaters

4 cups all-purpose flour

5 teaspoons baking powder

½ teaspoon salt

½ teaspoon freshly ground black pepper

¼ teaspoon dry mustard

10 tablespoons (1¼ sticks) cold unsalted butter

1½ cups finely shredded cheddar cheese (6 ounces)

1¾ cups milk

3 bacon slices, cooked until crisp (page 195)

A warm, homey snack like these bites served alongside some steaming cider at a winter affair makes partygoers of every stripe happy, helping them to take off the chill. (We like to spike the cider with rum and cinnamon schnapps and garnish it with cinnamon sticks and a few cloves, but you can make it virgin if you'd like.)

1. Preheat the oven to 400°F.

2. In a large bowl, sift together the flour, baking powder, salt, pepper, and mustard. Cut in the cold butter with a pastry blender (or, if you don't have one, use two knives). Keep working with the butter until the mixture is crumbly. Add the cheese to the bowl, and stir until the cheese is combined with the other ingredients. Add the milk and stir with a spoon until it is completely mixed into the dough.

3. Split the dough into equal parts, and transfer one part to a new bowl. Crumble the bacon and add it to the dough in one of the bowls. Using a spoon, mix the bacon into the dough.

4. Wash your hands, if necessary, to remove any bacon, and lightly grease two baking sheets. Starting with the bacon-free dough, form the dough into small rounds using a spoon or your hands, then place the rounds on one of the baking sheets. Repeat the process using the dough with bacon and the second baking sheet.

5. Place the baking sheets in the oven and bake for 10 minutes. If you had the sheets on different racks in the oven, carefully switch the position of the sheets. Bake for 10 more minutes, until the bites are golden brown and a toothpick comes out clean when inserted into one of the bites. Serve warm.

 MAKE IT ALL VEGETARIAN: Omit the bacon, and skip step 3. Form the dough into rounds and bake as directed.

 MAKE IT ALL MEAT: Increase the amount of bacon to 6 slices. In step 3 don't divide the dough before adding the bacon. Form the dough into rounds and bake as directed.

Pigs in a Blanket

Makes 16 pieces · 8 for vegetarians and 8 for meat-eaters

4 vegetarian hot dogs

4 hot dogs

One 8-ounce package refrigerated crescent rolls (8 rolls)

Condiments of your choice for dipping

Call them what you will (pigs in a blanket, franks-in-jackets, coated Chihuahuas, kilted sausages, wiener winks, or happy hounds), these suburban cocktail-hour favorites have ridden waves of popularity but never gone completely out of fashion. That's because they're so darn scrumptious. And they're a breeze to make, especially if you do as we suggest and use refrigerated crescent rolls and vegetarian and meaty hot dogs (which taste better than cocktail sausages, in our opinion). It's an excellent idea to serve these with an array of condiments to cover the range of party palates: Ketchup, different flavored mustards, barbecue sauce, sweet chili sauce, hot sauce, and mayonnaise can all be tempting.

1. Preheat the oven according to the package directions for the crescent rolls.

2. Cut each vegetarian hot dog in half.

3. Open the package of crescent rolls. Spread out the dough for one roll and cut it in half so you have two triangular pieces. Place one vegetarian hot dog half into the corner of one crescent roll half. Wrap the dough around the hot dog and place it on a baking sheet, with the tailing end of the dough down on the sheet. Repeat with the remaining vegetarian hot dog halves.

4. Cut the hot dogs in half, and wrap each half in some crescent-roll dough as in step 3. Place these on a separate baking sheet.

5. Bake according to the package directions for the crescent rolls (checking once about three-quarters of the way through the cooking time to avoid overcooking). Serve hot, with your chosen array of condiments.

Notes: The proportions are best if you use regular-size hot dogs and vegetarian dogs here and not the giant or sausage-style dogs. Placing a slice of cheddar cheese between either kind of "pig" and its "blanket" before cooking is an excellent idea.

 MAKE IT ALL VEGETARIAN: Use 8 vegetarian hot dogs and no meaty dogs.

 MAKE IT ALL MEAT: Use 8 meaty hot dogs and no vegetarian dogs.

Speared Savories

¾ cup honey

¼ cup pineapple juice

2 tablespoons vegetable
oil

1 tablespoon minced
fresh ginger

2 teaspoons soy sauce

1 teaspoon freshly
ground black pepper

1 teaspoon sriracha sauce

1 garlic clove, minced

12 ounces pork loin, cut
into 1-inch chunks

12 ounces vegetarian
chicken breast, cut into
1-inch chunks

One 16-ounce can
pineapple chunks,
drained, or fresh
pineapple cut into
chunks (1¾ cups)

Feel no need to don any sort of loin cloth, centurion skirt, or other outfit that you think might be traditional for hunting your nibbles with a spear. The spear here is, between us, a skewer, and the items on it aren't as hard to pin down as your average saber-toothed tiger, or even your average runaway soybean. This doesn't mean you can't talk a good game about how you speared down the eats for your soiree. That's just good party patter.

1. Using a whisk or slotted spoon, combine the honey, pineapple juice, oil, ginger, soy sauce, pepper, sriracha, and garlic in a medium-size bowl. Mix until everything is well combined. Reserve ¼ cup of the marinade in a separate container.

2. Put the pork in a casserole dish and pour half of the remaining marinade over the pork. Put the vegetarian chicken in another casserole dish and pour the rest of the marinade over it. Marinate the pork and vegetarian chicken in the refrigerator for at least 1 hour (but don't leave them in longer than overnight).

3. Near the end of the marinating process, preheat the broiler, build a hot fire in a charcoal grill, or preheat a gas grill to medium-high.

4. Thread 1 vegetarian chicken chunk, then 1 pineapple chunk, then 1 cherry tomato onto a skewer, repeating until there is about 3 inches left at the bottom of the skewer (so you have room to hold on to it). Place the skewer on a plate. Repeat using 5 more skewers.

5. Thread 1 pork chunk, then 1 pineapple chunk, then 1 cherry tomato onto a skewer, repeating until there is about 3 inches left at the bottom of the skewer. Place the skewer on a separate plate. Repeat using the remaining 5 skewers.

6. If using the broiler, place the vegetarian chicken skewers on one broiling pan and the pork skewers on another broiling pan, and place both pans

36 cherry tomatoes

12 wooden skewers, soaked in water for 30 minutes before cooking

in the oven, 3 to 4 inches from the broiler. Cook for 5 minutes, turning twice. If using a grill, place the vegetarian skewers on one half of the grill with a pair of tongs, and use a separate set of tongs to place the pork skewers on the other half, making sure each stay on their own side of the grill. Grill for 10 minutes, turning once. Keep an eye on the vegetarian skewers, as they may cook more quickly on the grill than the pork skewers.

7. Transfer the vegetarian skewers to one platter and the pork skewers to another. Pour half of the reserved marinade over the vegetarian skewers, and the other half of the reserved marinade over the pork skewers, and serve.

 MAKE IT ALL VEGETARIAN: Omit the pork and increase the amount of vegetarian chicken breast to 1 1/2 pounds. In step 2, use one dish for marinating, watch your grilling time in step 6, and feel free to use one larger platter in step 7.

 MAKE IT ALL MEAT: Omit the vegetarian chicken breast and increase the amount of pork to 1 1/2 pounds. In step 2, use one dish for marinating, watch your grilling time in step 6, and feel free to use one larger platter in step 7.

Sweet Meatballs

Makes 50 meatballs
• 25 for vegetarians
and 25 for meat-
eaters

12 ounces vegetarian
ground sausage (such
as Gimme Lean)

12 ounces vegetarian
beef crumbles (such as
Yves Ground Round)

2 large eggs

1 cup milk

1 cup rolled oats (not
instant)

12 ounces ground ham

12 ounces ground pork

⅔ cup dark brown sugar

2 tablespoons all-purpose
flour

1 teaspoon dry mustard

1 cup pineapple juice

2 tablespoons rice wine
vinegar

⅓ cup honey

What little marvels these meatballs are, served with toothpicks sticking up in the air, waiting to be plucked and popped into mouths. While these make charming cocktail bites, they are also ideal as part of an Easter buffet or dinner. At least around our Easter tables, they sidle up right alongside the ham, macaroni and cheese, and salads (well, we mostly are just putting the salads in there so you don't completely doubt our healthiness). The recipe calls for ground ham, which can be hard to come by pre-made. If you happen to have a meat grinder and can grind your own, then go that route. If not, ask your butcher to grind it for you, or just finely chop it in the food processor instead. Be sure to mark the serving plates clearly to ensure that no one ends up with a meatball when they were going for an imitation meatball, and vice versa.

1. In a large bowl, combine the vegetarian sausage, vegetarian beef crumbles, 1 of the eggs, 1/2 cup of the milk, and 1/2 cup of the oats using a spoon or, for serious mixing, your hands. Once everything is combined, form the mixture into 1- to 1 1/2-inch-diameter balls, and place them in a shallow baking pan. Don't forget to wash those hands afterward.

2. In another large bowl, combine the ground ham, ground pork, and the remaining egg, 1/2 cup milk, and 1/2 cup oats, using a spoon or your hands. Form into 1- to 1 1/2-inch-diameter balls, and place in a second shallow baking pan (again washing those hands afterward). Place both pans in the refrigerator and let sit for 30 minutes to 1 hour.

3. Meanwhile, preheat the oven to 300°F. In a medium-size bowl, whisk together the brown sugar, flour, and dry mustard until well combined. Add the pineapple juice, vinegar, and honey, whisking steadily until completely combined.

4. Remove the two pans of meatballs from the refrigerator. Pour half of the brown sugar sauce over each pan of meatballs. Bake for 1 hour. Serve hot with toothpicks.

MAKE IT ALL VEGETARIAN: Omit the ground ham and ground pork, and increase the amount of vegetarian ground sausage and beef to 1 1/2 pounds each. In step 1, combine the vegetarian ground sausage and beef with all of the eggs, milk, and oats. Form into meatballs and skip step 2.

MAKE IT ALL MEAT: Omit the vegetarian ground sausage and beef, and increase the amount of ground ham and pork to 1 pound each. Combine the ground ham and pork with all of the eggs, milk, and oats. Form into meatballs and proceed with the rest of the recipe.

Stuffed 'Shrooms

Makes 18
mushrooms · 9 for
vegetarians and
9 for meat-eaters

18 large button
   mushrooms (the
   bigger, the better)

1 garlic clove, crushed

½ cup bread crumbs

2½ tablespoons finely
   chopped fresh basil

1 tablespoon finely
   chopped fresh oregano

½ teaspoon freshly
   ground black pepper

⅛ teaspoon salt

¼ cup grated Parmesan
   cheese (1 ounce)

5 tablespoons extra-
   virgin olive oil

¼ cup loose pork sausage

Whether you think the word *snack* is a variant of the Middle English word *snak*, coming from *snacche*, which translates as "to snap or bite," or instead believe it traces back to the Dutch word *snacken*, which means "to snap at" or "to bite," if you're like us, you forget any sort of linguistic musings when you notice these stuffed mushrooms on the table. Because once you pop one into your mouth, who really cares about any other words besides *mmmm* and *yum*?

1. Preheat the oven to 350°F. Grease two medium-size casserole dishes.

2. Prudently, so you don't destroy the caps, remove the stems from the mushrooms. Finely chop half of the stems and set aside (compost the remaining stems, or use them to make stock). If, after removing the stems, you think that you'll need more room for the stuffing, you can also scrape out the gills. Put 9 of the mushroom caps in each of the prepared casserole dishes, making sure that the mushrooms are gill side up.

3. In a medium-size bowl, combine the chopped mushroom stems, garlic, bread crumbs, basil, oregano, pepper, salt, Parmesan, and 4 tablespoons of the olive oil. Stir well. Transfer half of the stuffing to a separate bowl and add the uncooked sausage. Stir the sausage into the mixture.

4. Using a clean spoon, place the sausage-free stuffing into the mushroom caps in one of the casserole dishes, making sure that each mushroom is stuffed with an equal (or close to equal) amount. You may need to use your fingers to pack the stuffing into the mushrooms.

5. Place the sausage-mushroom stuffing into the mushroom caps in the second casserole dish.

6. Drizzle the remaining 1 tablespoon oil over the mushrooms in both casserole dishes. Cover each with aluminum foil, and bake for 20 minutes.

7. Remove the foil and bake for 10 more minutes (take this time to make "meat" and "no-meat" labels for your serving platters). Serve hot.

MAKE IT ALL VEGETARIAN: Omit the sausage and increase the amount of grated Parmesan to 1/2 cup (2 ounces). If you like, you can bake all of the mushrooms in one large casserole dish.

MAKE IT ALL MEAT: Increase the amount of sausage to 1/2 cup. If you like, you can bake all of the mushrooms in one large casserole dish.

Rillettes

Serves 8
vegetarians and
8 meat-eaters

3 ounces fresh pork fat
or leaf lard, cut into
1- to 2-inch dice

2 cups dry white wine

2 sprigs fresh rosemary

2 sprigs fresh thyme

2 bay leaves

2 medium-size onions,
thinly sliced

1 pound boneless pork
shoulder (the fattier
the better), cut into
1-inch dice

¼ cup olive oil

2 pounds chanterelle,
lobster, or other
light-colored wild
mushrooms, finely
chopped

Rillettes (meaning "planks," most likely referring to their appearance when spread across some crusty bread) are a pâté-like meat preserve, traditionally using inexpensive and delicious pork shoulder. In our vegetarian version, we use wild mushrooms to mimic the light color of its porky counterpart. Heavily seasoned and unconscionably high in delectable fat (usually pork fat, but some butter here for the vegetarians among us), *rillettes* work well as a thin spread on crackers or crusty bread or even as a condiment on a sandwich that needs a rich bit of sprucing up. Although these are easy to make and can be made ahead, *rillettes* do take some time to prepare, so plan accordingly.

1. In a heavy pot over low heat, combine the pork fat, 1 cup of the wine, one sprig of the rosemary, one sprig of the thyme, one of the bay leaves, and one of the onions. Cook until the fat is melted.

2. Add the pork to the pot. Cover and cook over very low heat, stirring occasionally. (The minutest amount of browning is acceptable here, but don't go crazy. Bear in mind that this is a "meat preserve"—browning, although delicious in almost all applications, is still an oxidative process leading to a less shelf-stable product.) This should take 3 to 4 hours.

3. After the pork *rillettes* have cooked for 2½ to 3 hours, heat the olive oil over medium heat in another pot and add the mushrooms, tofu, capers, and the remaining onion. Stir to mix everything together. Continue cooking over medium heat, stirring occasionally, until the mushrooms and tofu have released most of their liquid, then add the remaining 1 cup wine, the remaining sprigs of rosemary and thyme, and the remaining bay leaf. Cover and cook for about 45 minutes.

4. When the pots are approaching doneness, check the clarity of the fat in each pan. If the fat is nice and clear, that means most or all of the water has been driven out. This is a good thing. If the fat is a little cloudy, continue cooking over low heat until the fat is clear. Fight the temptation to raise the heat to expedite the process, especially in the pork pot. Because of the higher smoking point of olive oil, the vegetarian pot could probably take a tiny bit more heat, but why rush perfection?

8 ounces silken tofu, squeezed through cheesecloth to achieve maximum dryness, then mashed finely

2 tablespoons capers

4 teaspoons salt

2 teaspoons freshly ground black pepper

½ cup (1 stick) unsalted butter, melted

5. Remove the herb sprigs and bay leaves from both pots.

6. Remove the pork from the pot with a slotted spoon and set aside. Strain the liquefied pork fat through cheesecloth and reserve the fat. Return the pork and one-third of the rendered fat to the pot and mash with a potato masher. It should practically melt into a meaty paste. Season the pork with 2 teaspoons of the salt and 1 teaspoon of the pepper and mix to combine. Feel free to adjust the seasoning to your taste. Spoon the paste into four 4- to 6-ounce glass or earthenware crocks, leaving about ½ inch of space at the top, then cover with a layer of the remaining pork fat.

7. Add one-third of the melted butter and the remaining salt and pepper to the pot with the vegetarian *rillettes*, and stir to incorporate. Adjust the seasoning to your taste as desired.

8. Spoon the vegetarian *rillettes* into four 4- to 6-ounce glass or earthenware crocks and cover with a layer of the remaining melted butter. The *rillettes* are ready to serve.

Note: Both versions of *rillettes* will keep in the refrigerator for a week or two. Because of their high fat content, they should also freeze well, especially if you have done a good job of ridding the *rillettes* of moisture.

 MAKE IT ALL VEGETARIAN: Omit the pork fat and pork shoulder. Increase the amount of olive oil to ½ cup, the amount of mushrooms to 4 pounds, the amount of tofu to 1 pound, the amount of capers to ¼ cup, and the amount of butter to 1 cup (2 sticks). Skip steps 1, 2, and 6. In step 3, use all of the onions, wine, rosemary, thyme, and bay leaves. In step 7, use all of the salt and pepper.

 MAKE IT ALL MEAT: Omit the olive oil, mushrooms, tofu, capers, and butter. Increase the amount of pork fat to 6 ounces and the amount of pork shoulder to 2 pounds. In step 1, use all of the wine, rosemary, thyme, bay leaves, and onions. In step 6, use all of the salt and pepper. Skip steps 3, 7, and 8.

Drain that Tofu

Tofu is a great vegetarian source of protein made from soy and is an ingredient in a variety of recipes. Unless you get it in fried, baked, or dried form (which would be specified if needed in any of the recipes in this book), it's going to come out of the package a little wet, maybe even surrounded by liquid. This is not only because some companies pack their tofu with water, but also because tofu itself contains a lot of moisture. You usually see tofu in three varieties, soft, firm, and extra-firm, but even the extra-firm has a little extra moisture. It's good to try and drain out as much of this moisture as possible.

Place your block of tofu on a flat, slightly slanted surface in the sink—such as a baking sheet. You don't want a ferocious angle, just a slight angle pointing down into the sink. Place another baking sheet on top of the tofu, then place a small weight on the upper baking sheet—a full can of chickpeas works, or anything that puts a little pressure on the tofu. Then leave it all in the sink for up to an hour. You'll see that moisture has been forced out of the tofu, making it drier and easier to work with.

Pâté Your Way

Serves 8
vegetarians and
8 meat-eaters

1 pound chicken livers

2 cups milk

½ cup (1 stick) unsalted
butter, at room
temperature

¼ cup olive oil

2 shallots, finely chopped

2 pounds mushrooms of
your choice, sliced

1 tablespoon salt

1 teaspoon freshly
ground black pepper

1 cup Cognac, brandy,
sherry, or Madeira

1 large carrot, shredded

2 thinly sliced scallions
(white and some of
the green part)

1 cup lightly toasted
and coarsely chopped
walnuts

The meaty version of this recipe is a classic but humble chicken liver pâté whose flavor is rich yet rustic. As for its vegetarian friend, mushrooms and walnuts lay down an earthy base that is accented by the savory and umami-laden miso and Marmite. Suffice it to say, we think both versions are fantastic and will class up any soiree. Serve with crusty bread, toast points, crackers, or whatever you like. Some nice cordial glasses filled with any of the alcohols listed in the ingredients would be a natural accompaniment for this pâté.

1. Combine the chicken livers and milk in a bowl. Refrigerate for 2 hours to remove any blood or other impurities from the livers.

2. Chill two empty, clean medium-size bowls in the refrigerator or freezer for 30 minutes to 1 hour. Heat 2 tablespoons of the butter and 2 table-spoons of the olive oil in a large skillet over medium-high heat. Add the shallots and cook for 1 minute, making sure they do not brown. Add the mushrooms to the skillet and sauté, stirring often, until the mushrooms have released their liquid, 8 to 10 minutes. Season the mushrooms with 2 teaspoons salt and 1/2 teaspoon pepper.

3. When the mushrooms have released most of their liquid, increase the heat to high and add the Cognac. Watch out for possible flare-ups. Cook, stirring often, until the liquid is almost completely reduced. Turn off the heat, add the carrot and scallions, and stir until the new veggies on the block are just warmed through. Set aside and cool to room temperature.

4. In a food processor, combine the walnuts, tofu, tempeh, miso, and Marmite. Pulse until the mixture is a smooth paste, then add 4 tablespoons of the butter and pulse just until combined.

5. Transfer the walnut mixture to one of the chilled bowls and add half of the mushroom mixture and 1/4 cup of the pistachios. Blend lightly with a wooden spoon, and spoon the mixture into four 4-ounce ramekins or a 5 x 9-inch loaf pan. Cover with aluminum foil or plastic wrap and refriger-ate to set.

CONTINUES ON P. 46

4 ounces firm tofu,
drained (page 44)

4 ounces tempeh,
coarsely chopped

1 tablespoon light miso
paste (see Notes)

1 tablespoon Marmite or
Vegemite (see Notes)

½ cup shelled, lightly
toasted pistachios

6. Remove the livers and milk from the refrigerator and drain. Blot the livers dry with paper towels.

7. Heat the remaining 2 tablespoons olive oil in a skillet over medium-high heat. Carefully add the livers and season with 1 teaspoon salt and ½ teaspoon pepper. Brown the livers on both sides for about 2 minutes, or until the centers retain the slightest blush of pink, then set aside to cool to room temperature.

8. Wipe out the bowl of the food processor and add three-quarters of the livers, reserving the rest. Pulse the livers until they are a smooth paste, then add the remaining 2 tablespoons butter and pulse until just incorporated.

9. Pour the liver mixture into the other chilled bowl. Slice the reserved livers into quarters and add to the bowl, along with the remaining mushroom mixture and pistachios. Mix until just combined and spoon into another four 4-ounce ramekins or another 5 x 9-inch loaf pan. Cover with aluminum foil or plastic wrap and place in the refrigerator to chill and set.

10. Remove the pâtés from the refrigerator 30 to 60 minutes before serving so they come to room temperature. If not serving immediately, you can store the pâtés in the refrigerator for up to 1 week. Be sure to keep them wrapped tightly with aluminum foil or plastic wrap or in a sealed container to prevent them from absorbing the odors of other foods in the refrigerator.

Notes: Miso paste is a savory product made by fermenting soybeans with salt for a highly flavored, almost meaty-tasting result. Miso may also be made from rice, barley, or any combination thereof and may be colored and flavored in various ways. Just think of something that is somewhat salty and nicely browned, or perhaps a meat that has been cured and aged, and you've got a good idea of the flavor of miso. Marmite and Vegemite are thick, dark brown pastes made from yeast extract, a byproduct of brewing beer. They are strongly flavored in a salty and savory way, similar to soy sauce and miso.

MAKE IT ALL VEGETARIAN: Omit the chicken livers and milk. Increase the amount of butter to 10 tablespoons, using 8 tablespoons in step 4. Increase the amount of tofu to 8 ounces, the amount of tempeh to 8 ounces, the amount of miso to 2 tablespoons, and the amount of Marmite to 2 tablespoons. In step 5, add all of the mushroom mixture to the walnut mixture. Skip steps 1, 6, 7, 8, and 9.

 MAKE IT ALL MEAT: Omit the walnuts, tofu, tempeh, miso, and Marmite. Increase the amount of chicken livers to 2 pounds and the amount of milk to 4 cups. Reduce the amount of butter to 6 tablespoons, using 4 tablespoons in step 8. Skip steps 4 and 5.

Bake
Your Own Tofu

While there are recipes that use regular tofu (see page 44 for more info on it and how to drain it), using baked tofu also adds a textured touch to dishes. You wouldn't want to sub it in every time for regular tofu (because sometimes the creaminess of regular tofu is needed), but the less-crumbly and less-creamy texture of baked tofu, along with its chewiness, gives it a more substantial mouthfeel that's really pleasant. You can buy baked tofu in many grocery stores and Asian markets, but you can also bake your own, which is nice because much of the baked tofu available is already seasoned, and thus unsuitable for recipes.

1/2 teaspoon vegetable oil
1 pound extra-firm tofu, drained and cut into 6 slices

1. Preheat the oven to 300°F.

2. Oil a baking sheet with the vegetable oil, and place the tofu slices on it. Bake for 1½ hours, turning the slices over every half hour. They should be brown and dry on all sides when finished. If not, bake them a bit longer. You can keep baked tofu, refrigerated, for a couple of weeks. With this in mind, it's something that can easily be made in advance—and it's also good in sandwiches.

a brunch
bunch

don't be fooled—brunch is a serious matter.

Often the main event on a Sunday, or the only spread before an afternoon event (a wedding perhaps, or a birthday, or another formal occasion), brunch must fortify and satisfy without overwhelming or causing too much kitchen-related chaos that could unravel the rest of the day. It's also often a family-centered meal, which can add just a touch of extra pressure (for some families, at least—which is why brunch is usually accompanied by a sparkling-wine type of drink).

But don't forget that brunch should always be fun, maybe more fun than any other meal, in our opinion, because it often means you've slept in, and because it might just mean you can have a nice post-brunch nap, or at least some leisurely couch time, before any other scheduled tasks. You can rest assured that brunch menus featuring the scrumptious selections in this chapter, such as Bacon and Cheese Tartlets, *Omelettes du Matin*, and *Pissaladière*, transcend the norm for eaters of all diets. These recipes deliver both meat and vegetarian versions without a lot of extra work, so any brunch worries are as last week as using the term *bruncheon*.

Bacon and Cheese Tartlets

**Makes 40 tartlets ·
20 for vegetarians
and 20 for
meat-eaters**

1 tablespoon unsalted
butter

2 shallots, finely chopped

1 tablespoon chopped
fresh basil

¾ teaspoon freshly
ground black pepper

¼ teaspoon salt

2 cups shredded
mozzarella cheese
(8 ounces)

7 bacon slices, cooked
until crisp (page 195)

7 vegetarian bacon slices,
cooked according to
package directions

40 store-bought tartlet
shells

Brunches, we believe, lend themselves to larger groups of people, but cooking for a crowd can be daunting. Which is why it's good to have a yummy little brunch dandy like this one on the menu, which uses pre-made tartlet shells that cut your prep time. Look for the tartlet shells in the freezer case of your local supermarket. This recipe is easy to double or triple.

1. Preheat the oven to 350°F.

2. Heat the butter in a large sauté pan over medium heat. Once the butter is hot and has stopped bubbling, add the shallots. Cook, stirring, for 3 to 5 minutes. Add the basil, pepper, and salt. Remove the pan from the heat.

3. Stir the mozzarella into the sauté pan quickly, then divide the mixture between two bowls.

4. Chop the bacon (both varieties—using separate cutting boards). Add the vegetarian bacon to one of the bowls with the cheese-shallot mixture, and add the bacon to the other bowl. Stir each to mix well.

5. Most tartlet shells are prebaked, but if yours aren't, prebake them for a few minutes before filling them. Portion the vegetarian bacon mixture into half of the tartlet shells, making sure that each shell gets an equal amount, and place them on a baking sheet. Portion the bacon mixture into the remaining tartlet shells, and place them on a second baking sheet.

6. Bake the tartlets for 5 to 8 minutes. Remove the tartlets from the oven, arrange them on two serving platters (one vegetarian and one not), and serve hot.

 MAKE IT ALL VEGETARIAN: Omit the bacon, and use 14 vegetarian bacon slices. You can leave everything in one bowl in step 3.

 MAKE IT ALL MEAT: Omit the vegetarian bacon, and use 14 bacon slices. You can leave everything in one bowl in step 3.

Blini and Caviar

**Serves 4
vegetarians and
4 meat-eaters**

½ cup buckwheat flour

½ cup all-purpose flour

1 teaspoon baking soda

½ teaspoon salt

1 large egg, lightly beaten

1 cup milk

1½ teaspoons unsalted
butter

½ cup sour cream

2 ounces caviar

¾ cup eggplant caviar
(see Note)

¼ cup finely chopped
fresh chives

Doesn't "blini and caviar" have a deliciously decadent sound to it? Much more charmingly snooty than "pancakes and fish eggs," though between us, that's the basic setup here. Of course, it's the kind of pancakes and the kind of fish eggs that make the meal. In this recipe, the pancakes are thin, made with two kinds of flour, and accent the flavor of the caviar without overwhelming it. For the caviar, choose one of good quality, either black or red, but please use domestic, as some kinds of imported caviar come from sturgeon from the Caspian Sea, which are endangered.

1. Preheat the oven to 250°F.

2. In a large bowl, combine the flours, baking soda, and salt, stirring well. Add the egg and milk and stir until completely combined. Set the batter aside.

3. Heat the butter in a medium-size skillet over medium heat. Once the butter has started to foam, use a spoon to drop batter into the pan in 1-tablespoon increments. Once the blini begin to bubble and reach a medium-brown color, turn them and cook until they are medium-brown on both sides.

4. Place a baking sheet in the oven. As each blini finishes cooking, place it on the baking sheet to keep warm. Once all the blini are made, remove the baking sheet from the oven.

5. Place the blini in a single layer on two platters. Spoon a small amount of sour cream on top of each blini. Top the blini on one platter with a dollop of caviar, and those on the other platter with a dollop of eggplant caviar (your dollops should be approximately 1 teaspoon's worth). Sprinkle the chives over both platters before serving.

Note: Eggplant caviar is a vegetarian version of caviar made from eggplant, onions, tomatoes, and a variety of spices, and is available in many gourmet and imported-food stores. Check the ingredients to be sure you get one that doesn't contain anchovies.

MAKE IT ALL VEGETARIAN: Omit the caviar, and increase the amount of eggplant caviar to 1 1/2 cups.

 MAKE IT ALL MEAT: Omit the eggplant caviar and use 4 ounces caviar if you want to have a full seafood platter.

Talk to Your Fruits and Vegetables

I know what you're saying. "Talk to your vegetables? I don't get it. Won't that make me look crazy?" And my reply is, "Crazy like a culinary fox, friend." Not that I believe the vegetables are going to talk back, by the way, nor do I sit around discussing Sartre with a satsuma or Bakhtin with a broccoli. What I'm referring to is getting up close and personal with your produce when picking it out at a store, farmers' market, or your own garden—checking it for bruising before buying, giving it a smell even, and maybe a shake. The underlying point is this: If you want to ensure better-tasting meals, you need to give your recipes the best ingredients to work with, and fruits and vegetables can be the most difficult items, because most of us just grab them without giving them a good once-over. If you do end up with blemished peppers and discover it only minutes before making Hungry Hungarian Stuffed Peppers (page 136), then I suggest removing the bad parts. It's much better to have a dish that has a little bit of its style ruined than having a dish whose very substance is compromised. To avoid this altogether, though, you must get over any fear of looking a touch nutty when in the produce section and start talking to (and touching, and prodding) your fruits and vegetables.

Eggs Benedict

Serves 3
vegetarians and
3 meat-eaters

3 English muffins, split
and lightly toasted

6 thin slices cooked ham

6 vegetarian Canadian
bacon slices or
vegetarian ham slices

¼ teaspoon white vinegar

6 large eggs

½ cup Hollandaise Sauce
(page 169), warmed

1 tablespoon chopped
fresh flat-leaf parsley

Not connected with the world's most famous traitor (though some may think of Mr. Benedict Arnold when consuming it), eggs Benedict actually has an interesting, though well-debated, history. According to the most popular version of the story, the dish was introduced at New York's Waldorf Hotel, when Lemuel Benedict, a stockbroker staying at the hotel, awoke with a hangover and ordered two poached eggs, bacon, buttered toast, and a pitcher of hollandaise sauce, then created the dish that bears his name. (The recipe was later modified, substituting ham for the bacon and English muffins for the toast.) Others believe that this is a younger relative of the French dish *oeufs à la bénédictine*, which is a cod mixture topped with poached eggs and hollandaise sauce and served on toast. Whichever story fits your morning mood, know that this is a great dish to make for mixed dietary company. Serve these accompanied by fresh fruit or Herbed Home Fries (page 204).

1. Preheat the broiler.

2. Place the English muffin halves, cut side up, on a baking sheet.

3. Place the ham slices on a broiler pan, and broil in the oven for 5 minutes—you want them hot and a little crisp. While the ham is cooking, place the vegetarian Canadian bacon on a separate broiler pan. Place it in the oven for the last 2 minutes of the ham's cooking time.

4. Reduce the oven temperature to 200°F. Place 2 ham slices each on 3 of the English muffin halves, and 2 vegetarian Canadian bacon slices each on the remaining 3 English muffin halves. Place this baking sheet in the oven to keep warm while you poach the eggs.

5. Place enough hot water in a large skillet to reach a 2½-inch depth. Bring to a simmer, and add the vinegar. Carefully crack one of the eggs, and drop it (without breaking the yolk) into a small heatproof bowl, cup, or ramekin. Gently slide the egg (again, without breaking the yolk) into the boiling water. Poach until set (a couple of minutes), gently spooning boiling water over the egg as needed. Remove with a slotted spoon, let the water drain off, and place on an English muffin half, on top of either the vegetarian Canadian bacon or ham slices.

6. Once all the eggs have been poached and placed on the English muffin halves, transfer each half to a plate, and top each with 1 tablespoon of the hollandaise sauce and a sprinkling of fresh parsley. Serve immediately.

 MAKE IT ALL VEGETARIAN: Omit the ham, and use 12 vegetarian Canadian bacon slices. Cook under the broiler for 2 minutes.

 MAKE IT ALL MEAT: Omit the vegetarian Canadian bacon, and use 12 ham slices. Cook under the broiler for 5 minutes.

Omelettes du Matin

Serves 2
vegetarians and
2 meat-eaters

¼ cup (½ stick) unsalted
butter

8 large eggs, at room
temperature

2 teaspoons salt

2 bacon slices, cooked
until crisp (page 195)
and coarsely crumbled

1 cup grated Gruyère
cheese or other melting
cheese of your choice
(4 ounces)

2 ounces fresh spinach,
blanched and squeezed
in a clean kitchen
towel to remove as
much moisture as
possible (see Notes)

A well-prepared omelet and a perfectly dressed salad on the side make for a noble, fast, and rather inexpensive meal for anyone anytime. As in many tasty French dishes, the ingredients in an omelet are simple, but the technique requires a little effort to master. To paraphrase the great chef Auguste Escoffier, an omelet is essentially scrambled eggs encased in a coating of coagulated egg. Preparing a perfect omelet can be tricky, but really, the worst that can happen is you end up with scrambled eggs. A glass of Chablis or a light, hoppy beer makes a fine balm to such an "insult."

1. Preheat a large plate in the oven at 225°F. For each omelet, heat 1 tablespoon of the butter in an 8-inch skillet over high heat. (Yes, this flies in the face of everything our high school home ec teachers told us, but who are you going to trust—Escoffier or them?) Quickly whisk together 2 of the eggs and 1/2 teaspoon of the salt. Avoid whisking too vigorously or the omelet will lose elasticity and won't rise in the pan.

2. When the butter has just barely stopped foaming and has turned the lightest amber color, add the eggs and stir briskly for 5 seconds with a fork to even out the curds.

3. For each meaty omelet, position half of the bacon and 1/4 cup of the cheese in a nice little line on the left-hand third of the eggs. For each vegetarian omelet, position half of the spinach and 1/4 cup of the cheese on the left-hand third of the eggs.

4. Here's the tricky part—a true French omelet is rolled, not folded, so, working left to right, roll the omelet over the filling ingredients. Tipping the pan slightly to the right, continue to roll the omelet into the shape of a chubby cigar. (When you have mastered this technique, the omelet will roll itself the second half of the way in the tipped pan.)

5. Transfer the rolled omelet to the preheated plate in the oven, and repeat steps 3 and 4 to make the remaining 3 omelets, working as quickly as possible. If there are a few people around, try getting more than one omeleteer in on the action. Remember—practice makes perfect. Serve immediately.

Notes: Choose a skillet with gently sloping sides for optimal omelet production. Also, avoid the temptation to "kitchen-sink" your omelet ingredients; limit yourself to no more than two ingredients (prewarmed or meltable) that have very little water content, like bacon or blanched/dried spinach. To blanch spinach, bring 1 quart water and 1 teaspoon salt to a boil. Add the spinach. Stir gently for 30 to 60 seconds, until the spinach is limp yet remains brilliantly emerald green. Drain through a strainer, then mound the spinach onto a clean dishtowel. Wrap the dishtowel tightly around the spinach and wring as much green water out as possible. The spinach is now ready to use.

 MAKE IT ALL VEGETARIAN: Omit the bacon, and use 4 ounces spinach. Or, to add a Mexican flair to your omelet, use Jeremy's favorite meat substitute, Soyrizo, a really spot-on imitation chorizo, instead of the bacon (use 1 ounce of Soyrizo per omelet). Be sure to heat the Soyrizo up in a pan or in the microwave first. Another idea is to use tempeh instead of the bacon: Fry 2 tempeh strips in 1/2 teaspoon vegetable oil in a skillet over medium-high heat. Drizzle 1/2 teaspoon liquid smoke (make sure it's vegetarian) over the tempeh strips. Fry the tempeh for 5 minutes, or until golden and crisp.

 MAKE IT ALL MEAT: What, you can't eat a little spinach? Feel free to also increase the amount of bacon to 4 slices.

Fantastic Frittatas

Serves 4
vegetarians and
4 meat-eaters

¼ cup (½ stick) unsalted
butter

2 cups chopped button
mushrooms

10 large eggs

⅔ cup chopped cooked
ham

1 cup grated Parmesan
cheese (4 ounces)

¼ teaspoon kosher salt

¼ teaspoon freshly
ground black pepper

Ah, the classics. They're classic for a reason, but sometimes they need a more modern interpretation to suit today's diners. Take the frittata, for example. In its classic Italian version, the frittata consists solely of eggs, salt, and pepper. Today, that might be considered a little minimalist (though, if done right, so scrumptious), and so adding a little Parmesan, mushroom, and ham (for the meat-eaters) ups the ante in a manner suitable to the modern "more is more" lifestyle. The key is to still end up with the classic frittata structure: dry on the outside and slightly soft on the inside. To accomplish this, you'll need to have two skillets going at once—but we have faith in you.

1. In a medium-size skillet over medium-high heat, melt 1 tablespoon of the butter. Once the butter has melted, add the mushrooms. Stirring continuously, sauté the mushrooms for 5 to 7 minutes. Transfer them to a medium-size bowl.

2. In a large bowl, lightly beat 5 of the eggs. Add the eggs to the bowl containing the mushrooms. Lightly beat the remaining 5 eggs in another bowl (of medium or larger size), and add the ham. Add ½ cup of the cheese, ⅛ teaspoon of the salt, and ⅛ teaspoon of the pepper to each bowl. Using different spoons for each bowl, stir briefly to combine.

3. Place the mushroom skillet back on the stovetop over medium-high heat. Place a second, similarly sized skillet on the stovetop over medium-high heat. Add 1½ tablespoons of the butter to each skillet. Once the butter has melted and bubbled, add the mushroom and egg mixture to the skillet in which the mushrooms were cooked, and add the ham and egg mixture to the other skillet.

4. Reduce the heat under both skillets to medium, and cook for 2 minutes. The eggs should be set around the edges but still slightly jiggly in the middle. Now comes the fun part. Carefully slide the first frittata onto a large flat plate. Then, holding both plate and skillet firmly, place the skillet on top of the plate, and flip the frittata back into the pan. Repeat for the second frittata.

5. Once the frittatas have made it safely back into their skillets, cook for another 3 to 5 minutes. The outsides of the frittatas should be dry, but the insides should still be slightly soft. Transfer the frittatas to separate plates, slice into wedges, and serve hot.

Note: The possibilities for frittata fillings are endless (a little Monterey Jack cheese and some chopped chiles would make for a nicely spicy frittata), but try to keep to the same egg-to-filling ratio as above. If you have a fear of flipping, you can use two ovenproof skillets, and finish cooking the frittatas for 5 minutes in a 400°F oven after cooking them on the stovetop for 2 minutes, instead of flipping them in step 4.

 MAKE IT ALL VEGETARIAN: Omit the ham, and increase the amount of mushrooms to 4 cups. You can combine everything in one bowl in step 2, but you'll probably still want to use two skillets.

 MAKE IT ALL MEAT: Unless you dislike mushrooms, we think it's nice to keep a few of them around, even when going all meat. With that in mind, reduce the amount of mushrooms to 1 cup, and increase the amount of ham to 1$\frac{1}{3}$ cups. You can combine everything in one bowl in step 2, but you'll probably still want to use two skillets.

Foolproof Quiche

Serves 2
vegetarians and
2 meat-eaters

It is truly sad that the phrase "real men don't eat quiche" ever entered the American lexicon. Jacques Pépin eats quiche, and we're pretty sure he can hold his own in a kitchen battle royal. So, fellas, just jump right in (ladies, we know you're already together enough to enjoy a good quiche like this one). To make it even more alluring, we've included a recipe for pastry dough, so you don't have to resort to store-bought. The dough recipe makes enough for two 8-inch regular crusts or one 9-inch deep-dish crust.

Universal pastry dough:

2½ cups all-purpose flour, sifted

1 teaspoon salt

1½ cups (3 sticks) unsalted butter, cut into small cubes and well chilled

3 tablespoons cold water

Filling:

4 large eggs

2 cups light cream

½ teaspoon salt

½ teaspoon freshly ground black pepper

2 cups shredded Swiss cheese (8 ounces)

3 bacon slices, cooked until crisp (page 195) and crumbled

1. Make the dough: On a clean, flat work surface, mix the flour and salt into a mound. Add the butter and begin gently working it together with the flour until the mixture takes on a flaky texture. It does not have to be thoroughly blended. When the flour and butter are mostly together, add the water, mix gently, and form into a ball. Wrap the dough in plastic wrap and refrigerate for 20 to 30 minutes. (The dough can be stored in the refrigerator for up to 1 week or in the freezer for up to 1 month. Thaw frozen dough in the refrigerator before using.)

2. Preheat the oven to 350°F.

3. Remove the dough from the refrigerator and divide it into 2 pieces. Gently form each half into a ball, and roll each ball into a circle that is ⅛ to ¼ inch thick. Lightly press each circle of dough into an 8-inch pie plate. Lay a piece of aluminum foil large enough to cover over the entire crust, and fill the pie plate with dried beans, rice, or pie weights. Bake the crusts for 20 to 35 minutes, then transfer to wire racks to cool.

4. While the crusts bake, make the filling: In a large bowl, beat together the eggs and cream, then add the salt and pepper.

5. Carefully remove the aluminum foil and weights from the cooled crusts. Sprinkle 1 cup of the cheese evenly over each of the 2 cooled crusts. Sprinkle the bacon over the cheese in one pie plate. Pour half of the egg mixture into each pie plate.

6. Bake on the center oven rack for 30 to 40 minutes, until a thin knife inserted into the middle of the quiche comes out clean. Remove from the oven and cool for 10 to 15 minutes before cutting and serving.

Note: You can put almost anything edible into quiches, which is one of the biggest reasons we love them so much. A quick word of advice, though—make sure all the ingredients are in their driest possible form, while maintaining their flavor integrity. For example, do not put handfuls of raw spinach into a quiche, as they will leach out water while baking. Instead, blanch the spinach quickly in salted simmering water, then gather it into a clean dishtowel and wring as much green water out of the leaves as possible. When using tomatoes, consider removing about half the moisture from them by oven-drying or oven-roasting. Caramelize onions to remove water and add more flavor. If using a high-fat protein component such as sausage, brown it and render some of the fat first. Remember, you worked hard to make a perfect crust, so don't ruin the quiche by filling it with a bunch of vegetable water or greasy runoff.

 MAKE IT ALL VEGETARIAN: For this one, simply omit the bacon. Easy peasy.

 MAKE IT ALL MEAT: Increase the amount of bacon to 6 slices, and divide it equally between the two pie plates in step 5.

Huevos Rancheros

**Serves 2
vegetarians and
2 meat-eaters**

2 ¼ teaspoons vegetable
   oil, plus more as
   needed

½ small yellow onion,
   chopped

1 jalapeño chile, seeded
   and chopped

3 garlic cloves, diced

One 14.5-ounce can
   chopped tomatoes

Pinch of salt

Pinch of freshly ground
   black pepper

¼ cup Mexican chorizo

8 corn tortillas

8 large eggs

½ cup shredded
   Monterey Jack cheese
   (2 ounces)

A south-of-the-border superstar that's hit it big all around the United States, huevos rancheros, or ranch-style eggs, are cheered like a bullfighter for their simplicity, slightly spicy taste, and ability to jump-start your day (even if your day, unlike that of most ranchers, doesn't start until noon). The basic dish is simply a well-balanced combination of tortillas, eggs, and sauce, but boosting the olé factor with a bit of Monterey Jack cheese and some chorizo isn't much extra work and adds a nice extra bit of flavor. This recipe includes the sauce, though you conceivably could use canned or bottled enchilada sauce or salsa. But what kind of ranch would that be?

1. Heat 1 teaspoon of the vegetable oil in a medium-size saucepan over medium-high heat. Once the oil is hot, add the onion. Cook for 3 to 5 minutes, stirring regularly.

2. Add the jalapeño and the garlic to the pan, and cook for 5 more minutes, stirring regularly.

3. Add the tomatoes, salt, and pepper to the pan and stir well. Cook until the sauce begins to boil, then reduce the heat to low. Simmer the tomato sauce for 10 to 15 minutes.

4. Preheat the oven to 200°F.

5. Heat ¼ teaspoon of the oil in a small skillet or sauté pan over medium heat. Crumble in the chorizo, and cook for 5 minutes. Set aside.

6. Heat the remaining 1 teaspoon vegetable oil in a large skillet over medium-high heat. Once the oil is hot, place 2 of the tortillas in the pan. Cook them for 30 seconds on each side, then pat dry on a paper towel and place in the oven on a baking sheet to keep warm. Repeat with the remaining tortillas, adding a little more oil to the pan if you think it's needed.

7. Fry the eggs in the skillet in which you cooked the tortillas. How much to cook your eggs depends on preference, but in the traditional version of huevos rancheros the eggs are a little runny (over medium works nicely).

8. Remove the tortillas from the oven, and place two of them on each of four plates. Top each tortilla with a fried egg. On two of the plates, top the egg with half of the chorizo. Spread some of the tomato sauce over all four plates, then sprinkle some of the cheese over the sauce. Serve immediately.

Note: Some think that a little sour cream, and even a dash or two of Mexican hot sauce (such as Cholula) adds something to the huevos. If you're one of those people, act accordingly.

 MAKE IT ALL VEGETARIAN: Omit the chorizo to make the meal completely vegetarian.

 MAKE IT ALL MEAT: Increase the amount of chorizo to $1/2$ cup. In step 8, divide the chorizo among all four plates.

Hot and Gooey Ham and Cheesers

**Serves 3
vegetarians and
3 meat-eaters**

¼ cup stone-ground
mustard

¼ cup mayonnaise

12 slices whole wheat
bread

6 smoked ham slices

6 vegetarian ham slices

9 slices smoked cheddar
cheese

Gooey is good. Hot and gooey is even better. Hot and gooey and cheesy and hammy is delectable. Hot and gooey and cheesy and hammy between two slices of hearty whole wheat bread is a doubly delish delight. Hot and gooey and cheesy and hammy between two slices of hearty whole wheat bread served to pals both vegetarian and omnivorous while sipping summer beers (equal parts cold lager beer and lemonade topped with an ounce of vodka and a fresh lemon slice) at a spring luncheon while sitting outside in the sun is so good there hasn't been a word created yet to describe the feeling.

1. Preheat the oven to 425°F.

2. In a small bowl, stir together the mustard and mayonnaise. Spread some of the mixture on one side of each of the bread slices.

3. Place 3 of the bread slices, dry side down, on a cutting board. Top each piece of bread with 2 slices of the smoked ham and 1½ slices of the cheese—you want the cheese to go to the edge, but not hang over. Place a slice of bread, mustard-mayo side down, on top of the cheese.

4. Repeat step 3 with the remaining bread slices and cheese, but substituting vegetarian ham slices for the smoked ham.

5. Grease a large jelly-roll pan or baking sheet. Put the 6 sandwiches on the pan, then place the pan in the oven (being sure to remember which are vegetarian and which aren't). Bake for 5 minutes. Using tongs or other helpful oven-safe utensils, turn each sandwich over. Bake for 5 minutes more. The sandwiches should be gooey. Transfer the sandwiches to individual plates or a serving platter and serve immediately, so you don't lose any of the gooey-ness.

 MAKE IT ALL VEGETARIAN: Omit the smoked ham, and use 12 slices of vegetarian ham.

 MAKE IT ALL MEAT: Omit the vegetarian ham, and use 12 slices of smoked ham.

Sformato

Serves 3
vegetarians and
3 meat-eaters

1 tablespoon unsalted
butter

1 cup bread crumbs

½ teaspoon salt

2¼ pounds fresh spinach

3 cups Béchamel Sauce
(page 168)

1 cup grated Parmesan
cheese (4 ounces)

⅛ teaspoon freshly
ground black pepper

6 large eggs, separated

4 ounces sliced prosciutto

Sformato **seems like** the epitome of a brunch dish, due to its inclusion of that brunch staple, eggs, but also because its flexibility matches up with brunch's relaxed nature. There are many different kinds of *sformato*, but most commonly it is a soufflé-like savory dish baked in a mold. This version is adapted from *The Silver Spoon* (Phaidon Press, 2005)—a mighty cookbook that's a must for anyone who loves Italian food.

1. Preheat the oven to 350°F.

2. Grease the insides of two 10-inch ring molds with the butter. Carefully spread ½ cup of the bread crumbs in each ring mold, working to cover all sides of the mold.

3. Fill a medium-size saucepan three-quarters full with water, and bring it to a brisk simmer over medium-high heat. Add ¼ teaspoon of the salt. Blanch the spinach by dropping it into the water for a few seconds. Gather it out of the water and into a clean dishtowel, and wring as much green water out of the leaves as possible. Chop the spinach finely.

4. In a large bowl, combine the béchamel with the spinach, cheese, the remaining ¼ teaspoon salt, and the pepper. Add the egg yolks, one at a time, and mix well.

5. In a separate bowl, whisk the egg whites until they are stiff. Using a spatula, fold them into the béchamel mixture.

6. Line the inside of one of the molds completely with the prosciutto.

7. Pour half of the béchamel mixture into each of the molds. Place each mold in a roasting pan, and fill each pan with enough water to reach halfway up the sides of the mold. Carefully place the roasting pans in the oven, and bake for 50 to 60 minutes, until a knife inserted into the *sformato* comes out clean. Carefully remove the molds from the water, and let stand for 5 minutes. Slice the *sformati* and serve.

 MAKE IT ALL VEGETARIAN: Omit the prosciutto and skip step 6.

 MAKE IT ALL MEAT: Increase the amount of prosciutto to 8 ounces. In step 6, line each of the molds with 4 ounces of the prosciutto.

No-Struggle Strata

Serves 3
vegetarians and
3 meat-eaters

¾ cup loose breakfast
sausage (about 8
ounces)

6 vegetarian breakfast
sausage patties

12 slices whole wheat
bread

12 large eggs

3 cups milk

1½ teaspoons paprika

¾ teaspoon freshly
ground black pepper

½ teaspoon salt

3 cups shredded cheddar
cheese (12 ounces)

½ cup chopped yellow
onion

Strata sounds like it would be a struggle to prepare—the word seems to imply that there are so many layers involved you'd need to be an archeologist. But it's a snap—or, at most, a couple of snaps. The strata does require a bit of cooking, so be sure to figure that time into your brunch planning. Strata for brunch is a favorite for both of our families that can be made in multiple ways—this version uses plenty of cheese, eggs, sausage, and bread for hearty results.

1. Preheat the oven to 350°F.

2. Place a small skillet or saucepan on the stove over medium-high heat. Crumble in the breakfast sausage, and cook completely.

3. While the sausage is cooking, heat the vegetarian sausage patties according to the package directions. Coarsely chop the patties into 1/4- to 1/2-inch pieces.

4. Cut the bread into 1/2-inch pieces.

5. Combine the eggs, milk, paprika, pepper, and salt in a large bowl. Using a whisk or slotted spoon, mix well.

6. Place a layer of the bread pieces in the bottoms of two 9 x 13-inch baking pans, using one-quarter of the bread in each pan. Top the bread layer in each pan with 3/4 cup of the cheese, then 1/4 cup of the onion, then a layer of the sausage, using the cooked sausage in one pan and the chopped vegetarian sausage in the other. In each pan, top the sausage with half of the remaining bread and 3/4 cup of the cheese.

7. Pour half of the egg mixture into each pan. It should cover the top layer of bread.

8. Bake the stratas for 1 hour. A knife inserted into the center of the strata (use a separate knife for each pan) should come out clean. If it does not, cook the stratas a little longer, checking for doneness at 5-minute intervals. Remove the pans from the oven and let rest for 5 minutes before cutting and serving.

 MAKE IT ALL VEGETARIAN: Omit the loose breakfast sausage and use 12 vegetarian breakfast sausage patties. In step 6, use half of the chopped vegetarian sausage in each pan.

 MAKE IT ALL MEAT: Omit the vegetarian breakfast sausage patties, and use 1 1/2 cups loose breakfast sausage. In step 6, use half of the cooked breakfast sausage in each pan.

Pipin' Pipérade

Serves 3
vegetarians and
3 meat-eaters

2 medium-size yellow
    onions

2 green bell peppers

2 red bell peppers

4 medium-size tomatoes

2 tablespoons olive oil

2 garlic cloves, diced

½ teaspoon chopped
    fresh flat-leaf parsley

½ teaspoon chopped
    fresh marjoram

½ teaspoon kosher salt

¼ teaspoon freshly
    ground black pepper

½ cup cubed smoked
    ham

8 large eggs

A Basque dish, *pipérade* traditionally contains bell peppers, onions, and tomatoes, spiced up and cooked in one big skillet, but different versions of it add other ingredients—for example, Basque shepherds in New Mexico tended to add eggs, while others add ham or other meats. We say, the more the merrier. This simple dictum applies also to the number of skillets used; we break with tradition here by using two skillets, one for the meat-eaters and one for the vegetarians. You want everyone to feel involved, so that way, no one shirks their duty when it comes time to herd those sheep. Serve with big chunks of hearty bread for sopping up all the juices.

1. Peel the onions and cut them in half, and core and seed the peppers. Slice the onions and peppers into long, thin, strips (one of the keys to a good *pipérade* is the vegetables being in strips). Core and chop the tomatoes, reserving their juice.

2. Add 4½ teaspoons of the oil to a large skillet over medium heat. Once the oil is hot, add the onions and cook for about 10 minutes, stirring, until softened.

3. Add the peppers to the skillet, and cook for about 10 more minutes, until the peppers are softened.

4. Add the tomatoes and their juice, the garlic, parsley, marjoram, salt, and pepper to the skillet. Simmer for 25 to 30 minutes, until the mixture has a fairly thick, almost puree-like consistency. Reduce the heat to medium-low.

5. Add the remaining 1½ teaspoons oil to another large skillet over medium-high heat. Add the ham, and cook for 5 minutes. Take half of the onion-pepper-tomato mixture and transfer it to the skillet with the ham. Reduce the heat to medium-low and mix well.

6. Beat the eggs in a large bowl, then pour half of the eggs into each skillet. Cook the eggs slowly, until they just start to get firm—they should be soft and not tough. Serve the *pipérade* immediately in bowls.

 MAKE IT ALL VEGETARIAN: Omit the ham, reduce the amount of oil to 4 1/2 teaspoons, and skip step 5, cooking everything in one skillet.

 MAKE IT ALL MEAT: Increase the amount of ham to 1 cup, reduce the amount of olive oil to 4 1/2 teaspoons, and in step 4 add the ham to the skillet with all of the veggies, making it a one-skillet meal.

A Bridging BLT

Makes 6 sandwiches · 3 for vegetarians and 3 for meat-eaters

12 slices hearty whole wheat bread, toasted

2 tablespoons mayonnaise

9 bacon slices, cooked until not quite crisp (page 195)

12 romaine lettuce leaves

2 large tomatoes, cut into ¼-inch-thick slices

9 vegetarian bacon slices (we like Morningstar Farms), cooked according to package directions

One doesn't think of opposing parties coming together over a plate of sandwiches, which typically are served at lunchtime. Who, after all, sees important decisions being made over lunch in a political thriller, or reads about a serious state lunch in the daily newspaper? Ah, but this is how they (the mysterious "they") have fooled you, because lunch is where people come together and are open to listening to others' opinions in a way that they are less willing to at breakfast (too early) or dinner (too rule-based). Perhaps the perfect item to serve in these situations (which may be only as serious as bringing siblings with different diets together) is the BLT. Simple yet tasty, crisp and warm, savory and subtle, the BLT is our nominee for the ideal lunch diplomat.

1. Place 6 slices of the toasted bread on a clean work surface. Smear ½ teaspoon of the mayonnaise on each of the slices. Top 3 of the bread slices with 3 of the bacon slices (breaking the slices in half to fit the bread as needed), 2 of the lettuce leaves, and 2 tomato slices.

2. Top the remaining 3 prepared bread slices with 3 vegetarian bacon slices (breaking to fit the bread as needed), 2 lettuce leaves, and 2 tomato slices.

3. Spread ½ teaspoon mayonnaise on each of the remaining 6 bread slices, and place them on top of the tomatoes, mayo side down.

4. Using a separate knife for the vegetarian and meaty sandwiches, carefully cut each sandwich in half (you don't want any of that bacon escaping), and serve.

Note: BLTs also make dandy finger foods for a party. Once you've constructed the sandwiches, put a toothpick in the center of each quarter. Cut each sandwich into 4 pieces. Place the mini sandwiches on serving platters (one meat, one vegetarian), and serve.

 MAKE IT ALL VEGETARIAN: Want to take the pig away from the party? Omit the bacon, and increase the amount of vegetarian bacon to 18 slices.

 MAKE IT ALL MEAT: Want your BLT to be a bridge just for meat-lovers? Omit the vegetarian bacon, and increase the amount of bacon to 18 slices.

Serious Soufflé

Serves 4
vegetarians and
4 meat-eaters

2½ tablespoons unsalted
butter

2 tablespoons all-purpose
flour

¼ teaspoon salt

⅛ teaspoon cayenne
pepper

¼ teaspoon freshly
ground black pepper

¼ teaspoon dry mustard

1½ cups milk

½ cup grated Parmesan
cheese (2 ounces)

1½ cups shredded
cheddar cheese
(6 ounces)

5 large eggs, separated

¾ cup chopped cooked
ham

Oh, the soufflé. It's the Headless Horseman of brunch favorites. Mention its name and a hush descends on the room, and everyone becomes so serious you'd think that cooking up a cheesy cloud-like creation was as dangerous as going up against that hellacious horse rider. But we're redirecting the "serious" here—as in, "Get serious." The soufflé is a fluffy dish, by golly, and one you shouldn't fear (though, we have to say, it did scare A.J. quite a bit before he actually tried making one; he had been accustomed to just slapping his signature on the check after eating one in a restaurant). You must keep a close eye on the soufflé as it cooks to keep it from caving in, and make sure your egg whites are folded in lightly, but don't get scared and lose your head over it.

1. Preheat the oven to 350°F.

2. Melt the butter in a large saucepan over medium heat. Once the butter is foaming, add the flour and whisk the butter and flour together until they make a smooth paste.

3. Whisk in the salt, cayenne, black pepper, and dry mustard, then whisk in the milk. Continue whisking until the milk is completely incorporated and the mixture has thickened, but do not allow it to boil.

4. Remove the pan from the heat, and stir in the cheeses. Set aside.

5. In a large bowl, beat the egg whites briskly until they form soft peaks.

6. In a separate large bowl, beat the egg yolks until they start to thicken but are still fluffy. Add the yolks slowly, a bit at a time, to the saucy cheese mixture, blending thoroughly, until all of the yolks have been incorporated.

7. Using a spatula, slowly and carefully fold the egg whites into the cheese mixture. Keep folding until all of the egg whites have been incorporated and no streaks of egg white remain.

8. Place the ham in a soufflé dish or other straight-sided baking dish. Pour half of the egg and cheese mixture over the ham, carefully (using that spatula again) mixing in the ham.

9. Pour the rest of the egg and cheese mixture into a second soufflé dish. Place both dishes in the oven and bake for 45 minutes. The soufflés should be a nice golden color on top, and be set but still fluffy. Serve immediately.

 MAKE IT ALL VEGETARIAN: Omit the ham.

 MAKE IT ALL MEAT: Increase the amount of ham to 1 1/2 cups. In step 8, place 3/4 cup of the ham in each soufflé dish.

Welsh Rabbit

Serves 2
vegetarians and
2 meat-eaters

1½ cups pale ale–style
beer

1½ teaspoons dry
mustard

2 dashes of Tabasco or
other hot sauce

3 cups shredded sharp
cheddar cheese
(12 ounces)

2 eggs

8 slices whole wheat
bread, toasted

8 bacon slices, cooked
until crisp (page 195)

½ teaspoon freshly
ground black pepper

There's no reason to lie—one of us (okay, the initialed one) for years thought that this contained actual rabbit. It doesn't, of course, contain meat as a rule, but since the term *Welsh rabbit* started being used to describe a bit of cheese sauce on toast (the first mention of it, according to the *Oxford English Dictionary*, was in 1725), there have been numerous variations on the theme. We like the versions that contain beer, and we're making our own up here to include a bit of bacon (which the omnivore among us thinks makes the meal). This dish also goes by the name *Welsh rarebit*.

1. Preheat the oven to broil.

2. In a medium-size saucepan, whisk together the beer, dry mustard, and Tabasco over medium-high heat.

3. Add the cheese to the pan in small batches, whisking well after each addition before adding the next batch. When all the cheese has been added, cook until the mixture is smooth, about 5 minutes, whisking continuously.

4. In a small bowl, lightly beat the eggs. When the yolks and whites are combined, slowly pour the eggs into the saucepan, whisking the whole time. Reduce the heat to medium and continue to whisk the mixture until it thickens, 5 to 7 minutes.

5. Place 4 slices of the toast in a large baking dish, and top each piece of toast with 2 bacon slices (if a little bacon breaking is needed to fit the bread, that's okay). Place the remaining 4 slices of toast in another large baking dish. Top all of the toast slices with the cheese sauce. Sprinkle some of the pepper on each piece of toast.

6. Place both baking dishes in the oven, and broil for 2 to 3 minutes, until the cheese sauce gets bubbly and a bit brown on top—keep an eye on it so nothing gets burned. Serve immediately, either by bringing the baking dishes right to the table or by transferring the slices to individual plates.

Note: Some people like a bit of broiled tomato on their Welsh rabbit. If you're one of them, just slice a whole tomato and broil the slices in the oven for a few minutes, then add them to the toast slices in step 5, before the cheese sauce.

 MAKE IT ALL VEGETARIAN: It's easy: Just omit the bacon.

 MAKE IT ALL MEAT: Increase the amount of bacon to 16 slices. In step 5, place 2 bacon slices on all 8 pieces of toast.

Pissaladière

Serves 2
vegetarians and
2 meat-eaters

5 tablespoons olive oil

4 medium-size onions,
sliced into rings

2 teaspoons sugar

All-purpose flour for
rolling the dough

1 recipe pizza dough
(page 148), divided
into quarters

1 teaspoon freshly
ground black pepper

¼ cup drained capers

½ cup good-quality black
olives, such as Niçoise
or Moroccan oil-cured,
pitted and halved

2 tablespoons plus 2
teaspoons fresh thyme
leaves

4 ounces anchovy fillets,
preferably white
anchovies packed in a
light brine or oil

1 bunch fresh flat-leaf
parsley, chopped, for
garnish

Who says the French can't make a good pizza—or at least a rather addictive flatbread with toppings that very closely resembles pizza? With Nice located just a stone's throw from Italy, is it any surprise that just such a delicacy should arise? *Pissaladière* is a specialty of Nice, based on a local condiment called *pissalat* or *pissala*, which is anchovy puree flavored with thyme, bay leaf, cloves, and pepper and blended with olive oil. *Pissaladière* is essentially a flatbread topped with (warning: buzzword ahead) a deconstructed *pissalat* as well as lightly caramelized onions, capers, and olives. Savory and salt freaks, this is the recipe for you; just be sure to have handy *un petit pichet* of a cool and lovely rosé, perhaps one from Nice's nice neighbors in Provence.

1. Place a pizza stone or inverted baking sheet in the oven and preheat the oven to 450°F. If your pizza stone or baking sheet is sufficiently large, you will be able to bake two *pissaladières* at a time.

2. To caramelize the onions, heat 1 tablespoon of the olive oil in a large sauté pan over medium-high heat. Add the onions and the sugar. Stirring frequently, cook until the onions are a deep brown, but have not become black or burned.

3. On a well-floured work surface, roll out the dough pieces into rectangles that are about 5 x 12 inches, leaving the edges slightly thicker than the middle. Prick the middle of the dough with a fork so it won't rise during baking.

4. Brush the top of each piece of dough with 1 tablespoon olive oil and sprinkle each with ¼ teaspoon pepper. Top each piece with one-quarter of the onions, 1 tablespoon of the capers, 2 tablespoons of the olives, and 2 teaspoons of the thyme.

5. Divide the anchovies between 2 of the dough pieces, arranging the anchovies in a latticework pattern.

6. Making sure the bottom of the dough is well floured, transfer one anchovy-topped *pis-saladière* onto the preheated pizza stone or inverted baking sheet with a pizza peel or other suitable tool (a thin, flexible plastic cutting mat also works well). Bake for about 10 minutes, until the crust is nicely browned. Repeat with the remaining three *pissaladières*.

7. Garnish each *pissaladière* with some of the parsley as it comes out of the oven. Serve hot.

Note: Got no time to make pizza dough, what with all the rising, punching, and waiting? Ask the proprietor of your favorite local pizzeria if you can buy some dough—they generally have tons on hand, especially around dinnertime, and are unlikely to say no.

 MAKE IT ALL VEGETARIAN: Omit the anchovies, and skip step 5.

 MAKE IT ALL MEAT: Increase the amount of anchovy fillets to 8 ounces, and divide them equally among all the *pissaladières* in step 5.

Sanitize Your Kitchen Situation

This book is all about putting aside petty differences between omnivores and herbivores; however, this book is not all about getting salmonella from the Salmagundi. Especially for brave vegetarians who have been inspired by this book to enter the world of cooking for omnivores, here are a few simple tips for keeping everyone happy and healthy.

In keeping with basic kitchen sanitation, wash your hands and cooking surfaces early and often. Not everyone agrees, but I'm a big fan of a good wipedown with a three-to-one water-bleach solution. I also like to clean with a good orange oil–based surface cleanser.

Consider purchasing extra cutting boards or earmarking current cutting boards for meat use only. Although a thorough scrubbing with soap and water will eliminate most harmful bacteria, be sensitive to vegetarians who may not want their tofu sliced on the same board as a T-bone. An old kitchen trick for wooden cutting boards that I like to employ is a good salt scrub done with half a lemon after the board has been washed with soap and water. Then give it another rinse with hot water and *poof*—you have a double-sanitized, lemony-fresh cutting board.

Keep your meat in tidy packages in the refrigerator until ready for use. If anything is a little leaky when you've brought it home from the butcher shop or grocery store, give it a quick rinse and repackage it in a zipper-top plastic bag or other sealable container. It's always a good idea to purchase your meat as close to the time you will use it as possible, for both taste and sanitation reasons.

Finally, prepare all meat items last whenever possible, especially chicken. When you encounter a recipe in the book that requires the meat portion of the dish to be started before the vegetarian portion, follow these steps: 1) prepare any necessary non-meat items and keep them in separate bowls with lids, 2) assemble any meat components as necessary and begin cooking according to the recipe instructions, and 3) while the meat dish is on the stovetop or in the oven cooking, give all surfaces and utensils a thorough cleaning.

soups, salads & sandwiches

what would the American table be without an

assortment of soups, salads, and sandwiches to provide a break from standard entrée fare and to serve as tasty options for lunch and dinner (and even, on occasion, breakfast) that aren't too time-consuming? It would be a much less fun place to be, that's what. Soups, salads, and sandwiches tend to be key players in everyday eating when you want something delicious (and maybe warming, in the case of soup) but don't want to sweat over it. These favorites are ideal when you're sitting around playing a marathon domino match with a few friends, or after an afternoon spent making snowmen on a chilly December day. And what about a spring picnic featuring all three of these indispensable friends? Envision a basket containing a thermos of hot soup, a fresh salad to be dressed while you're sitting on a checkered blanket, and some nice sandwiches that have been pressed to perfection under some dishware and that half-bottle of Beaujolais you cleverly brought along.

This chapter aims to help you live out these idyllic scenes and myriad others. Salmagundi is an ideal offering for a brunch party at any time of year or for a summer wing-ding, even for a larger group—throw some slices of bread alongside this salad and you have an amazing sandwich bar/buffet. Anyone who is not seduced by a bubbling crock of French Onion Soup served fireside on a cold winter's night might need to have their pulse checked. And for a cheap ticket to the Big Easy, cook up a mess of Gumbo and some Po' Boys. No matter which recipe in this chapter you choose, it will surely transport you to somewhere special.

Year-Round Minestrone

Serves 2 to 3 vegetarians and 2 to 3 meat-eaters

3 tablespoons olive oil

1 medium-size yellow onion, finely chopped

2 medium-size carrots, chopped

2 celery stalks, chopped

2 garlic cloves, minced

One 14.5-ounce can diced tomatoes

1 pound mixed chopped vegetables

5 sprigs fresh oregano, leaves only

One 15-ounce can cannellini or other white beans, drained

1 quart chicken stock or broth, homemade (page 100) or store-bought

1 quart vegetable stock or broth, homemade (page 100) or store-bought

4 ounces pasta shells

1 cup grated Parmesan cheese (4 ounces)

British art-rock band 10cc had it right: "Life is a minestrone, served up with Parmesan cheese. . . ." Minestrone recipes, like life, have a few common elements (onions, carrots, celery, beans, starch in the form of pasta or rice, and tomatoes more often than not), but then the rest of the story is up to the individual, a story heavily shaped by time and place. Traditionally in the milieu of Italian *cucina povera* ("poor kitchen" or "cooking of the poor"), this "big soup" (from *minestra* = soup and *-one* = large) would be made with water, taking most of its flavor from the ingredients added to it. Here we'll cook from the "*cucina* middle class" and use some stock. Use whatever seasonal vegetables you like, and serve with toasted crusty bread.

1. Heat 1½ teaspoons of the olive oil in each of two large soup pots over medium heat. Add half of the onion, carrots, celery, and garlic to each pot, and cook for about 5 minutes, stirring occasionally. Add half of the tomatoes, mixed vegetables, oregano, and beans to each pot.

2. Add the chicken stock to one pot and the vegetable stock to the other pot. Raise the heat to medium-high and simmer lightly for about 10 minutes to allow the flavors of the vegetables to infuse the soup.

3. Meanwhile, cook the pasta in salted boiling water for 4 minutes. Drain, divide between the pots, and simmer for another 5 minutes.

4. Ladle the soups into bowls, and sprinkle each bowl with some of the Parmesan. Serve immediately.

 MAKE IT ALL VEGETARIAN: Omit the chicken stock, and use 2 quarts vegetable stock.

 MAKE IT ALL MEAT: Omit the vegetable stock, and use 2 quarts chicken stock.

Chicken or No-Chicken Noodle Soup

2 tablespoons olive oil

1 large yellow onion,
chopped

2 medium-size carrots,
chopped

2 celery stalks, chopped

2 teaspoons salt

½ teaspoon freshly
ground black pepper

6 ounces roasted chicken
(page 115), cut into
bite-size pieces

1 quart chicken stock
or broth, homemade
(page 100) or store-
bought

2 bay leaves

1 quart vegetable stock
or broth, homemade
(page 100) or store-
bought

Origin of Chicken Noodle Soup, Hypothesis #303: An atheist chicken, a priest, and a rabbi walk into a bar. They order their respective drinks and before long the talk turns, naturally, to the subject of religion. The rabbi and the priest are having a convivial debate about the nature of the Holy Trinity along the usual well-established lines. Meanwhile, the atheist chicken, without much to say on the subject, is just getting soused. After a while, the chicken, fully in his cups by this time, turns to the other two and proclaims loudly in drunken-chicken speak, "There is no God," then promptly passes out. When the chicken finally comes to, he finds himself in a pot on the stove. A fatalist at heart, the chicken, resigned to his demise, says, "I could have guessed when I walked into a bar with a priest and a rabbi I'd get into some hot water—I just didn't know there were that many nonbelieving carrots, too."

1. In a large soup pot, heat the oil over medium-high heat for 1 minute.

2. Add the onion, carrots, and celery, and reduce the heat to medium. Season with the salt and pepper. Cook the vegetables, stirring constantly, for 2 to 3 minutes. Do not allow them to become brown.

3. Transfer half of the vegetable mix to a second large soup pot, and add the roasted chicken, the chicken stock, and one of the bay leaves to the second pot. Bring to a simmer only; do not boil or you'll end up with a cloudy-looking soup. Simmer for 30 minutes.

4. Meanwhile, add the vegetable stock and the remaining bay leaf to the first pot. Bring to a simmer only; do not boil or you'll end up with a cloudy-looking soup. Simmer for 30 minutes.

5. Add half of the parboiled noodles to each pot, and simmer for another 2 minutes.

6 ounces dried egg noodles, parboiled for 5 minutes and drained, or 1 recipe Spaetzle (page 162), parboiled for 1 minute and drained

1 vegetarian chicken breast, cooked according to package directions and sliced

6. Add the vegetarian chicken to the first pot and simmer until it is heated through. Serve the soups piping hot.

 MAKE IT ALL VEGETARIAN: Omit the roasted chicken and chicken stock. Increase the amount of vegetable stock to 2 quarts, and use 2 vegetarian chicken breasts.

 MAKE IT ALL MEAT: Omit the vegetarian chicken breast and the vegetable stock. Increase the amount of roasted chicken to 12 ounces and the amount of chicken stock to 2 quarts.

Cream of Mushroom Soup

Serves 2 to 3 vegetarians and 2 to 3 meat-eaters

½ cup (1 stick) unsalted butter

¼ cup olive oil

1 pound mushrooms of your choice, sliced

1 medium-size white onion, finely chopped

2 sprigs fresh thyme, leaves and stems separated

1½ teaspoons salt

½ teaspoon freshly ground black pepper

2 tablespoons all-purpose flour

2 tablespoons cornstarch

¼ cup dry sherry

1 cup vegetable stock or broth, homemade (page 100) or store-bought

Dateline: Friday, November 23, 1973, White Bear Lake, Minnesota—the day after Thanksgiving. A package of Tater Tots thaws on the counter alongside remnants from yesterday's turkey, a bag of frozen peas and carrots, and a familiar-looking red and white can. The whir of the electric can opener signals that our heroes are to endure another turkey-and-processed-potato hot dish, just one more in a seemingly endless parade of cream of mushroom–based casseroles. The contents of another red and white can have already found their way into a slow cooker, along with a block of Velveeta and a can of Ro-Tel tomatoes, re-creating a recipe from an aunt in Texas that was written on the back of a postcard depicting the Alamo. But fear not, readers—it is a new millennium, and we are here to put the "soup" back in cream of mushroom soup. Any mushrooms will work here, but why not delve a little deeper into the mycological magic shop? Chanterelle, cremini, lobster, morel, porcini, matsutake, hen-of-the-woods—go crazy! (P.S.: Good ol' button mushrooms will also do the job.) Serve with some crusty bread.

1. Heat the butter and oil in a medium-size stockpot over medium-high heat. When the butter is melted, add the mushrooms, onion, and thyme stems. Reduce the heat to medium. Add the salt and pepper.

2. Continue cooking over medium heat, stirring occasionally, for 15 to 20 minutes, until the mushrooms take on a slightly bronzed look and any liquid in the pan is clear. If there are some bits of stuff stuck to the bottom of the pot, do not fret as long as they aren't overly brown or burned. This is mushroom *fond*, and it equals good flavor for your soup.

3. Add the flour and cornstarch to the pot, and stir constantly for 1 minute. Add the sherry, stirring constantly for 30 seconds to scrape up any sticky bits from the bottom of the pot. This deglazing will create an unsightly thick and gooey mass, but not to worry as long as the stirring continues and your stock is ready nearby.

1 cup chicken stock or broth, homemade (page 100) or store-bought

2 cups heavy cream

2 cups whole milk

2 generous pinches of freshly grated nutmeg

White truffle oil for garnish

½ bunch fresh flat-leaf parsley, chopped, for garnish

4. Take half of the contents of the pot and transfer to a second medium-size stockpot.

5. Add the vegetable stock to the first pot and the chicken stock to the second pot, and stir both (using different spoons). Your gooey masses will thin out nicely—be sure every bit on the bottom of the pots gets mixed in. Raise the heat to medium-high and cook until the contents of the pots are reduced by one-half, 5 to 10 minutes, stirring occasionally. Discard the thyme stems.

6. Add 1 cup of the cream to each pot, and continue to cook until the mixture returns to a light bubble; continue cooking for about 5 minutes, adjusting the heat as needed to keep a light simmer.

7. Add 1 cup of the milk to each pot, and bring to a slow simmer only, then simmer for 5 to 10 minutes. (Bringing the mixture to a boil after adding the milk runs the risk of "breaking" or slightly curdling the soup. It will not taste bad, but it will not be as smooth as the beautiful creation one might have hoped for.) Add a pinch of the nutmeg and half of the thyme leaves to each pot, and stir.

8. Ladle the soup into bowls, garnish each bowl with a few drops of white truffle oil and a dash of parsley, and serve.

 MAKE IT ALL VEGETARIAN: Omit the chicken stock, and use 2 cups vegetable stock.

 MAKE IT ALL MEAT: Omit the vegetable stock, and use 2 cups chicken stock.

French Onion Soup

Serves 2
vegetarians and
2 meat-eaters

¼ cup (½ stick) unsalted
   butter

¼ cup olive oil

4 large yellow onions,
   thinly sliced

1 teaspoon sugar

1 teaspoon salt

½ teaspoon freshly
   ground black pepper

2 tablespoons all-purpose
   flour

1 cup white wine or dry
   vermouth (see Note)

2 cups chicken stock
   or broth, homemade
   (page 100) or store-
   bought, or beef broth

2 cups vegetable stock
   or broth, homemade
   (page 100) or store-
   bought

One rumor has it that King Louis XV of France created this soup one night upon discovering he had only onions, butter, and champagne at his man-shack in the hunting woods. Interestingly, the accounts never mention where the beef stock might have come from. Others credit the soup's invention to Louis XIV—perhaps because some people think the Sun King was behind everything in France. Another funny food legend says that Napoleon created the soup on the battlefield, having only onions, wine, and a French proclivity for the eating of horse meat. This confusion leads to the refrain "Lou-ie, Lou-ie, Fourteen or Fifteen—who-made-the-soup-in-this-tureen?" You know what, though? When serving this soup on a cold day, it doesn't even matter who invented it.

1. Preheat the oven to 450°F.

2. Heat the butter and oil over medium-high heat in a medium-size soup pot until the butter is melted. Add the onions and sugar (the sugar will assist in the caramelization of the onions). Add the salt and pepper. Reduce the heat to medium. Stir the onions frequently until they take on a nice cappuccino color. This may take 15 minutes or so of rather constant stirring.

3. Add the flour and stir for another minute. Raise the heat to high and add the wine. Stir to deglaze, being sure to scrape any sticky bits from the bottom of the pot. Stir for another minute.

4. Transfer half of the mixture to a second soup pot.

5. Heat both of the stocks (microwaving is fine), then add the meat stock to one pot and the vegetable stock to the other. Stir both pots (with different spoons), and bring them to a simmer.

6. While the soup is simmering gently, place the bread slices on a baking sheet and slide them into the oven. Bake until they're lightly golden brown on each side. When they are nicely toasted, remove from the oven and rub each with one of the garlic halves. Preheat the broiler.

Eight ½- to 1-inch-thick slices French bread

4 garlic cloves, halved

2 cups shredded Emmenthaler cheese (8 ounces)

7. Ladle the soup into individual ovenproof bowls. Place one of the toasted bread slices in each bowl and sprinkle each with 1/2 cup of the cheese.

8. Remembering which bowls are meaty and which are vegetarian, place them on a baking sheet to catch any drips or spills, then place the sheet under the broiler until the cheese is nicely browned, about 5 minutes. Serve immediately with the remaining toasted bread slices.

Note: Much fuss is made over the quality of wine one should use for cooking. The only rule we follow is that we cook with what we drink, but that doesn't mean we wouldn't keep a bottle of wine that's been opened for drinking purposes in the fridge for a week or so to use for cooking purposes. Trust us, it doesn't matter whether you've just popped the cork on a magnificent bottle of wine moments ago or it's been open for several days— if you are applying heat to it in the sauté pan or oven, it's going to oxidize, changing the flavor of the wine enough so that any subtleties are lost. So save the fresh stuff for drinking and use your leftovers for cooking.

Variation: For an Italian twist, omit the Emmenthaler, and add 2 minced garlic cloves and one 15-ounce can of crushed tomatoes to the soup when simmering in step 5. Just before serving, gently crack 2 eggs into each pot of simmering soup, being careful to not break the yolks, and poach the eggs for 3 to 4 minutes. Gently ladle the soup into bowls, toss in a toasted bread slice, and slide a poached egg atop the bread. Garnish with some grated Parmesan and fresh parsley, and serve the remaining bread slices on the side. You now have a simple version of the superb Tuscan soup called *acqua cotta*.

 MAKE IT ALL VEGETARIAN: Omit the meat stock, and use 4 cups vegetable stock.

 MAKE IT ALL MEAT: Omit the vegetable stock, and use 4 cups meat stock.

Reducing Stock

One of the basic tenets of any kitchen, whether home or professional, omnivore or vegetarian, should be waste avoidance. There is probably no more delicious an example of this than *glace de viande*, which is French for "meat glaze." After a meat stock is made, there's still a whole lotta love to be extracted from that somewhat unsightly bony detritus. *Glace de viande* can be used to thicken pan sauces, giving them a more luxurious texture, or to coat a piece of meat. You can buy small containers of *glace de viande* (often labeled *demi-glace*, which is actually a reduction of Espagnole sauce and brown stock with sherry added) for a pretty penny, but you can also make it at home for practically no pennies.

Vegetables lack the gelatin required to give a *glace de viande* its silky-smooth shine and appealing mouthfeel. With the help of the natural complex carbohydrates found in vegetables, aided by some concentrated vegetable-based protein sources, our recipe for vegetarian *glace* is an elegant and inexpensive technique sure to improve the flavor of that next tofu steak or vegetarian pan sauce.

Vegetable Glace

MAKES ABOUT 1 CUP

2 quarts vegetable stock or broth, homemade (page 100) or store-bought

3 ounces tomato paste

3 tablespoons Marmite or Vegemite

3 tablespoons light miso paste

Combine all of the ingredients in a stockpot and simmer over low heat. Strain the mixture into consecutively smaller pots, reducing the heat as the mixture thickens. Reduce until the mixture will coat the back of a spoon without quickly dripping. This *glace* won't be as thick as the meat version, but it will be very close. You can store the *glace* in a glass jar in the freezer for up to 3 months.

Glace de Viande

The heat will need to be lowered gradually and continuously through the cooking process to avoid scorching the ever-thickening *glace*. Feel free to strain the mixture into consecutively smaller pots, as this will also help prevent overheating. Some occasional skimming of the surface is helpful, too.

MAKES ABOUT ¼ CUP

Leftover bones from chicken stock (page 100)
2 carrots, peeled and broken into a few large pieces
1 celery stalk, broken into a few large pieces
1 medium-size onion, cut in half
10 peppercorns
1 tablespoon tomato paste

1. Place the bones, carrots, celery, onion, and peppercorns, plus enough cold water to cover them, in a large stockpot, and bring it to a simmer. Simmer for 3 to 4 hours.

2. Strain the stock into a clean pot. Discard the solids.

3. Reduce the stock over medium-low heat until there is about 1 quart of liquid. Whisk in the tomato paste.

4. Reduce the heat to low, and continue reducing until a spoonful dropped onto a plate and refrigerated sets up like your Aunt Glenda's Jell-O salad. You now have *glace de viande*. This can be poured into a small glass jar while still quite warm, then cooled in the refrigerator and stored in the freezer. A warmed spoon is all you'll need to remove a little from the jar. This can keep for 3 to 4 weeks in the refrigerator or up to 1 year in the freezer.

Gumbo

Serves 4 to 5 vegetarians and 4 to 5 meat-eaters

4 quarts chicken stock or broth, homemade (page 100) or store-bought

4 quarts vegetable stock or broth, homemade (page 100) or store-bought, warmed

1 pound shrimp (any size), peeled and deveined, with the heads, shells, and tails reserved

6 tablespoons (¾ stick) unsalted butter

6 tablespoons flour, preferably whole wheat

1 pound chicken thighs, skinned and cut into 2-inch pieces

8 ounces andouille sausage links, cut into ¼- to ½-inch slices

We both are big fans of Southern cooking, especially the Cajun and Creole cuisines of Louisiana (and we both are a bit wary of folks who aren't fans of such). Jeremy's wife, Megan, lived in New Orleans for five years, and they spent the first 18 months of their courtship in a long-distance relationship between the Crescent City and the Twin Cities. Many stars aligned, and he was able to spend a week or so monthly down South visiting Megan and her awesome friends (as well as our mutual awesome friends and Bywater denizens Ed, Jill, Erik, and Laura). All this visiting and sharing of meals led to the creation of a meat/no-meat gumbo long ago, making it one of the first *Double Take* recipes. Serve with a scoop of long-grain white rice, a pinch of filé powder if that's your thing, and some nice vinegary Louisiana hot sauce. If you had a cold Dixie beer to go with it, that would be heaven.

1. Put one large pot on the stovetop, and add the chicken stock. Throw the reserved shrimp heads, peels, and tails into the pot. Bring to a low simmer and simmer for 1 hour, then strain the stock into a bowl and set aside.

2. Over low to medium-low heat, melt 3 tablespoons of the butter in each of two stockpots. Add 3 tablespoons of the flour to each pot and whisk to incorporate. Although not technically difficult, this step takes patience, paying close attention to the pot. The color (and hence flavor) of the roux being created here is a matter of personal preference, but we're shooting for a medium-beige. This should take 5 to 10 minutes of stirring.

3. When the roux is approaching its desired color, add the chicken and andouille to one stockpot and the mushrooms to the other pot. Stirring rather frequently, allow these new kids in the pot to contribute their flavors to the roux. This should take another 5 to 10 minutes. If you perceive that the roux is getting too dark, reduce the heat or remove the pot from the heat altogether.

4. Add half of the chopped onion, chopped celery, bell pepper, and garlic to each pot. Sweat these aromatics in the roux mixtures for 5 to 10 minutes, stirring often, until the vegetables are softened. Adding the aromatics

1 pound button mushrooms, halved

1 large onion, chopped

3 celery stalks, chopped

1 green bell pepper, seeded and chopped

4 garlic cloves, minced

1 pound mixed crab legs and lump crabmeat, legs separated at the joints

1 pound fresh okra, chopped into ½ -inch pieces

1 pound smoked tofu, oven-dried to remove moisture (page 48)

1 pound vegetarian chicken, cut into 2-inch pieces

will all but halt any further browning of the roux as long as the low temperature is maintained.

5. Add the strained chicken stock to the pot with the chicken and sausage, and add the vegetable stock to the pot with the mushrooms. Using separate whisks for each pot, whisk the contents and bring to a simmer. Things may look a little unsightly until the stocks come to a simmer, but don't fret—it'll all come together. Add the crab to the meaty pot, and continue to simmer both pots for 10 to 15 minutes. Add half of the okra to each pot and simmer for another 10 minutes.

6. Add the shrimp to the meaty pot, and add the tofu and vegetarian chicken to the vegetarian pot. Stir to incorporate everything, turn off the heat, cover the pots, and allow the residual heat to cook these last ingredients for 5 minutes. Serve immediately.

 MAKE IT ALL VEGETARIAN: Omit the chicken stock, shrimp, chicken, sausage, and crab. Use 8 quarts vegetable stock, 2 pounds tofu, and 2 pounds vegetarian chicken. If you have a large enough pot, you can cook everything together.

 MAKE IT ALL MEAT: Omit the vegetable stock, tofu, and vegetarian chicken. Use 8 quarts chicken stock, 2 pounds shrimp, 2 pounds chicken, 1 pound sausage, and 2 pounds crab. If you have a large enough pot, you can cook everything together.

Lamb and Lambless Stew

Serves 2 to 3
vegetarians and
2 to 3 meat-eaters

There are so many ways to go with lamb stew: How about Greek-style, with tomato and mint? Or perhaps give it a Moroccan flavor with olives and preserved lemon? What about an Indian curry with some lentils? Any way you spice it, lamb stew is great, but it seems that more often than not we picture it in a pub, nourishing woolen sweater–clad folks by an inviting hearth providing protection against the gales of an unforgiving North Sea.

3 tablespoons olive oil

1 pound boneless lamb shoulder, cut into bite-size pieces

4 large portobello mushrooms, chopped (stems included)

½ teaspoon salt

½ teaspoon freshly ground black pepper

1 medium-size yellow onion, coarsely chopped

1 medium-size carrot, coarsely chopped

1 celery stalk, coarsely chopped

1 leek (white part only), thinly sliced into rounds

8 ounces waxy potatoes, such as Yukon gold, coarsely chopped

1. Preheat the oven to 400°F.

2. Heat 1½ teaspoons of the oil in each of two medium-size, heavy, flameproof casserole dishes over medium-high heat. Add the lamb to one dish and the mushrooms to the other, and brown, stirring frequently, for about 5 minutes.

3. Season each dish with ¼ teaspoon of the salt and ¼ teaspoon of the pepper. Add half of the onion, carrot, celery, leek, and potatoes to each dish. Add 1½ teaspoons of the flour, 1½ teaspoons of the cornstarch, and 1½ teaspoons of the curry powder to each dish, and cook, stirring continuously, for 1 to 2 minutes.

4. Add 8 ounces of the Guinness and the vegetable stock to the dish with the mushrooms, and 8 ounces of the Guinness and the beef broth to the dish with the lamb. Raise the heat to high. Using separate spoons, scrape the bottom of each dish to lift all the tasty browned bits into the stew.

5. Add half of the peas to each dish, and continue cooking until the stews begin to bubble.

6. Taste (carefully—it's hot), and adjust the seasoning with extra salt and pepper if needed. Add 2 thyme sprigs to each dish.

1 tablespoon all-purpose
flour

1 tablespoon cornstarch
or arrowroot

1 tablespoon Madras
curry powder

16 ounces Guinness or
another hearty dark
beer of your choice

1 cup vegetable stock
or broth, homemade
(page 100) or store-
bought

1 cup beef broth

One 8-ounce package
frozen peas or 1 cup
freshly shelled peas

4 sprigs fresh thyme

7. Cover the dishes loosely with lids or aluminum foil and bake in the oven until a stew-like consistency is reached, 30 to 45 minutes. Remove from the oven, and serve hot.

Note: Give this stew the special treatment by portioning it into individual ramekins and topping it with creamy mashed potatoes (page 200), flaky pastry crust (page 60), or store-bought puff pastry. Place the ramekins in a 400°F oven and bake for 15 to 25 minutes, until nicely browned. Cool for 5 to 10 minutes before serving to avoid the dreaded "lava mouth."

 MAKE IT ALL VEGETARIAN: Omit the lamb and the beef broth. Use 8 mushrooms and 2 cups vegetable stock.

 MAKE IT ALL MEAT: Omit the mushrooms and the vegetable stock. Use 2 pounds lamb and 2 cups beef broth.

Potage Parmentier

Serves 2 to 3 vegetarians and 2 to 3 meat-eaters

8 ounces waxy potatoes, such as Yukon gold, peeled and coarsely chopped

2 leeks (white and tender green parts), sliced into ¼- to ½-inch rings

2 tablespoons olive oil

½ teaspoon salt

½ teaspoon freshly ground black pepper

1 quart chicken stock or broth, homemade (page 100) or store-bought

1 quart vegetable stock or broth, homemade (page 100) or store-bought

3 tablespoons minced fresh herb of your choice (such as flat-leaf parsley, chives, chervil, or tarragon), for garnish

This is undeniably a mighty fine soup, and on the merits of simplicity, economy, and taste, it rates an A+ in our book. Its components are nearly as elemental as air and water, and it would be impossible to nail down the first time these humble ingredients were transformed into a wonderful soup. For added flavor, we roast the vegetables in a hot oven first. This soup tastes wonderful served piping hot, but if you like, you can cool it down and serve with a splash of heavy cream on top.

1. Preheat the oven to 475°F.

2. On a baking sheet, toss the potatoes and leeks with the oil and season with the salt and pepper. Place the sheet in the oven, and roast until the vegetables are very lightly browned, 7 to 10 minutes.

3. Divide the roasted vegetables between two medium-size stockpots, and place them on the stovetop over medium-high heat. Add the chicken stock to one pot and the vegetable stock to the other.

4. Blend the vegetable stock mixture with a handheld blender until smooth, then do the same with the chicken stock mixture. Continue to heat until the soups begin to bubble.

5. Adjust the seasoning with additional salt and pepper if desired. Ladle the soup into bowls, garnish with the fresh herbs, and serve.

Note: For an added treat, add a splash of heavy cream or a pat of butter to each bowl and stir into the soup.

 MAKE IT ALL VEGETARIAN: Omit the chicken stock, and increase the amount of vegetable stock to 2 quarts.

 MAKE IT ALL MEAT: Omit the vegetable stock, and increase the amount of chicken stock to 2 quarts.

Season It, Season It

The single greatest difference between blasé home-cooked food and good restaurant food is not cost, exotic ingredients, fancy technique, or technologically advanced kitchen equipment. No, the single biggest difference is the judicious use of salt and pepper, especially salt. Once the home cook masters the proper use of these two elemental seasonings, all other facets of excellent home cooking are secondary. (Okay, a good handle on some simple techniques goes a long way, too.) For the salt, we recommend using plain kosher salt. Iodized salt, which was a nutritional godsend in the first half of the twentieth century, is mostly unnecessary now, as people have a more iodine-replete diet. Depending on the sensitivity of one's taste buds, iodized salt will often have a slightly metallic taste, especially if you are accustomed to kosher salt. For the pepper, use freshly ground peppercorns whenever humanly possible. The goodness of pepper resides in aromatic essential oils that degrade over time with exposure to air. Preground pepper has a lot of surface area for exposure to air, so these oils will dissipate more quickly, leaving a less flavorful product. To really go the extra mile, lightly toast your whole peppercorns just before using them. This will activate these essential oils, giving a more delightfully peppery aroma to whatever dish you are making. As a chef I once worked under, Etienne Jehl, used to say, "*Assaisonnez! Assaisonnez!*"—"Season it! Season it!"—so with those words ringing in your ears, here are a few tips for proper seasoning:

- **Season lightly multiple times**: You can always add seasoning, but it is impossible to remove it.
- **Season early and taste often**: Bearing the previous tip in mind, get some "S and P" in the dish from the get-go. In addition to flavor enhancement, salt will draw liquid out of food and quicken any sweating or browning process, especially with vegetables. But remember, after the first addition of a small amount of salt and pepper, taste first, and then re-season with successive small amounts of salt and pepper. Also drink some nice palate-cleansing water between tastings so your taste buds don't become "salt-fatigued," which may lead to improper final seasoning. One exception to this edict would be in the boiling of dried legumes. If you salt the ol' bean boil, the water will want to stay where the salt is hanging out—the pot, that is, and unfortunately not the bean. And without the water entering the beans, it's exceedingly difficult to get them soft.
- **Be mindful of "hidden" salt in your ingredients**: Are you using capers, olives, anchovies, cured meats, or other salt-preserved goodies in your recipes? These have a lot of salt in them, so be conservative when adding salt to these dishes. Also, your tongue perceives acids like lemon juice or vinegar in a similar way to salt. If these are part of the ingredient list, chances are small that extra salt will be needed.
- **Bear in mind the starting and ending volume of the dish**: If you are making a long-simmered soup or stew, overly aggressive seasoning at the outset will become more concentrated over time, leading to an overly seasoned end-product.
- **Last but not least**: Re-taste and re-season right before the dish goes to the table.

Cappelletti en Brodo

Serves 2 to 3
vegetarians and
2 to 3 meat-eaters

2 tablespoons unsalted
butter

1 small carrot, finely
chopped

1 small onion, finely
chopped

½ celery stalk, finely
chopped

4 ounces finely ground
pork

4 ounces finely ground
chicken

8 ounces finely chopped
firm tofu, drained
(page 44)

1 teaspoon salt

¼ teaspoon freshly
ground black pepper

1 cup well-drained
whole-milk ricotta
cheese

½ cup grated
Parmigiano-Reggiano
cheese (2 ounces), plus
more for garnish

If this doesn't become one of your favorite pasta dishes, we'll eat our hats, especially if those hats are these cappelletti (which means "little hats") in broth. Traditionally served around Christmas in Italy, particularly in the Emilia-Romagna region in the northern part of the country, this pasta is shaped to resemble a miter, or Pope-style hat. The shaping of the pasta might seem a little daunting. But it's not that tough, and after you start you'll wonder why you've never made (or eaten) hats before.

1. Combine 1 tablespoon of the butter and half of the carrot, onion, and celery in each of two saucepans, and cook over medium heat until the vegetables are quite soft, 7 to 10 minutes.

2. Add the pork and chicken to one of the saucepans and the tofu to the other. Continue to cook until the meat is no longer pink and the tofu is heated through. Season each mixture with ½ teaspoon of the salt and ⅛ teaspoon of the pepper.

3. Place the contents of the tofu pan, the ricotta, ¼ cup of the Parmigiano-Reggiano, half of the lemon zest, and ¼ teaspoon of the nutmeg in a food processor. Pulse the mixture until combined. Taste the mixture and add salt and pepper if desired. Transfer the mixture to a bowl.

4. Wipe out the food processor, then repeat step 3 with the contents of the meaty pan, the remaining ¼ cup Parmigiano-Reggiano, the remaining lemon zest, and the remaining ¼ teaspoon nutmeg. Again, taste and adjust the seasonings if desired. Our pasta fillings are now ready.

5. Lay the pasta squares out on a clean work surface. Place 1 teaspoon or so of filling in the middle of each pasta square, using the meaty filling for half of the squares and the vegetarian filling for the other half. Be careful to segregate the meaty ones from the vegetarian. Do not put too much filling on the pasta squares, or the cappelletti might explode when cooked.

6. To form the cappelletti, brush the edges of each square lightly with the egg, then fold two opposite corners together, pinching and pressing the edges of the pasta together to seal into a triangle. Next, fold the two cor-

Zest of 1 lemon

½ teaspoon freshly
grated nutmeg

1 recipe fresh pasta (page
172), rolled thin and
cut into 1½- to 2-inch
squares

1 large egg, beaten

2 cups chicken stock
or broth, homemade
(page 100) or store-
bought

2 cups vegetable stock
or broth, homemade
(page 100) or store-
bought

ners on the long side of the triangle together snugly under the ball of stuffing and pinch together. It should now look like a miter, or Pope-style hat. The cappelletti can be cooked immediately, or you can store them in the refrigerator for up to 1 week or in the freezer for up to 1 month.

7. Bring the stocks to a simmer, the chicken stock in one pot and the vegetable stock in another. Slide 12 to 18 cappelletti per person, plus a few "tester" cappelletti, into their corresponding pots (the vegetarian cappelletti in the vegetable stock, and the meat-filled cappelletti in the chicken stock), and cook at a simmer for 2 to 3 minutes, until al dente.

8. Serve the cappelletti in warmed bowls with about 1 cup of broth per serving. Garnish with a sprinkling of Parmigiano-Reggiano.

 MAKE IT ALL VEGETARIAN: Omit the pork, chicken, and chicken stock. Use 1 pound tofu, 2 cups ricotta, and 4 cups vegetable stock. Cook the filling all in one pot.

 MAKE IT ALL MEAT: Omit the tofu, ricotta, and vegetable stock. Use 8 ounces pork, 8 ounces chicken, and 4 cups chicken stock. Cook the filling all in one pot.

Tuscan Soup with Cannellini and Black Kale

Serves 2 to 3 vegetarians and 2 to 3 meat-eaters

2 tablespoons extra-virgin olive oil, plus more for drizzling

1 pound Italian pork or turkey sausage, loose or removed from casings

2 medium-size onions, finely chopped

2 garlic cloves, minced

2 teaspoons red pepper flakes

2 tablespoons all-purpose flour

2 tablespoons cornstarch

1 quart chicken stock or broth, homemade (page 100) or store-bought

1 quart vegetable stock or broth, homemade (page 100) or store-bought

Ah, Italy! If you're ever in the mood to be talked at for an hour or so, just engage us in a conversation about Italy. Having been there together twice with our respective wives, including our shared honeymoon with A.J.'s mom (who was, funnily enough, Jeremy's wedding officiant) and two other couples, we love Italy. This soup is reminiscent of cool late fall days in Florence and is absolutely great prepared either with meat or without. Black kale is not really black, by the way, but a very deep green. It also goes by the names "dinosaur kale" and "Tuscan kale."

1. Heat 1 tablespoon of the olive oil in a medium-size soup pot over medium heat. Add the sausage and brown well, 5 to 10 minutes.

2. Place another medium-size soup pot on the stove over medium heat, and add the remaining 1 tablespoon olive oil. Add to each pot half of the onions and garlic and 1 teaspoon of the red pepper flakes. Sweat these over medium heat for 3 to 5 minutes (you don't want them to color).

3. Add 1 tablespoon of the flour and 1 tablespoon of the cornstarch to each pot and stir continuously for 1 minute to mix well.

4. Add the chicken stock to the pot with the sausage and the vegetable stock to the other pot. Increase the heat to high, and bring both pots to a simmer.

5. Reduce the heat to medium and add 1 teaspoon of the salt, 1/4 teaspoon of the pepper, half of the kale, and 1 cup of the cream to each pot. Keep at a low simmer for about 15 minutes, stirring occasionally. Add 1 can of beans to each pot and simmer for another 5 minutes.

2 teaspoons salt

½ teaspoon freshly ground black pepper

2 bunches black kale, stems removed and leaves coarsely chopped

2 cups heavy cream

Two 15-ounce cans cannellini beans, drained

6. Ladle the soup into shallow wide bowls. Garnish with a small drizzle of extra-virgin olive oil, and serve.

 MAKE IT ALL VEGETARIAN: Omit the sausage and the chicken stock, and use 2 quarts vegetable stock. Skip step 1, and cook everything in one pot.

 MAKE IT ALL MEAT: Omit the vegetable stock, and use 2 pounds sausage and 2 quarts chicken stock. Cook everything in one pot.

Basic Chicken and Vegetable Stock

Makes 2 quarts of each stock

4 pounds chicken carcasses, or 1 stewing chicken cut into 8 pieces

6 tablespoons neutral-tasting cooking oil, such as canola

3 large onions, peeled and each studded with 3 cloves

12 carrots, cut into large pieces

12 celery stalks

3 leeks (white part only), sliced in half lengthwise

10 sprigs fresh thyme

10 sprigs fresh flat-leaf parsley

4 bay leaves

20 peppercorns

6 gallons cold water, plus more as needed

No doubt, we like to have fun with food, but there's one area of study where we're dead serious—the love of a well-made stock. The freshness and flavor of a well-executed homemade stock or broth are incomparable. A good stock is a melodious composition of a major, usually protein-based, chord, such as chicken, reinforced by several minor, usually vegetal or herbal, chords. A broth is generally a simple unified note showcasing a subtle but predominant flavor. The same gentle techniques must be used to achieve the clearest and highest-quality broth or stock. Making stock is a time- and space-consuming endeavor, so if you're short on one or both of these, by all means use some store-bought broth instead. We do all the time, without a single iota of guilt. Commercially packaged broths are just fine for everyday use, especially as their quality and availability have improved in recent years (always purchase low-sodium or salt-free, and we prefer organic, by the way). A good compromise between homemade and store-bought is to purchase a quality broth from the store and then simmer some fresh onion, carrots, and celery in the broth for 30 to 60 minutes to liven up the taste.

1. Preheat the oven to 400°F.

2. To make the chicken stock, toss the chicken parts in 3 tablespoons of the oil, place in a large roasting pan (do not crowd the pan), and roast for 45 to 60 minutes, turning the contents every 15 to 20 minutes for even browning. (This is a great way to render some of the fat, which will lead to less skimming of your stock down the road.) Add 1 of the onions, 4 of the carrots, and 4 of the celery stalks halfway through the browning.

3. To make the vegetable stock, toss the remaining 2 onions, remaining 8 carrots, and remaining 8 celery stalks with the remaining 3 tablespoons oil in a separate roasting pan, and roast for 30 minutes. For both stocks, this roasting/browning is not an absolutely necessary step.

4. When the chicken is nicely browned, drain off any excess fat from the pan. It should be a clear golden color. (You have just made schmaltz. It is great for cooking potatoes or flavoring stews, or for a hundred other applications, so don't just throw it away.)

5. Transfer the contents of both roasting pans to separate stockpots, and add 3 gallons of cold water to each pot, making sure there is sufficient water to cover the ingredients.

6. For the chicken stock, tie 1 of the leeks, 5 of the thyme sprigs, 5 of the parsley sprigs, and 2 of the bay leaves together with kitchen twine. Add to the pot with the chicken, along with 10 of the peppercorns.

7. For the vegetable stock, tie the remaining 2 leeks, remaining 5 thyme sprigs, remaining 5 parsley sprigs, and remaining 2 bay leaves together with kitchen twine. Add to the other pot, along with the remaining 10 peppercorns.

8. Place the pots over medium heat and bring to a whispering simmer, with only a few small bubbles per second coming to the top. This is absolutely necessary for a clear stock. A rolling boil will force any protein component of the stock into a cloudy suspension that is all but impossible to clarify. Go slowly. Skim any froth that develops with a large spoon or mesh strainer. This is far more important with the chicken stock. Skim often in the first 15 to 30 minutes of simmering; you can skim less often as the process goes on.

9. Continue simmering and skimming, adding more water to keep things covered as needed. Simmer for 2 to 3 hours for the chicken stock, and 45 to 60 minutes for the vegetable stock.

10. Strain each stock through several layers of cheesecloth or unbleached coffee filters (save what does not go through the cheesecloth to make *glace*, page 88) into separate containers. The stock is now ready to use. If you are not using it the same day you make it, cool the stock in its container in a sink full of cold water before storing it for future use. Fresh stock will keep for up to 1 week in the refrigerator or for several months in the freezer.

Note: You can usually obtain chicken carcasses from your butcher for very little money. If you don't see carcasses in close proximity to the fresh chicken products at your local store, check in the freezer section or ask your butcher. Or, if you ever buy whole roasted chickens from the grocery store—don't be ashamed; we (well, Jeremy at least) do, too— the leftover carcasses are a great source for stock fixings. Just remove all of the meat for your immediate eating needs, then freeze the carcass until you have enough carcasses to make stock.

Cobb Salad

Serves 2 to 3
vegetarians and
2 to 3 meat-eaters

Dressing:

¼ cup red wine vinegar

¼ cup sherry vinegar

¼ teaspoon sugar

1 teaspoon freshly
squeezed lemon juice

2 teaspoons kosher salt

¾ teaspoon freshly
ground black pepper

¾ teaspoon vegetarian
Worcestershire sauce

¼ teaspoon dry mustard

1 small garlic clove,
minced

¼ cup olive oil

¾ cup neutral-tasting
cooking oil (such as
canola, safflower, or
grapeseed)

Salad:

½ head iceberg lettuce,
chopped

½ head romaine lettuce,
chopped

Far be it from us to spread rumors, but it has been said that the Cobb salad is named for former-boxer-turned-actor Randall "Tex" Cobb and was created in 1986 by a young Nicolas Cage from random craft-service supplies on the set of the movie *Raising Arizona*. Knowing Cobb's affinity for playing brutish, hirsute character roles, combined with certain expectations of a hearty lunch fit for Leonard Smalls (Cobb's character in the movie), Cage thought he'd put one over on the gentle giant by creating a light repast for Cobb. Starting with well-chopped lettuces and adding tomato and avocado, Cage's efforts were adorned by Holly Hunter's addition of sliced chicken breast, chives, and Roquefort cheese. It was the Coen brothers (who wrote the screenplay for the film) who suggested the bacon. If that story strikes a false note, you may choose to believe one of many revisionist-history versions of the salad's creation. According to one, Robert H. Cobb, owner of the famous Los Angeles eatery The Brown Derby, created the salad in 1937 as a late-night nosh for himself and a toothache-inflicted Sid Grauman, owner of the landmark Grauman's Chinese Theater.

1. For the dressing, combine the vinegars, sugar, lemon juice, salt, pepper, Worcestershire sauce, dry mustard, and garlic in a blender and blend well. Slowly add the oils and blend until emulsified. Thin with water, if needed, to your desired consistency.

2. In a large bowl, combine the lettuces, watercress, and chicory. Toss with 1/2 cup of the dressing. Arrange the dressed greens in a large shallow serving bowl. Arrange the tomato, avocado, eggs, and Roquefort in discrete sections atop the salad. Sprinkle the chives over the top.

1 bunch watercress, chopped

1 bunch chicory, chopped

1 ripe tomato, seeded and chopped

1 avocado, pitted and sliced

3 hard-boiled eggs, peeled and halved

¾ cup crumbled Roquefort cheese (3 ounces)

2 tablespoons chopped fresh chives

One 4-ounce chicken breast, cooked and sliced

1 vegetarian chicken breast, cooked according to package directions and sliced

3 bacon slices, cooked until crisp (page 195) and crumbled

3 thin slices smoked seitan, baked until crisp and chopped

3. Serve the salad with the chicken, vegetarian chicken, bacon, and seitan alongside in separate smaller bowls.

 **MAKE IT ALL VEGETARIAN**: Omit the chicken and bacon. Use 2 vegetarian chicken breasts and 6 slices of seitan.

MAKE IT ALL MEAT: Omit the vegetarian chicken and seitan. Use 2 chicken breasts and 6 slices of bacon.

Double Take Caesar Salad

**Serves 2
vegetarians and
2 meat-eaters**

Croutons:

Two 1-inch-thick slices
day-old bread of your
choice, cut into 1-inch
cubes

½ cup plus 2 tablespoons
extra-virgin olive oil

¼ teaspoon salt

½ teaspoon freshly
ground black pepper

Salad:

1 small garlic clove,
minced

Salt

2 egg yolks, preferably
organic (pasteurized
if you prefer)

1 tablespoon Dijon
mustard

2 tablespoons freshly
squeezed lemon juice

1 teaspoon vegetarian
Worcestershire sauce

Is there any salad that has captured as much American menu acreage in the past three decades as the Caesar salad? From honest, keepin'-it-real versions to ghoulish Franken-salads, the Caesar is undoubtedly here to stay. Although the ingredient list in many modern Caesars would lead you to believe that it was named after an orgiastic Roman emperor, and certainly its origins are somewhat debatable, here's what is generally accepted: Caesar Cardini, a restaurateur in Tijuana, Mexico, most likely created the dish in the 1920s, perhaps fashioning it after a salad his brother Alex (a pilot in the Italian air force) created, called the Aviator Salad. The main difference between the two is that the Aviator most likely contained anchovy fillets, while the true Caesar did not. All arguments aside, we certainly aren't calling this salad an "Alex" or an "Aviator." We say, "To the king go the spoils—salad, thy name is Caesar!"

1. Preheat the oven to 400°F.

2. Toss the bread cubes with 2 tablespoons of the olive oil and season with the salt and pepper. Spread the bread out on a baking sheet and bake for 10 to 12 minutes, turning once or twice during the baking time. (We like our croutons a little on the soft side, so as to avoid any dangerously sharp crouton edges.)

3. In a large wooden salad bowl, use a fork to mash the garlic together with a pinch of salt. Add the egg yolks, mustard, lemon juice, and Worcestershire sauce to the bowl and mix with a fork. Slowly drizzle in the remaining ½ cup olive oil, whisking constantly until the dressing is well emulsified (with the egg yolk and mustard in there, it should be easy-cheesy). And speaking of cheesy, add the grated cheese to the dressing and mix.

4. Add the romaine and endive leaves to the bowl and toss to coat. Divide the salad among four individual plates, and serve, garnished with the cheese curls. (If using the anchovies, reserve half of the dressing in a ramekin or small bowl, then toss half of the romaine and endive in the dressing remaining in the salad bowl. Remove the dressed vegetarian salad to

½ cup grated
Parmigiano-Reggiano
cheese (2 ounces), plus
more shaved into large
curls for garnish

1 head romaine lettuce,
cored and separated
into whole leaves

2 heads endive, cored and
separated into whole
leaves

4 oil-packed anchovy
fillets (optional;
though not strictly
traditional, one of
us loves them)

two individual plates. Add the anchovies to the salad bowl and mash with a fork. Add the reserved dressing to the mashed anchovies and mix. Add the remaining romaine and endive to the bowl and toss to coat. Portion the anchovy-enhanced salad between two individual plates.)

5. Garnish each salad with a smattering of fresh croutons and curls of Parmigiano-Reggiano.

Note: As this recipe uses raw egg yolks, it should not be served to the elderly or anyone with a compromised immune system. Using pasteurized eggs eliminates most, if not all, of the health risk associated with consuming raw eggs.

 MAKE IT ALL VEGETARIAN: It couldn't be easier: Omit the anchovies.

 MAKE IT ALL MEAT: Double the number of anchovy fillets to 8. Yum, says Jeremy.

Salade Niçoise

Serves 2
vegetarians and
2 meat-eaters

1 garlic clove, minced

2 tablespoons finely
chopped fresh basil

1 tablespoon Dijon
mustard

2 tablespoons red or
white wine vinegar

1 tablespoon freshly
squeezed lemon juice

½ teaspoon salt

½ teaspoon freshly
ground black pepper

6 tablespoons extra-
virgin olive oil

2 medium-size tomatoes,
seeded and chopped

1 small cucumber, peeled,
seeded, and chopped

2 ounces canned or jarred
artichoke hearts

1 cup baby green beans,
blanched briefly, dried,
and chopped

This Niçoise niece of Salmagundi (page 108) has endured more interpretations than its New World cousin, the Caesar salad (page 104). Perhaps this variety is due to the geography of the Niçoise salad: Given Nice's proximity to the beaches of the French Riviera, anything prepared à la Niçoise should be fresh and light, with crispy, mostly raw, vegetables; should contain some seafood and salty elements; and should feature garlic and olive oil. Easy peasy.

1. Make the vinaigrette by combining the garlic, basil, mustard, vinegar, lemon juice, salt, and pepper in a medium-size bowl. Slowly drizzle in the olive oil, whisking constantly until emulsified.

2. In a large bowl, lightly dress the tomatoes, cucumber, artichokes, and green beans individually with a small amount of the vinaigrette. Set aside.

3. On each of two medium-size serving platters, arrange a bed composed of half of the lettuce and endive.

4. Drain the onion slices and dry them off using paper towels. Arrange half of the tomatoes, cucumber, artichokes, green beans, onions, eggs, and olives in discrete groupings atop the lettuce to allow diners to select their ingredients. Add the anchovies to one of the trays.

5. Pour the remainder of the dressing over both platters of salad, dividing it equally.

1 small head of lettuce, cored and coarsely chopped (Bibb is our favorite, but romaine works well, too)

2 heads endive, cored and coarsely chopped

1 small white onion, thinly sliced and reserved in ice water

3 hard-boiled eggs, peeled and halved

12 pitted Niçoise or other good-quality black olives

12 anchovy fillets (oil-packed or rinsed salt-packed)

Note: Stuff some rather heavily dressed Niçoise salad into a hollowed-out portion of crusty bread, compress this sandwich with your hand, a book, a brick, or an unheated panini press, and enjoy another Niçoise nicety, the *pan bagnat*.

 MAKE IT ALL VEGETARIAN: Simply banish the anchovy fillets.

MAKE IT ALL MEAT: Simply double the number of anchovy fillets to 24.

Salmagundi, Made on Sunday

Serves 4 to 5
vegetarians and
4 to 5 meat-eaters

1 cup plus 1½ teaspoons
extra-virgin olive oil

4 large portobello
mushroom caps, sliced

½ teaspoon salt

½ teaspoon freshly
ground black pepper

1½ teaspoons balsamic
vinegar

2 heads butter lettuce,
leaves separated
and sliced in half
lengthwise

6 hard-boiled eggs,
peeled and quartered
lengthwise

2 large ripe tomatoes,
thinly sliced

3 medium-size carrots,
peeled, then peeled
into long curls

One 6-inch daikon
radish, peeled, then
peeled into long curls

2 small cucumbers,
peeled and sliced into
wheels

Salmagundi is an old English dish that takes its etymology from the French word *salmigondis*, which roughly means "something composed of disparate individual articles to create a coherent whole." A type of composed salad (meaning one whose ingredients are arranged carefully instead of tossed together), salmagundi is a real crowd-pleaser, with potential for an opulent visual presentation. There are infinite ingredient combinations possible with salmagundi, but in our composed-salad dreams, this is it. Try serving this dish at your next dinner party or outdoor barbecue, and wait for the kudos to flow your way.

1. In a medium-size sauté pan, heat 1½ teaspoons of the oil over medium heat. Add the portobellos, ¼ teaspoon of the salt, and ¼ teaspoon of the pepper. Sauté the mushrooms for 5 minutes, remove from the heat, and transfer to a small bowl. Add the balsamic vinegar, toss, and let cool completely.

2. Arrange half of the lettuce on each of two large serving platters.

3. Arrange half of the eggs, mushrooms, tomatoes, carrots, daikon, cucumbers, and fennel in an artful fashion on each platter. Arrange the ham, chicken, beef tongue, and anchovies on one of the platters.

4. Make the vinaigrette by combining the vinegar, shallot, and mustard, then slowly drizzling in the remaining 1 cup olive oil, all the while whisking like mad.

5. Lightly drizzle the vinaigrette over the ingredients on both platters, making sure both platters get an equal amount of the dressing.

6. Garnish each platter with the some of the tarragon, chopped parsley, chopped fennel fronds, and nasturtiums.

7. Sprinkle the remaining ¼ teaspoon salt and ¼ teaspoon pepper over both of the platters (adding more, if desired).

2 medium-size fennel bulbs, thinly sliced perpendicular to the root, fronds chopped and reserved for garnish

¾ cup chopped cold ham

¾ cup chopped cooked chicken or turkey

2 ounces beef or lamb tongue, sliced (see Notes)

2 ounces marinated white anchovies (20 to 25 anchovies)

½ cup sherry vinegar

1 small shallot, minced

1 tablespoon Dijon mustard

1 bunch fresh tarragon, leaves only, for garnish

1 bunch fresh flat-leaf parsley, leaves only, chopped, for garnish

½ to 1 cup nasturtium flowers (or other edible flowers), for garnish

Notes: Butter lettuce is our fave in this salad, but sub in other varieties if necessary or desired and you'll still be just fine. If you're not eager to procure, scrub, boil, peel, and slice some beef tongue (and Jeremy grudgingly admits that even some carnivores may not be into this), any self-respecting kosher deli should be able to provide it for you.

 MAKE IT ALL VEGETARIAN: Omit the ham, chicken, beef tongue, and anchovies. If the salad feels a little insubstantial, feel free to double the amounts of the eggs, mushrooms, and veggies.

 MAKE IT ALL MEAT: Mmm, meat salad . . . Increase the amount of ham to 1½ cups, the amount of chicken to 1½ cups, the amount of beef tongue to 4 ounces, and the amount of anchovies to 4 ounces. Feel free to omit any vegetables that don't appeal to your tastes, but please keep some of them!

Warm Escarole and Romaine Salad

Serves 2 vegetarians and 2 meat-eaters

¼ cup olive oil

2 thick-cut bacon slices, chopped

1 small white onion, sliced

4 ounces mushrooms of your choice, sliced

1 teaspoon salt

¼ teaspoon freshly ground black pepper

2 ounces smoked seitan, chopped

1 tablespoon Dijon mustard

1 tablespoon sherry or sherry vinegar

Juice of 1 lemon

½ bunch escarole, chopped into bite-size pieces

1 head romaine lettuce, cored and chopped into bite-size pieces

Warm and wilted salads are very underrated and under-served. Most people have probably had a salad of raw spinach dressed with a warm, bacon-y vinaigrette, but few have gone further than that in the world of wilted salads—which is a shame. Remember that, nutritionally speaking, it's a good idea for the acid in your dressing to contain vitamin C (such as the lemon juice used here), as vitamin C improves the amount of iron your body will absorb from leafy greens like escarole, kale, or spinach.

1. Heat 1 tablespoon of the oil in a sauté pan over medium heat. Add the bacon and cook until it is crisp. Being careful not to get burned by the hot fat, remove all but 1 tablespoon of the bacon fat from the pan. Set the pan aside off the heat.

2. Heat 1 tablespoon of the oil in a second sauté pan over medium heat. Add the onion, mushrooms, salt, and pepper and sauté until the onion browns slightly and the mushrooms have released most of their liquid.

3. Transfer half of the mushroom-onion mixture to the bacon-filled pan, and place it on the stovetop over medium heat. Add the seitan to the bacon-free pan, and cook for a few minutes to crisp it.

4. Mix the mustard, sherry, and lemon juice together in a small bowl. Pour half of the mixture into each pan, and cook slightly to deglaze the pans.

5. Turn off the heat under the pans and add half of the escarole and romaine to each pan. Working quickly, and using different spoons for each pan, toss the greens with the contents of the sauté pans to coat.

6. Transfer the wilted salads to two serving bowls, add 1 tablespoon olive oil to each bowl, and give each a quick toss (using separate spoons again) before serving.

 MAKE IT ALL VEGETARIAN: Omit the bacon and increase the amount of seitan to 4 ounces. Skip step 1, and cook everything in one sauté pan.

 MAKE IT ALL MEAT: Omit the seitan, increase the amount of bacon to 4 slices, and cook everything in one sauté pan.

Carolina-Style Barbecue Sandwiches

Makes 6 sandwiches · 3 for vegetarians and 3 for meat-eaters

¾ cup rice wine vinegar

¾ cup distilled white vinegar

1 cup apple cider vinegar

4 ½ teaspoons brown sugar

1 ½ teaspoons Tabasco or other Louisiana-style hot sauce

½ teaspoon salt

½ teaspoon freshly ground black pepper

¾ teaspoon dry mustard

6 country-style sandwich buns, cut in half

One 5 ½-ounce package deli-style sliced vegetarian ham

5 ½ ounces roasted pork shoulder or loin, cut into ¼-inch-thick slices

The key to good barbecue is not the meat, it's the sauce. For a Carolina-style sauce, the key (which makes it the key to the key to this tangy lock) is a strong vinegar component, accomplished by using three different vinegars, which may seem excessive but tastes just right. Creamy-style coleslaw (page 190) is the ideal accompaniment to these sandwiches and is especially good on the sandwich itself. If you need a bit more to round out a nice lunch, Vinegar Greens (page 198) are a great choice.

1. Preheat the broiler.

2. Combine the vinegars, brown sugar, Tabasco, salt, pepper, and dry mustard in a medium-size saucepan over medium-high heat, stirring continually. Cook until the brown sugar is completely dissolved and the sauce has started to thicken. Reduce the heat to low and leave the sauce on the stove, stirring occasionally.

3. Place the sandwich buns on a baking sheet (cut side up), and broil until toasted, checking regularly.

4. While the buns are toasting, put the vegetarian ham on a small plate and the sliced pork shoulder on a second plate. Place the plates in the microwave, and heat for about 1 minute on high power, until warm, but not smoking hot.

5. To assemble the sandwiches, place the bottom halves of the buns on individual serving plates, and top 3 of them with a few (3 seems right) slices of vegetarian ham and the remaining 3 with a few slices of pork. Top the ham and pork with a nice spoonful of sauce and then the top halves of the buns. Serve immediately.

 MAKE IT ALL VEGETARIAN: Increase the amount of vegetarian ham to 11 ounces, and omit the pork shoulder.

 MAKE IT ALL MEAT: Increase the amount of pork shoulder to 11 ounces, and omit the vegetarian ham.

Po' Boys

Makes 4 sandwiches • 2 for vegetarians and 2 for meat-eaters

Two 12-inch baguettes

1 cup milk

1 large egg

½ cup all-purpose flour

½ cup cornmeal

3 tablespoons vegetable oil

8 ounces medium-size shrimp, peeled

2 tablespoons mayonnaise

One 7-ounce package plain baked tofu, sliced

8 romaine lettuce leaves

1 large tomato, cut into 8 slices

1 kosher dill pickle, cut into 8 slices

Tabasco, Frank's RedHot, or other Louisiana-style hot sauce

Coming from a city like New Orleans—which is full of stories, songs, folklore, and magnificent cuisine—it's not a wonder that the famous po' boy sandwich has numerous possible histories (including one derived from the French *pour boire*, which supposedly referred to the large sandwich filled with oysters and other goodies that men used as a peace offering when coming home late from a night on the town). Getting the traditional Louisiana-style French bread is admirable and ideal, but if you aren't anywhere near Louisiana, make sure you get baguettes that are very thin and crispy on the outside but soft and airy on the inside. The sandwiches are usually served as a "half," about 6 inches long (sometimes called a "shorty"), or a "full," about a foot long. Toppings may include fried shrimp, oysters, roast beef, or crayfish, dressed with lettuce, tomato, mayonnaise, and sometimes pickles and onions. For the vegetarians in the house, we're subbing in some baked tofu for the shrimp; its chew goes well with the tradition. Serve with a side of Vinegar Greens (page 198).

1. Slice each baguette in half crosswise, then make a horizontal slice three-quarters of the way through each half-baguette.

2. Mix the milk and egg together in a small bowl. Mix the flour and cornmeal together in another small bowl.

3. Heat the oil in a small, straight-sided skillet over medium-high heat. Dunk the shrimp into the milk-egg mixture, then roll in the flour-cornmeal mixture until coated. Place the shrimp carefully in the hot oil, and fry until golden brown, about 5 minutes. Remove the shrimp from the oil and place on a paper towel–lined plate. (You may have to fry the shrimp in batches.)

4. Open the baguette halves like a book. Spread 1 ½ teaspoons mayonnaise on the inside of each half-baguette. Top 2 of them with half of the fried shrimp and the other 2 with half of the tofu. Top each of the sandwiches with 2 lettuce leaves, 2 tomato slices, and 2 pickle slices. Serve with lots of hot sauce.

 MAKE IT ALL VEGETARIAN: Use two 7-ounce packages of baked tofu, and omit the shrimp.

 MAKE IT ALL MEAT: Use 1 pound shrimp, and omit the tofu.

Selecting Shrimp

Ever overwhelmed by the number of shrimp choices out there these days? Peeled versus shell-on, raw versus precooked, Gulf versus tiger, and what the heck does "31-35" or "U-16" mean? First and foremost, unless held at gunpoint, never buy precooked shrimp, either frozen or thawed, at the grocery store. Still-hot, spicy boiled shrimp from a seafood vendor in New Orleans is okay; frozen and re-thawed cooked shrimp in a bag or a ring at the grocery store is not. As to the question of peeled or not peeled, this is a matter of price and application.

Peeled shrimp are generally more expensive since someone (or some machine) has done this work for you. I generally buy unpeeled shrimp so I can use the shells to make a court bouillon, or "short stock," that I can cook the shrimp in. If going for a clean, totally shrimpy taste, this is the best possible vehicle to cook the little fellas in. But if you're not into peeling shrimp (a Zen activity really, if there's enough around that need to be dispatched), just buy them with the shells off, making sure they are always raw.

Raw, frozen shrimp is also an option, but be sure they have only been frozen once. Multiple thaw/freeze cycles are death for the texture of shrimp. Shrimp are generally taken live from the boat to a processor, where they will eventually be frozen. This is the one and only time they should be frozen before use. A closer examination of so-labeled "fresh raw shrimp" will most likely reveal the words "previously frozen." This is okay, but again, be sure they've only been frozen once.

Unless I've come into a recent windfall and want to splurge on live whole shrimp, which are not widely available, I usually opt for frozen, shell-on shrimp. When buying shrimp, numbers like "31-35" simply refer to the number of shrimp per pound, so "31-35" means that there will be 31 to 35 shrimp per pound, and hence, each shrimp will be about a half an ounce. The "U" in "U-16" or "U-10" means "under," so each pound will have under 16 or under 10 shrimp per pound. These are the big daddies, or the classic oxymoron, jumbo shrimp.

Chop-Chop Chicken Salad Sandwiches

Makes 4 sandwiches • 2 for vegetarians and 2 for meat-eaters

6 hard-boiled eggs

½ medium-size yellow onion

1 whole dill pickle

1 cup mayonnaise

¼ teaspoon freshly ground black pepper

¼ teaspoon paprika

½ vegetarian chicken breast, chopped into ¼-inch pieces (see Notes)

1 cup chopped roasted chicken (opposite page), cut into ¼-inch pieces

8 slices whole-grain bread

Chicken salad and its close relative, egg salad, are often found among the sad bins of pre-made sandwiches in convenience stores. Unless you have access to an honest-to-goodness old-fashioned diner, your best bet for great-tasting chicken salad is to make it yourself. This recipe does require a bit of chopping (hence the name), but once you've got your rhythm down, the chopping flies by. We generally take our chicken-and-egg salad between a couple of slices of bread or toast, but it's tasty enough to go solo served atop a few leaves of crisp lettuce, or even as a party snack served in a bowl with sturdy crackers alongside.

1. Peel and chop the eggs into roughly ¼-inch pieces. Place them in a large bowl.

2. Chop the onion and pickle into ⅛- to ¼-inch pieces. You should have about ½ cup of each. Add the chopped onion, chopped pickle, mayonnaise, pepper, and paprika to the bowl with the eggs. Mix well to combine.

3. Place the vegetarian chicken in a medium-size bowl and the roasted chicken in a second medium-size bowl.

4. Add half of the egg mixture to the bowl with the vegetarian chicken. Add the remaining egg mixture to the bowl with the roasted chicken. Mix both well (using separate spoons for each).

5. Place 2 slices of the bread on a clean work surface. Spread half of the vegetarian chicken salad on each slice, then top with a second slice of bread. Place the sandwiches on plates and cut them in half. Repeat with the remaining bread and the roasted-chicken salad. Serve.

Notes: When picking up vegetarian chicken for this chicken salad, you want to stay away from the breaded variety. If you can't find unbreaded vegetarian chicken, then use the breaded, but only as a fallback. If you're feeling that there's an unhealthy amount of mayo used here, you could sub in a mixture of ¾ cup nonfat yogurt and ¼ cup mayo.

MAKE IT ALL VEGETARIAN: Omit the roasted chicken, and use a whole vegetarian chicken breast. You can combine everything in a single bowl in step 4.

 MAKE IT ALL MEAT: Omit the vegetarian chicken, and use 2 cups chopped roasted chicken. You can combine everything in a single bowl in step 4.

How to Roast a Chicken

A finely roasted and seasoned chicken is always a thing of sublime comfort and flavor. In *Mastering the Art of French Cooking*, the grande dame of cooking, Julia Child, rightly says, "You can always judge the quality of a cook or a restaurant by its roast chicken." Luckily, you can roast well following this method: Poultry shears in hand, remove the neck, spine, and tail of the bird by cutting on either side of the spine. In doing so, you will be separating the spine from the bird's collarbone, ribs, and hip joint. Save this piece in the freezer for the next time you make stock (page 100). With the bird skin side down, give it a few good whacks with a cleaver or other heavy implement at the neck opening to break the wishbone—or use two hands protected by a kitchen towel, and press the bird open firmly until the collarbone breaks. You now have a bird that will lay almost completely flat. Sprinkle ¼ to ½ cup of kosher salt all over the bird, rubbing it in lightly, and let it sit for 30 minutes.

While the bird is enjoying the salty spa treatment, place a rack in the middle of the oven and preheat to 400°F. Rinse the salt off the bird and dry completely with paper towels. On the stovetop, heat 1 tablespoon unsalted butter and 1 tablespoon olive oil over medium-high heat in a large cast-iron skillet just large enough to completely contain the bird—it's okay if it's a little snug, as this will help retain the chicken's juicy goodness. Place the bird skin side down in the skillet to sear the skin—this will prevent it from sticking to the pan when it must be flipped in the oven later on. Cook for 5 minutes on the stovetop, then slide the skillet into the oven and cook for 40 minutes. Flip the bird over so the skin side is up. Cook for another 20 minutes, then check the thickest part of the thigh to be sure it is 160°F (it will reach the target 165° temperature while resting out of the oven). Voilà, a perfect bird with a minimum of fuss.

Powerful Panini for the Populace

Makes 4 panini · 2 for vegetarians and 2 for meat-eaters

1 large eggplant, zucchini, or yellow squash, ends removed and cut lengthwise into 1¼-inch-thick slices

2 tablespoons olive oil

Salt and freshly ground black pepper

4 medium-size ciabatta rolls, sliced in half

4 ounces fresh mozzarella cheese, sliced

2 ripe plum tomatoes, thinly sliced

2 ounces prosciutto, mortadella, sopressata, or other Italian cured meat

1 bunch arugula

1 tablespoon balsamic vinegar

Is it possible that John Montagu, the Fourth Earl of Sandwich, spread the gospel of his eponymous meat and bread creation to Florence, Italy, in 1737—a feat necessarily accomplished between winning hands of whist and wooing his first wife, Dorothy Fane? History is inconclusive, but the artifactual evidence known collectively as panini endures. As its name suggests, a *panino* (the singular of *panini*) refers to the bread portion of the sandwich, and the traditional bread used would be a ciabatta (named for the bread's "house slipper" shape). Certainly any bread will do, but it is hard to beat the light texture and crispy crust of a well-made, well-grilled ciabatta panino.

1. Brush the eggplant with 1 tablespoon of the olive oil, sprinkle with ½ teaspoon salt and ½ teaspoon pepper, and grill using an indoor grill or panini press, about 5 minutes. Alternatively, preheat the broiler and broil the eggplant on a baking sheet until lightly browned on both sides.

2. To assemble the sandwiches, lay the bottom halves of the ciabatta rolls on a clean work surface. Place one-quarter of the mozzarella and one-quarter of the tomatoes on each of the 4 halves, then top 2 of them with the grilled eggplant and the other 2 with the prosciutto. Grill the sandwiches using a panini press or stovetop grill pan for 3 to 4 minutes. Flip the panini over and press firmly to create grill marks. Grill for 3 to 4 more minutes.

3. While the panini are cooking, toss the arugula with the remaining 1 tablespoon olive oil and the balsamic vinegar in a medium-size bowl. Season the greens aggressively with salt and pepper.

4. When the panini are done grilling, open them up and add some of the dressed arugula to each. Serve immediately.

Note: As much as we like mustard, one rarely sees it in Italy near any panini. Occasionally there's a swipe of mayonnaise to be found on the bread. Grilled or not, hot or room temperature, panini are great picnic food and travel well, especially when made with crusty ciabatta rolls.

 MAKE IT ALL VEGETARIAN: Omit the prosciutto and use 2 eggplant.

 MAKE IT ALL MEAT: Use 4 ounces prosciutto, and omit the eggplant.

comfort entrées

Ah, memories. They're what make this chapter glow.

From the lush mac and cheese you lived for when you were a kid to the fish sticks you had every other Friday at school to regional favorites that start you salivating every time you hear them mentioned (such as shrimp and grits or bierocks), the whole idea of "comfort foods" is driven by the memories of beloved dishes from days past. If only it were possible to make those same dishes today for both meat-eating and vegetarian family members or the posse of pals coming over for a big weekend dinner (because it's not too "comfortable" if you can't bring everyone to the table at the same time, right?).

If you're finding yourself with this same wish, then this chapter is going to fit you like a favorite sweater. The comfort foods on the next pages cover truck-stop top-tens like The Best Biscuits and Sausage Gravy as well as international favorites such as Pizza *Quattro Stagioni* and Hungry Hungarian Stuffed Peppers (well, maybe the latter isn't quite so international, but when growing up in Kansas it sure seemed to generate thoughts of other countries where hearty and yummy fare was the norm). The recipes in this chapter fit perfectly with this book's aim of making dishes to serve both vegetarians and meat-eaters at the same time, because these are the dishes that bring many of us together with shared memories of communal meals. So turn the pages and start creating even more comfort-food experiences.

Mighty Mac and Cheese

Serves 3 to 4 vegetarians and 3 to 4 meat-eaters

4 cups elbow macaroni

¼ cup (½ stick) unsalted butter

¼ cup all-purpose flour

4 cups milk

¼ teaspoon cayenne pepper

¼ teaspoon freshly grated nutmeg

½ teaspoon freshly ground black pepper

½ teaspoon salt

4 cups shredded cheddar cheese, preferably white cheddar (1 pound)

1 cup cubed cooked ham (½-inch cubes)

5 slices whole wheat bread, chopped into ½-inch pieces

There are comfort foods, and then there's macaroni and cheese, the queen of comfort foods (it seems more of a lady, or at least motherly, otherwise it would be the king). Made many, many different ways around the country, mac and cheese always has a few constants, including pasta, cheese (or, in many cases, cheeses), and a hearty helping of love and care, because that, friends, is what comfort foods are really about.

1. Preheat the oven to 400°F.

2. Cook the pasta according to the package directions. While the pasta is cooking, place a large saucepan on the stove over medium-high heat. Melt the butter in the pan, stirring occasionally. Once the butter is melted and hot, add the flour, and whisk to combine. Cook the roux for 2 minutes, whisking continuously.

3. Slowly add the milk to the roux, about 1 cup at a time, stirring or whisking continuously. Once all the milk has been added, continue stirring until the mixture thickens to the consistency of a thin gravy.

4. Take the pan off the stove and add the cayenne, nutmeg, pepper, salt, and cheese. Stir until well combined.

5. When the pasta has finished cooking, drain it, then return it to its cooking pot. Pour the cheese sauce over the pasta, and stir to combine. Pour half of the pasta and sauce mixture into a 9-inch square baking dish.

6. Add the ham to the remaining pasta and sauce in the pot, stir to combine, and pour it into a separate 9-inch square baking dish.

7. Top each dish with half of the bread pieces. Cover the dishes with aluminum foil, and bake for 30 minutes. Remove the foil and bake for another 15 minutes. The mac and cheese is done when it's slightly brown on top and hot all the way through (use a knife to check the middle). If this is not the case, bake for 15 more minutes. Serve hot.

 MAKE IT ALL VEGETARIAN: Simply omit the ham.

 MAKE IT ALL MEAT: Use 2 cups ham, and add the ham to the pasta and sauce in step 5, then transfer everything into a large baking dish.

Chili con/non Carne

3 fresh jalapeño chiles

3 garlic cloves, unpeeled

1 tablespoon vegetable
oil

1 large onion, chopped

2 medium-size to large
tomatoes, chopped
(save the juice that
spills out when you
chop them)

1½ teaspoons ground
cumin

1 teaspoon chili powder

¼ teaspoon salt

¼ teaspoon freshly
ground black pepper

2 cups vegetable stock
or broth, homemade
(page 100) or store-
bought

One 15-ounce can red
kidney beans

Boy, oh boy, there probably isn't another recipe in this book more apt to start a fistfight than this one. Even the mere suggestion of vegetarian chili can make people go off their rockers; add to this our love of beans in any chili and we could be tried for crimes against the Chili Purity Act of 1902. Okay, that Act of the Texas Congress is fictitious, but nevertheless, we are pro-*frijol* and find the all-meat-no-beans argument a bit elitist. Even in the most robust days of the Texas cattle trade, beans were still cheaper than beef, while today, we would gently recommend a closer examination of your eating practices if you're consuming beef that's cheaper than beans. Roasting the jalapeños and the garlic brings out a fuller flavor in both and tames the heat of the chiles a bit. (By the way, when working with the chiles, please remember either to wear gloves or wash your hands thoroughly right after touching them.) Serve this chili with corn tortillas or Delish Drop Biscuits (page 208).

1. Heat a small skillet or sauté pan over medium-high heat. Add the jalapeños and garlic, and roast them together in the pan. Roast the jalapeños for 8 to 10 minutes and the garlic cloves for 10 to 12 minutes, turning often with tongs. You don't want the chiles or garlic to blacken, though you'll probably end up with some charred areas. Once they're done and the garlic is slightly soft, transfer the chiles and garlic to a bowl and cover with a clean kitchen towel. Let them cool a little, then chop the jalapeños and peel and dice the garlic.

2. Heat a large saucepan or stockpot over medium-high heat. Add the oil and let it heat up a bit (but not to the point of smoking). Add the onion and sauté over medium heat, stirring occasionally, until the onion is just well-browned, about 10 minutes.

3. Add the jalapeños and garlic to the pan, and sauté for about 5 more minutes, until the chiles are just beginning to get soft and the kitchen is really starting to smell good.

4. Add the tomatoes and their juice to the pot, along with the cumin, chili powder, salt, and pepper, and sauté for 7 to 10 minutes, stirring every few minutes. The mixture should be bubbling a bit.

4 hamburger-style vegetarian patties, chopped into ¼- to ½-inch pieces (see Note)

8 ounces skirt steak, sliced into 1-inch-wide strips, then sliced into ¼-inch strips

½ cup shredded cheddar cheese (2 ounces; optional)

Sour cream (optional)

Chopped fresh cilantro (optional)

5. Add the vegetable stock and beans. Once everything comes up to a consistent simmer, stir, then transfer half of the mixture to a second pot.

6. Add the chopped vegetarian patties to the first pot, and add the steak to the second pot. Cook at a simmer for 10 minutes, stirring each pot occasionally (using different spoons for each). Taste, and adjust the seasonings if you desire. Cook for 5 more minutes. The chili should be thick, but still have a little juice.

7. Serve in bowls, and top with cheese, sour cream, and cilantro, if desired.

Note: In a pinch, you could substitute 12 ounces vegetarian beef crumbles for the vegetarian patties, but the crumbles don't provide the same nice texture as the patties.

 MAKE IT ALL VEGETARIAN: Omit the skirt steak, and use 8 vegetarian patties.

 MAKE IT ALL MEAT: Omit the vegetarian patties and use 1 pound skirt steak. If you like, substitute beef stock for the vegetable stock.

Spaghetti alla Carbonara

Serves 2 to 3
vegetarians and
2 to 3 meat-eaters

1 recipe fresh pasta (page
172), formed into
spaghetti, or 1 pound
dried spaghetti

6 tablespoons olive oil

2 ounces guanciale
or pancetta, finely
chopped (see Notes)

4 ounces white or cremini
mushrooms, sliced

2 large egg yolks

½ cup grated Pecorino
Romano cheese
(2 ounces), plus extra
for garnish

1 teaspoon coarsely
ground black pepper

1 tablespoon fresh flat-
leaf parsley, plus more
for garnish

Like almost all classic Italian dishes, spaghetti alla carbonara is accompanied by various stories about its history. Was it originally a sturdy dish meant to sustain the *carbonari*, Italian charcoal workers? Did it get its name because the coarse pepper in the dish resembles charcoal or because the dish was first made over charcoal grills? We're not sure, but one thing we do know is that this dish gets some pretty rough treatment at times with the addition of a lot of extraneous ingredients, the end result being more like a freakish, heavy Alfredo than the lovely, satisfying carbonara it should be. Simplicity is really best here, so use the best possible ingredients in the simplest possible way.

1. Preheat the oven to 200°F, and place two large serving bowls in the oven to warm.

2. Bring a large pot of salted water to a boil for the pasta. If using dried pasta, begin cooking it according to the package directions. If using fresh pasta, do not cook it until after the guanciale and mushrooms have been cooked.

3. Heat two medium-size sauté pans over medium-high heat, and add 1 tablespoon of the olive oil to each pan. Add the guanciale to one pan and the mushrooms to the other. Cook until the guanciale is lightly crisped and the mushrooms are lightly bronzed, 7 to 10 minutes. Remove from the heat. If using fresh pasta, add it to the boiling water and cook for 2 to 3 minutes, until al dente. This is one of the few instances where we will not be cooking the pasta further in a bit of sauce, so be sure it is done to your liking.

4. While the pasta is cooking, beat together the remaining 4 tablespoons olive oil, the egg yolks, and Romano cheese in a bowl.

5. Drain the pasta, reserving 1 cup of the pasta water, and place half of the cooked pasta in each of the two warmed serving bowls. While the pasta is still very hot, pour the contents of the guanciale pan over the pasta in one of the bowls and the contents of the mushroom pan over the pasta in the other bowl.

6. Pour half of the egg-and-cheese mixture over each bowl, add $1/2$ teaspoon of the pepper and $1 1/2$ teaspoons of the parsley to each bowl, and toss until the spaghetti is well coated. If the pasta sauce seems too thick and gummy, thin it with some of the reserved pasta water.

7. Garnish each bowl with a light sprinkling of parsley and cheese, and serve immediately.

Notes: Opinions vary, but an unsmoked pork product is the preferred meat here. Guanciale, which is cured pork jowl, is traditional in Rome. Use bacon if you prefer or if you can't find guanciale or pancetta. As this recipe uses raw egg yolks, it should not be served to the elderly or anyone with a compromised immune system. Using pasteurized eggs eliminates most, if not all, of the health risk associated with consuming raw eggs. Another option is to hard-boil the eggs and remove the yolks, then press the yolks through a sieve with a wooden spoon until they are like a fine powder. Mix the dry yolks with the oil and cheese and follow the rest of the recipe as written. The end result will still be quite good, we promise.

 MAKE IT ALL VEGETARIAN: Omit the guanciale, and use 8 ounces mushrooms.

 MAKE IT ALL MEAT: Increase the amount of guanciale to 4 ounces. Though mushrooms are not a traditional ingredient in carbonara, why not leave them in? Cooked together with the guanciale, they will make an even more delicious sauce for your pasta.

Beefy Bierocks

Serves 2 vegetarians and 2 meat-eaters

2 tablespoons vegetable oil, such as canola

8 ounces lean ground beef

1 medium-size onion, finely chopped

½ medium-size head cabbage, shredded

1 cup vegetarian beef crumbles

¼ cup all-purpose flour

Two 8-biscuit packages jumbo-size refrigerated biscuits

You don't usually think about giving the rock salute (hand raised with the two outside fingers up, thumb up or out depending on preference and geography) to food; instead, it's usually saved for AC/DC concerts or to demonstrate general good feeling among people who have been known to play their music a bit loud. But in the case of bierocks (or bieroch, biroux, or beerock), a tasty meat-filled pastry well known to Midwesterners and fans of easily constructed, filling fare, the gesture is entirely appropriate. Because, truth be told, bierocks rock.

1. Preheat the oven to 350°F.

2. Heat 1 tablespoon of the oil in a large skillet or sauté pan over medium heat, and add the ground beef. Cook until browned. Turn off the heat and drain off any excess grease, but leave the meat in the skillet.

3. Heat the remaining 1 tablespoon oil in a second large skillet or sauté pan over medium heat. Add the onion, and, stirring continuously, cook until the onion is soft and a light golden color, 7 to 8 minutes. Add the cabbage and cook until soft, stirring regularly (this should take about 5 more minutes).

4. Carefully transfer half of the onion-cabbage mixture to the skillet containing the beef. Add the vegetarian crumbles to the beef-free skillet, and cook over medium heat until warmed through.

5. Lightly flour a cutting board and a rolling pin. Open the biscuit tubes. Place one biscuit on the cutting board, and gently use the rolling pin to flatten it to a ¼-inch thickness. Place about ¼ cup of the vegetarian filling in the middle of the biscuit. Fold the biscuit over so the filling is covered and the edges of the biscuit touch each other. Using a fork, press the edges together to seal the biscuit package. Place the filled biscuit on a baking sheet. Repeat with 5 more biscuits and the remaining vegetarian filling.

6. Repeat step 5 using another 6 biscuits and the beef filling, and place the beef-filled biscuits on a separate baking sheet.

7. Bake the bierocks for 15 minutes, or until lightly brown on the outsides. Serve warm. Feel free to cook the remaining 4 biscuits while cooking the bierocks (perhaps saving the biscuits for dessert, topped with a little honey).

Notes: We use pre-made biscuits for the dough here, because it's easy, because they fit around the filling perfectly, and because, well, they're pretty tasty. If you feel you must make your own dough, we won't stop you. Another thing to know about bierocks is that folks like to top them differently. Some like a bit of ketchup, some a splash of hot sauce or barbecue sauce, and some prefer them without any extra topping. Set out a few extra condiments and let folks experiment.

 MAKE IT ALL VEGETARIAN: Omit the ground beef, and use 2 cups vegetarian beef crumbles. Skip step 2, and cook everything in one skillet.

 MAKE IT ALL MEAT: Omit the vegetarian beef crumbles, and use 1 pound ground beef. In step 3, cook the onions and cabbage in the same skillet with the ground beef, and skip step 4.

The Best Biscuits and Sausage Gravy

Serves 2
vegetarians and
2 meat-eaters

4 ounces loose pork sausage

¼ cup (½ stick) unsalted butter

½ cup all-purpose flour

1 vegetable bouillon cube, crushed

4 cups milk

¼ teaspoon salt

½ teaspoon freshly ground black pepper

2 vegetarian sausage patties, chopped (we like Morningstar Farms)

8 biscuits (either the Delish Drop Biscuits on page 208 or 1 package jumbo-size refrigerated biscuits, baked)

Biscuits and gravy was a Saturday staple at our houses during middle school in the middle of Kansas—actually making it exciting to get out of bed on the weekends. This version may make you feel a little sad, though, when you have to clean the pan of those last little trails of gravy sticking to the sides. This B&G is just like what you'd find in better truck stops throughout the Midwest, and it would make the longest-haul trucker proud. If you don't already love B&G, this recipe will make you a believer real quick. Yes, it uses a lot of butter. But the fat content is brought down a little by the imitation sausage, and you'll get plenty of exercise with all the whisking needed to get the gravy smooth.

1. Cook the pork sausage in a small skillet over medium heat. Remove the pan from the heat and set aside. Drain away the precious sausage drippings, if you're the sort of person who does such a thing.

2. To make the gravy, melt the butter in a large saucepan over medium heat. Once the butter is foaming, add the flour and the crushed bouillon cube. This is where the whisking starts, so take a deep breath. Whisk the butter, flour, and bouillon together until they make a smooth paste, or roux (pronounced ROO). Keep whisking the mixture until it becomes a nice, even tan color.

3. Add ½ cup of the milk to your roux. Keep whisking until the milk is completely blended in and the mixture has thickened (you want it to be about the texture of glue). Once you reach the desired consistency, whisk in another ½ cup milk. Whisk in the remaining 3 cups milk, 1 cup at a time, letting the mixture thicken up after each addition. When you add the last cup of milk, also add the salt and pepper and stir to combine. Whisking in all of the milk should take around 15 minutes. When the mixture reaches a consistency just thinner than honey, taste the gravy and add more salt and pepper if desired.

4. Transfer half of the gravy to the skillet with the pork sausage, and stir to combine.

5. Raise the heat on the saucepan with the remaining gravy to medium-high, and stir the gravy well. Add the chopped vegetarian sausage to the pan, and stir to mix well. Keeping an eye on both pans, cook, stirring occasionally, until the gravy in each reaches your desired degree of thickness.

6. Place 2 biscuits in each of four shallow bowls. Into two of the bowls, spoon some of the vegetarian sausage and gravy over the biscuits. Spoon some of the pork sausage and gravy over the biscuits in the other two bowls. Serve immediately.

MAKE IT ALL VEGETARIAN: Omit the pork sausage, and use 4 vegetarian sausage patties. Skip steps 1 and 4, and cook everything in one pan in step 5.

MAKE IT ALL MEAT: Omit the vegetarian sausage, and use 8 ounces pork sausage. Skip steps 4 and 5. Add the cooked sausage to the saucepan with the gravy.

Gorgonzola Polenta with Mushrooms and Sopressata

Serves 2
vegetarians and
2 meat-eaters

3 tablespoons olive oil

1 medium-size onion,
finely chopped

3 garlic cloves, minced

4 cups vegetable stock
or broth, homemade
(page 100) or store-
bought

1 cup Italian-style
polenta or coarsely
ground cornmeal

1 teaspoon salt

½ teaspoon freshly
ground black pepper

8 ounces mushrooms,
sliced (any variety will
work, so be creative)

2 sprigs fresh rosemary,
leaves only

¼ cup (½ stick) unsalted
butter

Although a seemingly mild slight by today's standards, "polenta eater" was a scathingly derogatory term southern Italians used in reference to the northern Italians of Lombardy and the Veneto way back when. Although porridge-like dishes had always been part of the Italian diet, polenta as we think of it today wasn't introduced into the Italian diet until the post-Columbian fifteenth and sixteenth centuries, when corn was transplanted from the New World to the Old World. Call us what you will, but "polenta eaters" is a moniker we'll take gladly.

1. Heat 2 tablespoons of the olive oil over medium heat in a large, heavy-bottomed pot—an enameled cast-iron vessel would be a good choice. Add the onion and garlic and cook for about 5 minutes, stirring constantly, until translucent. Add the vegetable stock, increase the heat to high, and bring to a boil.

2. When the stock is boiling, add the polenta slowly, stirring constantly to avoid lumps. Add the salt and pepper. Reduce the heat to medium-low and cook for 45 minutes to 1 hour, stirring every 10 minutes or so. Don't worry if the polenta on the bottom of the pot gets slightly browned—this is actually an expected and welcome outcome when making a classic polenta.

3. While the polenta is bubbling away, heat the remaining 1 tablespoon olive oil in a sauté pan over medium-high heat and add the mushrooms. Cook until the mushrooms have released most or all of their liquid, about 10 minutes, then add the rosemary and stir to combine. Remove the pan from the heat, cover, and set aside.

4. After the polenta has been cooking for about 45 minutes, give it a taste for texture and seasoning. If it seems too gritty, add some warm water or more stock and cook a bit longer. You want a nice, smooth, slightly loose consistency. Adjust the seasonings if desired.

4 ounces Gorgonzola cheese, sliced into 4 equal slabs

2 ounces sopressata or other hard, dry Italian salami, sliced into thin strips

4 teaspoons Marsala (optional)

5. A few minutes before serving, warm four shallow serving bowls in a 200°F oven. In the meantime, raise the heat under the polenta to medium-high and add the butter. Stir until incorporated. If there's any brown goodness stuck to the bottom of the pot, endeavor to scrape up and incorporate it into the rest of the polenta.

6. When the polenta is piping hot, divide it among the warmed serving bowls and smooth the top with a spoon or spatula. Add 1 slab of the Gorgonzola and one-quarter of the mushrooms to each bowl. Top each of two bowls with half of the sopressata. Sprinkle 1 teaspoon Marsala, if you are using it, over each bowl. Serve immediately as the Gorgonzola begins to enrich your humble polenta with its melting blue-cheesey goodness.

Note: In our hustle-bustle world we don't always have an extra hour or so to dedicate to polenta making, so what's a body to do? Go without polenta's creamy, corny goodness? We say, heck no—just find some instant polenta online or at your local Italian specialty shop. It takes only about 5 minutes to make, and if the alternative is the drive-thru, which is the better option? Given the relative abundance of delicious Italian-made instant polentas, we'd say those adamant anti-instant-polenta purists out there can just hush, puppies.

 MAKE IT ALL VEGETARIAN: Omit the sopressata; add more mushrooms, if you like.

 MAKE IT ALL MEAT: Increase the amount of sopressata to 4 ounces so that everyone gets some.

Chicken and Dumplings

**Serves 3
vegetarians and
3 meat-eaters**

4 cups vegetarian stock
or broth, homemade
(page 100) or store-
bought

1 pound roasted chicken
(page 115), coarsely
chopped

1 recipe Spaetzle (page
162)

1 pound vegetarian
chicken breast,
coarsely chopped

¼ cup chopped fresh
flat-leaf parsley

Dumplings just sound kindly, like they'll call to you on a cold winter's day, when the wind's been pelting your chin during the long walk home, and all day long you've only been able to think about a bowl filled with a bit of hearty hotness. Come on in, the dumplings say, and warm right up. What a good feeling, and how quickly all that cold and chill are left outside.

1. Heat 2 cups of the vegetable stock in a large saucepan over medium heat. Add the chicken and half of the spaetzle, and stir well.

2. In a second large saucepan, heat the remaining 2 cups vegetable stock, the vegetarian chicken, and the remaining spaetzle over medium heat, and stir well with a different spoon. Cook both for 5 minutes.

3. Ladle the chicken and dumplings into shallow bowls (you'll need to ladle the vegetarian version first if you only have one ladle). Garnish with the parsley, and serve with big spoons.

 MAKE IT ALL VEGETARIAN: Omit the roasted chicken, and use 2 pounds vegetarian chicken breast. You can cook everything together in one pot.

 MAKE IT ALL MEAT: Omit the vegetarian chicken breast, and use 2 pounds roasted chicken. You can cook everything together in one pot.

Make the Most of Your Meat

This book isn't intended to be a political manifesto, but any modern discussions of meat consumption or "organic versus conventional farming" inevitably bear the smell of political and ethical predilections. It is no secret that factory farmed livestock don't have a great life. Most commercially raised animals are exposed to myriad antibiotics and other potions, which an ever-growing body of science indicates may be impacting both human and environmental health. Moreover, have you ever taken and tasted your or your child's antibiotics? Being a pharmacist, I can tell you that very few taste good at all, and is that how you want dinner to taste? And really, I think we should just focus on taste, because fine food almost always leads to friendly discussion; if only the reverse were more reliably true. In the simple matter of taste, fresh food is almost always better when consumed soon after picking, or slaughter, for that matter. For a crazy pork fan like myself, that means getting some good chops from Wooly Pigs (a company in Washington State that raises a special breed of pig called the Mangalitsa and sells the meat at farmers' markets in Seattle and elsewhere), or ordering a whole pig to go into my Caja China (a Cuban pig-roasting box) from the guys at Better

Meat, who get them from Kapowsin, Washington—an hour's drive from Seattle. As far as beef goes, it's my humble opinion that grass-fed beef rocks the party. Although generally more expensive than the more common corn-fed beef, I like the flavor exponentially more, and it's higher in omega-3s and lower in saturated fat than corn-fed beef.

But the biggest motivation to buy organic and/or local has got to be found in the chicken department. The growing American appetite for boneless, skinless chicken breast over the past 20 years has had the unfortunate result of adding "flavorless" to chicken's list of "-less" descriptive adjectives. Because chicken is a rather mild meat to begin with, the difference is subtle, but the best way to describe the difference between chickens raised by the large poultry producers and chickens you would get from a smaller, more local farmer is that they are just more "chicken-y." And pound for pound, a whole organic chicken isn't much more expensive than conventional boneless, skinless breasts. Being the grandson of a postal worker who moonlit as a meat cutter in a super-old-school neighborhood grocery store, I would encourage you to find a good butcher and patronize the shop as much as possible.

Frisky Fish Sticks

Serves 3
vegetarians and
3 meat-eaters

1 pound extra-firm tofu,
   drained (page 44)

1 pound cod or halibut
   fillets

2 cups all-purpose flour

4 large eggs

½ cup milk

1 cup bread crumbs

1 garlic clove, minced

2 tablespoons minced
   fresh flat-leaf parsley

½ teaspoon cayenne
   pepper

½ teaspoon paprika

3 tablespoons vegetable
   oil

We have not-so-fond memories of those cardboard-ish rectangular lumps called fish sticks that were trotted out once a month in the school cafeteria (sorry, cafeteria ladies and gentlemen, we appreciated your efforts, but those fish sticks were a bit hard to swallow). Don't let similar memories scare you away from these friskier fish sticks, which are delish, with a hint of spice. Using some extra-firm tofu instead of fish in half the recipe allows the vegetarians to also put those scary school-fish-stick memories away for good. Serve with French fries, of course.

1. Preheat the oven to 200°F.

2. On separate cutting boards, cut the tofu and the cod into approximately 4 x ½-inch pieces. Set both aside.

3. Put the flour in a shallow bowl. In another shallow bowl, combine the eggs and milk, mixing well. In a third shallow bowl, mix the bread crumbs, garlic, parsley, cayenne, and paprika.

4. Heat the oil in a medium-size, high-sided skillet over high heat. Once the oil is good and hot, coat a tofu piece with the flour, dip it into the egg mixture, dredge it in the bread crumbs, then carefully place it in the hot oil. Fry for 2 to 3 minutes, then turn and fry for 2 to 3 minutes longer (it should be golden brown on both sides). Place the fried tofu on paper towels to drain for a few seconds, then transfer it to a baking sheet and place in the oven to keep warm. Repeat for all the tofu pieces, doing a few at a time if you feel comfortable with it.

5. Repeat the process in step 4 using the fish pieces instead of the tofu, and using a separate baking sheet to keep the cooked fish warm while frying the rest. Once all the tofu and fish have been fried, serve them up hot with some tartar sauce (see Note).

Note: For a quick and tasty tartar sauce, mix together 1 cup mayonnaise, ¼ cup chopped dill pickle, 2 tablespoons chopped yellow onion, ½ garlic clove (minced), ½ teaspoon freshly squeezed lemon juice,

$^1/_2$ teaspoon salt, and $^1/_2$ teaspoon freshly ground black pepper. Jeremy thinks that adding $^1/_8$ cup drained capers is also a great idea, though A.J. isn't so sure.

 MAKE IT ALL VEGETARIAN: Omit the cod, and use 2 pounds tofu.

 MAKE IT ALL MEAT: Omit the tofu, and use 2 pounds cod.

A.J. SAYS:

Doubling Up

Once you get into the swing of the *Double Take* setup and are making meals for meat-eaters and vegetarians on a regular basis, a couple of things will probably happen. First, you'll be amazed at how easy it can be. Second, more and more friends and family will start showing up at meal time, or coyly inviting themselves over for dinners and brunches, because they know you'll have entrées and sides for everyone, and that everyone will be able to come together at the same table. When this starts to happen, you'll probably need to make larger quantities, which might seem daunting but which can be an awful lot of fun. All of the recipes in this book can be doubled (some more easily than others, sure), but there are a few things to remember when increasing the yields. First, watch the spices. Some spices (pepper, for example) can quickly take over a dish if upped to higher levels. Keep an easy hand, and increase spice amounts in slightly smaller increments, and taste, taste, taste and season accordingly, and you'll end up in delicious-town. Second, figure out before you start cooking how many pans, bowls, and dishes you'll need, so that you don't run short. And third, don't be shy about asking those folks coming over to pitch in and lend a hand in the kitchen—cooking together is a great way to start an evening.

Hail the Chicken à la King

Serves 2
vegetarians and
2 meat-eaters

¼ cup (½ stick) plus 1½ teaspoons unsalted butter

2 cups chopped button mushrooms

½ cup all-purpose flour

1 vegetable bouillon cube, crushed

3 cups milk

¼ teaspoon salt

½ teaspoon freshly ground black pepper

¼ teaspoon cayenne pepper

1 cup cubed roasted chicken (page 115)

1 cup cubed vegetarian chicken breast

4 English muffins, split and toasted

1 teaspoon chopped fresh flat-leaf parsley

It's a little-known fact that kings worldwide love chicken à la king, so much so that they have it for their coronation ceremonies, and sometimes even on their birthdays and other royal holidays. This (we think) has been true throughout history, as certain lesser-known reports show that Arthur, as well as Charles VII of Sweden, King Lear (in a passage deleted in later editions of the play), and Billie Jean King were all avid consumers of the dish. And who can blame them? Chicken à la king's easy-to-construct-and-delicious-to-eat nature is ideal for kings and, lucky for us, commoners alike.

1. Heat 1½ teaspoons of the butter in a small skillet over medium-high heat. Once the butter is foaming, add the mushrooms. Cook for 5 minutes, remove from the heat, and set aside.

2. Melt the remaining ¼ cup butter in a large saucepan over medium heat. Once the butter is foaming and hot, add the flour and the bouillon cube. Whisk the butter, flour, and bouillon together until they make a smooth roux. Keep whisking the mixture until its color is an even tan, about 5 minutes.

3. Add ½ cup of the milk to the saucepan, whisking all the while, until the milk has been completely combined with the roux. Whisk in another ½ cup of the milk until well combined. Whisk in the remaining 2 cups milk, 1 cup at a time. When all of the milk is mixed in well, add the salt, pepper, and cayenne, and stir until well combined. Cook, stirring, until the sauce is about as thick as honey. Add the mushrooms to the pan, and stir once again.

4. Transfer half of the sauce to a medium-size saucepan set over medium heat. Add the cubed chicken to the pan and stir well.

5. Add the vegetarian chicken to the pan with the remaining sauce, and stir well (using a separate spoon).

6. Place two English muffin halves on individual plates, and top the English muffins on two of the plates with a good ladleful of vegetarian chicken and sauce. Top the English muffins on the remaining two plates with a good ladleful of the roasted chicken and sauce. (Either use two ladles or ladle the vegetarian mix first.) Sprinkle a bit of parsley over each plate and serve immediately.

 MAKE IT ALL VEGETARIAN: Omit the roasted chicken, and use 2 cups vegetarian chicken. Combine everything in one saucepan.

 MAKE IT ALL MEAT: Omit the vegetarian chicken, and use 2 cups roasted chicken. Combine everything in one saucepan.

Hungry Hungarian Stuffed Peppers

Serves 3 vegetarians and 3 meat-eaters

Two 15-ounce cans
tomato sauce

½ teaspoon freshly
ground black pepper

½ teaspoon kosher salt

1 tablespoon minced
fresh flat-leaf parsley

1 teaspoon dried thyme

½ teaspoon cayenne
pepper

3 teaspoons vegetable oil

1 large yellow onion,
chopped

12 ounces lean ground
beef

2 cups cooked white or
brown rice

These stuffed peppers pack quite a punch—not in a violent way, but in a stomach-filling kind of way, which is why they are the perfect meal on those days when you've been partaking in athletic activity (or those sad days when you've subbed in an oddly tasteless nutty bar or some such for a real lunch because you were too busy at the office). So whip these up when you have a serious hankering for some rib-sticking vittles. We're not saying Al Hrabosky (the former Major League Baseball relief pitcher and mustache enthusiast better known as the Mad Hungarian) would become instantly happy after eating these, but he'd at least smile.

1. Combine the tomato sauce, pepper, salt, parsley, thyme, and cayenne in a medium-size saucepan over medium-low heat; stir well, and cover.

2. Add 1½ teaspoons of the oil to each of two medium-size skillets or sauté pans over medium heat. When the oil is hot, add half of the onion to each skillet. Add the ground beef to one of the skillets. Stirring regularly, cook until the onions have reached a light golden color and are soft and the ground beef is browned, 5 to 7 minutes.

3. Add 1 cup of the rice to each skillet, and add the vegetarian crumbles to the skillet without the beef in it. Cook the contents of both skillets for 5 minutes, stirring occasionally.

4. Cut the tops off of the green peppers (about ¼ inch from the top is good), and scrape out the membranes and seeds. Using a spoon, fill 3 of the peppers with the vegetarian crumble–rice mixture, and fill the remaining 3 peppers with the beef-rice mixture.

5. Transfer half of the tomato sauce to a second medium-size saucepan. Place the 3 peppers stuffed with the vegetarian filling into one saucepan, making sure that the tops of the peppers are facing skyward (this may take a touch of balancing). Place the beef-stuffed peppers into the other sauce-

One 12-ounce package vegetarian beef crumbles (such as Morningstar Meal Starters)

6 medium-size green bell peppers

pan in the same manner. Cover both saucepans, and raise the heat under each to medium-high. Cook for 15 minutes, then reduce the heat to medium. Cook for 20 more minutes, then check the peppers for doneness with a fork. If the fork goes easily into the peppers, they're done—if not, cook for 10 more minutes.

6. Serve each pepper in a shallow bowl, pouring some of the tomato sauce over the top.

 MAKE IT ALL VEGETARIAN: Omit the ground beef, and use two 12-ounce packages vegetarian beef crumbles, cooking everything in one large skillet.

 MAKE IT ALL MEAT: Omit the vegetarian beef crumbles, and use 1 1/2 pounds ground beef, cooking everything in one large skillet.

Meat-and-Not-Meat Loaf

1½ pounds lean ground beef

1½ pounds vegetarian beef crumbles (such as Yves Ground Round)

½ cup finely chopped onion

1½ teaspoons freshly ground black pepper

1½ teaspoons salt

1½ cups bread crumbs

1 teaspoon chopped fresh flat-leaf parsley

1 teaspoon dried thyme

4 dashes of Tabasco or other Louisiana-style hot sauce

4 large eggs

½ cup ketchup

2 tablespoons water

There was a time when every family had its own version of meat loaf. You'd find some using eggs, some topping it with bacon, a few slipping in barbecue sauce, and most adding a grain product to the mixture (a practice that began after the Great Depression, to stretch the family's food dollar). Nowadays, you don't see meat loaf on the family table as much. A sorry state of affairs, especially when you consider that a) it's simple to make for both meat-eaters and vegetarians, and b) not only is it good on the first serving, but meat loaf sandwiches are one of the best uses of leftovers ever (especially when made with toasted bread and a little mayo). So when making this recipe, save a little meat loaf for tomorrow, too.

1. Preheat the oven to 350°F.

2. Place the ground beef in a large bowl, and the vegetarian beef crumbles in another large bowl. Place half of the chopped onion in each bowl.

3. In a small bowl, combine the pepper, salt, bread crumbs, parsley, and thyme. Place half of this mixture in each of the larger bowls.

4. Add 2 dashes of the Tabasco, 2 of the eggs, ¼ cup of the ketchup, and 1 tablespoon of the water to each bowl. Mix the contents of each bowl until thoroughly combined (you'll want to use different spoons for each bowl, or wash your hands between mixing each if going with the traditional hands-on mixing style).

5. Transfer the contents of each bowl to its own loaf pan. Bake both loaves, uncovered, for 1 hour. The beef meat loaf should be 160°F in the middle. They should both have a bit of crispness on top. Let cool slightly, then slice and serve.

Variation: As mentioned, there are many, many meat loaf variations. Want to add a little more pork pizzazz? Top the meat loaf with 3 bacon slices, and the vegetarian loaf with 3 vegetarian bacon slices. Want a bit more sizzle? Add ½ cup sliced jalapeño chiles to each loaf. Want a bit more juice and flavor? Add 4 tablespoons red wine instead of the water. See, it's fun to experiment a bit with a classic. Just don't forget to save some slices for sandwiches the next day.

MAKE IT ALL VEGETARIAN: Simply increase the amount of vegetarian beef crumbles to 3 pounds and omit the ground beef. Feel free to use just one large bowl in step 2, but still use two loaf pans.

 MAKE IT ALL MEAT: Increase the amount of ground beef to 3 pounds and omit the vegetarian beef crumbles. Again, use just one large bowl in step 2, but use two loaf pans.

Organic Is Good

Okay, it may be that there haven't been any definitive tests by teams of scientists huddled in tall buildings with clipboards aplenty verifying that organic fruits, vegetables, grains, and meats taste better than their non-organic counterparts. And maybe our regulations here in the United States on what actually qualifies as "organic" could be a bit better defined and enforced. And, conceivably, there are some folks out there using the term *organic* solely as a marketing device. But I still think organic carrots (not to mention most every other vegetable I've tried, which includes most everything you can think of) always taste better than conventional, and there's no question that less unwanted chemical intake is a good thing. So, if you can get organic and farm-fresh ingredients, I suggest using them. Luckily, there are many delivery services popping up that will bring organic produce to your doorstep—a fantastic way to save time and eat tastier food—and there are many more farmers' markets showing up where you can pick out produce and meat while talking about it to the folks who grew or raised it. The way I see it, there's just no reason not to take advantage of this bounty.

Shrimp and Grits

Serves 2
vegetarians and
2 meat-eaters

4½ cups vegetable stock
or broth, homemade
(page 100) or store-
bought

1 cup grits (regular or
quick-cooking, not
instant)

2 tablespoons unsalted
butter

½ medium-size yellow
onion, chopped

2 medium-size green bell
peppers, seeded and
chopped

1 medium-size red bell
pepper, seeded and
chopped

2 garlic cloves, minced

¼ teaspoon salt

½ teaspoon freshly
ground black pepper

The state food of South Carolina and the official prepared food of Georgia, grits are an essential element in the Southern comfort-food category, often eaten for a late breakfast, frequently with shrimp or another topping. The regionality of grits shouldn't keep you away from this dish if you're a Northerner, though, because it tastes fine no matter where it's prepared—and for that matter, though it's a traditional morning dish, it tastes fine no matter what time of day you make it. Finding a vegetarian substitute for shrimp is difficult, though. Those few products on the market calling themselves "vegetarian shrimp" tend to be too tough to chew. Instead of forcing the issue, we think the way to go vegetarian with this dish is shrimp-size pieces of portobello mushroom, which have a texture that gives vegetarians something to chew on without making them feel like they're eating rubber. Grits tend to like being partnered up with a vegetable, so serve this dish with Vinegar Greens (page 198) or a little coleslaw (page 190).

1. Heat the vegetable stock in a large saucepan over medium-high heat. When the stock starts to boil, slowly add the grits while stirring to combine. Reduce the heat to low. Cook for 30 minutes, stirring regularly (at least every minute or two) to avoid scorching. The grits should have the consistency of oatmeal, having soaked up the stock. If the grits seem too thick, add a little water to thin them. Remove the pan from the heat and set aside.

2. Heat 1 tablespoon of the butter in a large skillet or sauté pan over medium-high heat. When the butter has bubbled and is hot, add the onion. Stirring regularly, cook for 5 minutes, then add the green and red peppers, garlic, salt, pepper, and hot sauce. Cook for 5 more minutes, or until the onions are soft and golden.

3. Heat the remaining 1 tablespoon butter in a second large skillet or sauté pan over medium-high heat. Once the butter is hot, add the shrimp, along with half of the onion-pepper mixture.

3 dashes of Tabasco or other Louisiana-style hot sauce, plus more to taste

12 ounces medium-size shrimp, peeled and deveined

3 large portobello mushrooms, stemmed and chopped into ½-inch pieces

4. Add the portobello mushroom pieces to the pan with the remaining onion-pepper mixture. Cook the contents of both pans over medium-high heat for 6 to 7 minutes, stirring regularly, until the shrimp are cooked through.

5. To serve, spoon a nice helping of grits onto a plate or into a bowl, and top with a helping of either the shrimp mixture or the mushroom mixture.

 MAKE IT ALL VEGETARIAN: Omit the shrimp, use 6 mushrooms, and skip step 3.

 MAKE IT ALL MEAT: Omit the mushrooms, use 1½ pounds shrimp, and cook the shrimp in the same skillet with the onion-pepper mixture.

Border-Busting Parmigiana

Serves 2
vegetarians and
2 meat-eaters

1 medium-size eggplant,
peeled and sliced
lengthwise into four
½-inch-thick slabs

¾ teaspoon salt

6 slices good-quality
white bread, crusts
removed

½ cup grated
Parmigiano-Reggiano
cheese (2 ounces)

6 sprigs fresh oregano,
leaves only

½ teaspoon freshly
ground black pepper

2 cups all-purpose flour

1 large egg beaten with
1 tablespoon water

Four 3-ounce veal
or chicken cutlets,
pounded to a ¼-inch
thickness

6 tablespoons olive oil

Don't get the wrong idea—we're not talking about an international incident here (we certainly don't want to get in trouble with any folks in the European regions). The borders we're interested in busting are those keeping meat-eaters and vegetarians from sitting down together at the same table to a parmigiana all can enjoy. Because this southern-Italian comfort food, with its heartiness and friendliness, is meant to be part of a communal affair, be sure to serve it with a sturdy Italian red wine, or else folks from both sides may actually start getting their feathers ruffled. And don't be afraid to have some garlic bread nearby.

1. Arrange the eggplant in a colander and sprinkle with 1/2 teaspoon of the salt. Allow the eggplant to drain over a bowl for 1 hour, then rinse and pat or press dry (this removes a lot of flavorless water and concentrates the eggplant-y goodness).

2. Pulse the bread in a food processor until it resembles bread crumbs. Add 1/4 cup of the Parmigiano-Reggiano and the oregano, and pulse briefly to mix. Season lightly with the remaining 1/4 teaspoon salt and the pepper.

3. Put the flour, egg wash, and bread crumb mixture into separate shallow dishes. Dredge an eggplant slice in the flour and gently slide it into the egg wash. Remove the eggplant slice from the egg wash by hand and gently lay it on the bread crumbs. Gently press more bread crumbs into the top of the eggplant slice. Transfer the breaded eggplant to a clean dish. Repeat the process for the remaining eggplant slices.

4. Bread the veal cutlets as in step 3, and place them on a separate dish from the eggplant.

5. Preheat the oven to 400°F. Meanwhile, heat 3 tablespoons of the olive oil in each of two large ovenproof sauté pans over medium-high heat until almost smoking, then add the breaded eggplant to one pan and the breaded veal to the other. Cook the eggplant and the veal for 3 minutes on each side.

1 recipe tomato sauce
(page 186) or 2 cups
store-bought marinara
sauce

8 ounces sliced
mozzarella cheese

1 tablespoon chopped
fresh flat-leaf parsley,
for garnish

6. Remove the pans from the heat. Top each piece of eggplant and veal with 2 tablespoons of the tomato sauce, some Parmigiano-Reggiano, and a slice or two of the mozzarella.

7. Bake for 8 to 10 minutes, until the mozzarella is bubbly and lightly browned.

8. Garnish with the parsley, and serve immediately to prevent your lovely bread crumb crust from becoming soggy.

Note: Experimentation is fun here, as almost anything is good when breaded, covered with a simple tomato sauce and mozzarella, and then baked: Try tofu, seitan, or Quorn. Heck, you can even pound out a little beef blade steak and have an Italian-inspired chicken-fried steak.

 MAKE IT ALL VEGETARIAN: Use 2 medium-size eggplants and omit the meat. Skip step 4 and the meat-referencing portion of step 5.

 MAKE IT ALL MEAT: Omit the eggplant and use 8 veal or chicken cutlets. Skip step 1 and the eggplant-referencing portions of steps 3 and 5.

Tortilla Pie

**Serves
3 vegetarians and
3 meat-eaters**

1 tablespoon vegetable
oil

½ medium-size yellow
onion, chopped

1 cup corn kernels, fresh,
frozen, or canned

½ teaspoon freshly
ground black pepper

¼ teaspoon salt

1 teaspoon chili powder

1 cup Mexican chorizo

1 cup Soyrizo (see Notes)

2 cups enchilada sauce
(see Notes)

12 corn tortillas

1 cup cooked black beans
(canned is fine)

2 cups shredded
Monterey Jack cheese
(8 ounces)

Mexican-style hot sauce,
such as Cholula, for
serving

This dish has a hint of Mexican flair to it, though not as much flair as wearing *taleguilla*, or bullfighter pants—which is really a bad idea after eating a full helping of this very filling pie. Tortilla pie owes more to the casserole movement of the 1970s than to traditional south-of-the-border fare, but by adding Mexican chorizo and Soyrizo, we're slipping in a little authenticity.

1. Preheat the oven to 350°F.

2. Place two medium-size skillets over medium-high heat. Heat 1½ teaspoons of the oil in each pan, then add half of the onion to each pan. Sauté the onion, stirring, until it is soft and light brown. Add ½ cup of the corn, ¼ teaspoon of the pepper, ⅛ teaspoon of the salt, and ½ teaspoon of the chili powder to each pan, and cook for 5 minutes.

3. Add the chorizo to one pan and the Soyrizo to the other. Cook, stirring occasionally (using separate spoons), until the chorizo and Soyrizo are cooked through, about 5 minutes.

4. Spread a thin layer of the enchilada sauce on the bottom of each of two 9-inch square baking pans. Layer 3 of the tortillas over the sauce, tearing as needed to fit, then top that with ¼ cup of the black beans and ½ cup of the cheese. Top one of the pans with about half of the chorizo mixture, and top the other with about half of the Soyrizo mixture. Add another layer of enchilada sauce to each pan, then repeat the layering process to make a second layer of tortillas, black beans, cheese, and chorizo or Soyrizo. Pour whatever sauce is left equally over the pans.

5. Bake for 45 minutes. Test for doneness by putting a knife into the center of each pan (using a separate knife for each)—the knife should come out fairly clean. If it doesn't, cook the tortilla pies a little longer.

6. Let the tortilla pies sit for 5 minutes to set. When serving, they should be dry enough to slice fairly neatly, but they'll still be oozing delicious sauce and cheese, too. Serve with a little Mexican hot sauce on the side.

Notes: Soyrizo is a chorizo substitute made of textured vegetable protein, and it's remarkably similar to chorizo in taste and consistency. It also cooks in the same way and can be used in any recipe calling for chorizo. You can find Soyrizo in gourmet and better grocery stores (Trader Joe's makes its own version), as well as online—it's Jeremy's favorite meat substitute. You could use store-bought enchilada sauce here, but why not whip up your own? A very quick but spicily delish version can be made by combining 1 1/2 cups tomato sauce and 1 1/2 cups vegetable broth in a medium-size saucepan over medium heat. Add 1 teaspoon freshly ground black pepper, 1/4 teaspoon salt, 1 tablespoon chili powder, 1 teaspoon ground cumin, and 1 teaspoon garlic powder, and stir well. Dissolve 1 tablespoon cornstarch in 2 tablespoons water and add this to the mix. Stirring occasionally, cook for 10 minutes, until the sauce thickens. Now you have your homemade enchilada sauce.

 MAKE IT ALL VEGETARIAN: Omit the chorizo, and use 2 cups Soyrizo. Cook everything in one skillet in steps 2 and 3.

 MAKE IT ALL MEAT: Omit the Soyrizo, and use 2 cups chorizo. Cook everything in one skillet in steps 2 and 3.

Pizza Quattro Stagioni

Makes four 10-inch pizzas to serve 4 vegetarians and 4 meat-eaters

1 recipe tomato sauce (page 186) or 2 cups store-bought marinara sauce

1 recipe pizza dough (page 148) or 30 ounces store-bought pizza dough

Cornmeal for dusting pizza peel or cutting board

8 ounces thinly sliced fresh mozzarella cheese

4 ounces marinated artichoke hearts, well drained and chopped

4 ounces button or cremini mushrooms, thinly sliced

2 ounces thinly sliced prosciutto

Without exception, no other foodstuff has upheld the *Double Take* lifestyle more than pizza. The ability to order different toppings on each half of your pizza has been a balm to the aching divide between herbivores and omnivores for years, and this Italian classic quite possibly could have been the blueprint. Pizza *quattro stagioni*, or four seasons pizza, is a "kitchen sink" pizza, with different combinations of ingredients arranged on the four quadrants of the pizza. A quick tip: For best results, cook the pizza on a pizza stone, and be sure your ingredients, especially the vegetables, don't contain a lot of extraneous moisture. If they do, consider oven-drying them for 15 minutes at 375°F. Otherwise a sad, soggy pizza could be the result.

1. Place an oven rack with a pizza stone on it in the lower third of the oven and preheat the oven to 450°F. If you don't have a pizza stone, a large baking sheet will work.

2. Heat the tomato sauce on the stovetop in a medium-size saucepan over medium heat. Cook until the sauce has very little liquid in it.

3. Divide the pizza dough into four portions.

4. Shape one portion into a ball and roll it out into a circle on a clean, well-floured work surface. Leave the edges a little thicker than the rest of the circle. Don't fret if it's not perfectly round—ours never are. We promise shape will not affect taste.

5. Transfer the dough onto a pizza peel or a sufficiently large, thin cutting board liberally dusted with cornmeal so that the pizza dough can slide off of it easily.

6. Spread a thin layer of tomato sauce over the pizza dough, and top with one-quarter of the mozzarella.

7. Envisioning the pizza in quadrants, arrange one-quarter of the artichoke hearts on one quadrant, one-quarter of the mushrooms on another, half of the prosciutto on another, and one-quarter of the olives on the last quadrant.

¼ cup pitted and sliced kalamata or other black olives

2 ounces jarred roasted red pepper slices, drained and patted dry

8. Gently slide the pizza from the pizza peel onto the pizza stone, and bake for 8 to 12 minutes, until the crust is nicely browned and perhaps even a little charred here and there.

9. While the first pizza is baking, repeat steps 4 through 8 using another portion of dough, and substituting half of the roasted peppers for the prosciutto. (You can bake two pizzas at once if you like, but we only have 1 pizza stone, so we bake our pizzas in succession.)

10. Repeat steps 4 through 9 with the remaining portions of dough and ingredients so that you end up with 2 hammy and 2 veggie pizzas.

Note: Although our first trip to Italy with our wives (still our live-in girlfriends at the time) in the summer of 2002 had occasional minor irritations (heat rash, allergic reactions to detergents, wasp stings), one of the many amazingly memorable things was Pizzeria Nestor in the minuscule Umbrian town of Verna. Their pizza is crazy good and astoundingly inexpensive. Nestor's was the first place Jeremy had pizza *quattro stagioni*, and they cracked a raw egg on top before putting the pizza into the oven, the end result being a sunny-side-up egg in the center of the pizza. Most home ovens do not get hot enough to cook both the egg and the crust underneath it properly. But the next time you're dining at a traditional Italian pizzeria with a wood-fired oven, give it a go. Alternatively, try pan-frying an egg separately and then sliding it onto the center of the pizza before serving.

 MAKE IT ALL VEGETARIAN: Omit the prosciutto, and use 4 ounces roasted red peppers.

 MAKE IT ALL MEAT: That's entirely missing the point of pizza *quattro stagioni*, but, as Jeremy says, more prosciutto never hurts.

Pizza Dough Pleasantries

MAKES ENOUGH DOUGH FOR FOUR 10-INCH ROUNDS

1 ounce fresh yeast or $1/2$ ounce (2 packets) dry yeast

1 cup lukewarm (100° to 115°F) water

$2^1/2$ cups all-purpose flour, plus extra for rolling and dusting

$1^1/2$ teaspoons salt

1. Mix the yeast and water in a large bowl. Stir well.

2. Combine the flour and salt in a bowl, and then mix into the yeast and water.

3. Dump this mass out onto a clean, well-floured work surface. Knead until the dough is smooth and elastic, 3 to 5 minutes. (Alternatively, do steps 1, 2, and 3 in a stand mixer equipped with a dough hook, being sure to keep the gadget running at slow speed only. This may make the dough a tad chewier, but it sure is easy! Don't worry—it will still taste great.)

4. Shape the dough into a ball, return the mass to your mixing bowl, cover with a clean kitchen towel, and let rise in a warm-ish place for 1 to 3 hours. You can create a warm-ish place in your oven by turning on the oven to broil for 3 minutes, then turning it off. Let the heat escape by opening the oven door, then put the dough in to rise. Remember: Yeast likes to be at "body temperature," so make sure the oven isn't much more than 105°F or so by checking with an oven or meat thermometer. Placing the bowl on top of the fridge (as long as you don't have the AC on) works, too. Halfway through your proofing time (30 to 90 minutes), remove the dough from the bowl and place it on a floured work surface. Give it a few good punches to deflate the initial rise and knead for 30 to 60 seconds. At this point you may want to split the dough into individual portions. Reshape into a ball (or balls, if divided) place on a baking sheet, re-cover with the cloth, and finish proofing.

entertaining
entrées

this is the chapter that pours the concrete for the

bridge that will connect the once impossibly divided communities of Veggieville and Carnivore City. The recipes are slightly more involved and may take a bit longer to prepare, but how can getting everyone together in the kitchen for some prepping and cooking be a bad thing? As the term *entrée* suggests, these are main courses, but they also fulfill another definition of *entrée* in that they are a means of entry, a path down which dissimilar styles of eating can walk comfortably arm in arm.

This chapter definitively lays to rest the idea (held by carnivores) that vegetarian cooking is mostly a collection of several side dishes served together to form a main course. Coq et Moq à la Bourguignonne couldn't be more classically French—adapted to our *Double Take* purposes, of course—and we would challenge anyone to be unimpressed by the heartiness of our Osso Buco, both the traditional and vegetarian versions. Throw in a couple of classic Italian pasta recipes, add a decidedly western European take on stroganoff, sprinkle in a fricassee and some hearty stuffed radicchio, and you've got a wide selection to suit any entertaining occasion.

Coq et Moq
à la Bourguignonne

½ cup (1 stick) unsalted
butter

10 ounces fresh pearl
onions, peeled, or one
10-ounce bag frozen
pearl onions, thawed

1 pound cremini or
button mushrooms,
quartered

2 teaspoons salt

½ teaspoon freshly
ground black pepper

2 ounces bacon or salt
pork, chopped

½ chicken cut into 5
pieces: wing, thigh,
drumstick, and breast
in 2 pieces

4 vegetarian chicken
breasts, halved
(8 pieces)

Coq au vin, or "rooster in wine," is one of the most classic and recognizable exports of French cuisine, but its roots are assuredly more humble than the vaunted food palaces of Paris might indicate. Typically an older rooster or stewing hen would be used in this dish, as they contain more connective tissue than other chickens, thus producing a richer sauce, but if you follow the simple steps below, any chicken will do—even vegetarian chicken. Serve with some simple rice or crusty bread on the side. Then again, maybe some spaetzle (page 162) would be good, too. Oh, and don't forget a nice glass of red wine.

1. Melt 4 tablespoons of the butter in a skillet over medium-high heat. Add the pearl onions, mushrooms, 1 teaspoon of the salt, and ¼ teaspoon of the pepper. Sauté until the onions are nicely browned and the mushrooms have released all of their liquid. Transfer the mixture to a bowl and set aside.

2. Melt another 2 tablespoons of the butter in a large Dutch oven or stockpot over medium heat, and add the bacon. Continue cooking until the bacon is lightly browned and crisp. Remove the bacon with a slotted spoon and set aside.

3. Raise the heat under the Dutch oven to medium-high, and add the chicken pieces. Brown the chicken, turning occasionally, until the pieces are browned on all sides. Season the chicken with the remaining 1 teaspoon salt and ¼ teaspoon pepper. When sufficiently browned, use tongs to transfer the chicken to a plate, but remember that the chicken is only browned, not fully cooked, so be sure to wash the tongs after this step to avoid contamination from raw chicken.

4. While the chicken is browning, melt the remaining 2 tablespoons butter in another Dutch oven or large skillet (or whatever cooking vessel is handy that can hold about 8 cups) over medium-high heat. When the butter has just stopped foaming, add the vegetarian chicken and brown,

CONTINUES ON P. 152

1 large onion, chopped

1 large carrot, chopped

¼ cup all-purpose flour

2 cups chicken stock
 or broth, homemade
 (page 100) or store-
 bought

2 cups vegetable stock
 or broth, homemade
 (page 100) or store-
 bought

4 cups medium-bodied
 red wine, such as
 a light Burgundy
 or Chianti

2 tablespoons tomato
 paste

4 garlic cloves, minced

4 sprigs fresh thyme or
 1 teaspoon dried
 thyme

2 bay leaves

turning occasionally, until golden. Transfer the vegetarian chicken with tongs to a separate plate.

5. Add half of the chopped onion and carrot to the chicken pot and the other half to the pot formerly containing the vegetarian chicken. Cook, stirring occasionally, for about 5 minutes.

6. Add 2 tablespoons of the flour to each pot and stir for a minute or two. Don't worry—it will probably get a little lumpy and ugly, but it will be fine. Increase the heat under each pot to high, and pour the chicken stock into the pot that once held the chicken and the vegetable stock into the pot that once held the vegetarian chicken. Add 2 cups of the wine, 1 tablespoon of the tomato paste, and half of the garlic to each pot. Whisking frequently, bring each pot to a low boil until the sauce just thickens, then reduce the heat to medium-low.

7. Return the chicken and cooked bacon to the chicken-y pot, and add half of the thyme and one of the bay leaves to each pot. Cover each pot loosely with its lid or aluminum foil, allowing some steam to escape. Cook the chicken until the thigh and drumstick read 165°F and the breast reads 180°F on an instant-read thermometer inserted into their thickest parts.

8. Transfer the chicken to a clean plate. Remove the bay leaves from both pots, and raise the heat under both pots to medium-high to concentrate and thicken the sauce. Taste the sauce and season lightly with salt and pepper if needed. Whisking occasionally, reduce the sauce in each pot to about 1½ cups, which should take 5 to 10 minutes.

9. Divide the pearl onion–mushroom mixture evenly between the pots, and return the chicken to the chicken pot and the vegetarian chicken to its pot to warm everything up. Serve immediately.

Variation: Substitute 1 pound top sirloin, cut into 2-inch cubes, for the chicken in this recipe, cooking in a Dutch oven or covered casserole dish for about 3 or so hours in a 325°F oven, and you will wind up with another French classic, beef bourguignon.

MAKE IT ALL VEGETARIAN: Omit the bacon and the chicken pieces, and use 8 vegetarian chicken breasts. Omit the chicken stock and use 4 cups vegetable stock.

 MAKE IT ALL MEAT: Omit the vegetarian chicken breasts, and use a whole chicken cut into 10 pieces. Omit the vegetable stock, and use 4 cups chicken stock.

A.J. SAYS:

Watch Your Vegetarian Chicken Pickin'

There are many, many vegetarian meat substitutes out on the shelves today (and by shelves, I mean the frozen foods aisle), but perhaps the most dangerous one to devotees of the *Double Take* approach to cooking is the vegetarian chicken. This is for one simple reason: Much of it is breaded, and for recipes, breaded vegetarian chicken doesn't work as well. I've certainly had a good chicken sandwich with the breaded vegetarian chicken out there, topped with a slice of melted mozzarella, some tomato sauce, and lettuce. But when using vegetarian chicken in recipes, double-check that you're getting the nonbreaded variety. Even some "vegetarian chicken breasts" come out breaded. You can find tasty nonbreaded options from Morningstar Farms, Quorn, and others (if you live near an Asian grocery store, be sure to check the frozen foods aisle for vegetarian chicken, because you can often find some more obscure—but still very delicious—brands there, and the chance of accidentally coming out with something breaded is much smaller). Be careful with your vegetarian chicken picking, and you'll end up with much better Chicken à la King (page 134) and other dishes.

Osso Buco

Serves 2
vegetarians and
2 meat-eaters

4 pieces cross-cut veal
shank, about 6 ounces
each

7 tablespoons olive oil

½ cup plus 2 teaspoons
all-purpose flour

Salt and freshly ground
black pepper

2 medium-size carrots,
finely chopped

1 medium-size onion,
finely chopped

1 celery stalk, finely
chopped

One 14.5-ounce can
crushed tomatoes

2 cups dry white wine

2 cups chicken stock
or broth, homemade
(page 100) or store-
bought, plus extra
if needed

2 bay leaves

Soul-in-the-hole is the way we always think about osso buco (*osso buco* translated literally from the Italian means "bone hole"). Jeremy's been hooked ever since the first time he had it at Lidia Bastianich's restaurant Lidia's Italy in the West Bottoms district of Kansas City, Missouri. *Braised*, *veal*, and *shank* are some of his favorite words in the culinary lexicon, so it was natural that he would fall in love with osso buco. A.J.'s been hooked since Jeremy came up with such an amazing vegetarian take on this meat-heavy classic. This recipe takes a little time and preparation, so save it for a weekend, but we guarantee your guests will be completely blown away, meat-eaters and vegetarians alike.

1. Preheat the oven to 350°F. Tie each veal shank individually with kitchen twine to prevent the shanks from falling apart during cooking.

2. Heat 2 tablespoons of the olive oil in a sturdy casserole dish or Dutch oven (enameled cast iron is ideal for this) over medium-high heat.

3. Place ¼ cup of the flour in a shallow bowl. Season the veal shanks on all sides with salt and pepper, then dredge in the flour on all sides. When the oil is hot, add the veal shanks and cook for 3 to 4 minutes per side, until they are a nice deep brown color, but certainly not burned. Transfer the veal shanks to a clean plate.

4. Reduce the heat to medium, add 1 tablespoon of the olive oil to the casserole dish, and add half of the carrots, onion, and celery. Cook, stirring frequently, for 4 to 5 minutes. Scrape up any tasty browned bits stuck to the bottom of the pan with a wooden utensil during this step.

5. Increase the heat to high, and add half of the tomatoes, 1 cup of the wine, and the chicken stock. Bring to a simmer, making sure all of the browned bits have been scraped up from the bottom of the pan and incorporated into the sauce. Season the sauce with salt and pepper to taste.

6. Return the veal shanks and any accumulated juices to the casserole dish. Add 1 of the bay leaves, 2 sprigs of the rosemary, and 2 sprigs of the thyme. Cover the dish with a tight-fitting lid or aluminum foil and place in the oven. Cook for 1 to 1½ hours.

12 sprigs fresh rosemary

4 sprigs fresh thyme

One 12-ounce Original
  Field Roast loaf, flavor
  of your choosing,
  cut into four 3-ounce
  portions

2 cups vegetable stock
  or broth, homemade
  (page 100) or store-
  bought, plus extra if
  needed

2 large egg yolks

⅓ cup heavy cream

¼ teaspoon freshly
  grated nutmeg

1 recipe Risotto Milanese
  (page 184; optional)

½ teaspoon white truffle
  oil or extra-virgin
  olive oil

Zest of 1 large lemon

½ bunch fresh flat-leaf
  parsley, chopped

2 large garlic cloves,
  minced

7. While the veal shanks braise, prepare the Field Roast "shanks." Begin by scooping out a 1-inch-wide well from each portion of the Field Roast, being sure not to go all the way through the bottom. This well will serve as a custard receptacle, thus mimicking the *buco*, or hole, in its meaty counterpart.

8. Heat 3 tablespoons of the olive oil in a nonstick sauté pan over medium-high heat.

9. Place ¼ cup of the flour in a shallow bowl, and dredge the Field Roast portions in the flour. Since the loaf is already rather highly seasoned, additional salt and pepper should be unnecessary.

10. Brown the Field Roast "shanks" lightly on all sides and remove to a lightly oiled pie plate. Cover with aluminum foil and place in the oven with the veal shanks.

11. Heat the remaining 1 tablespoon oil over medium-high heat in the sauté pan that held the Field Roast, then add the remaining carrots, onion, and celery and sauté until tender—4 to 5 minutes, stirring frequently, being sure to incorporate any browned bits into the sauce.

12. Add the remaining tomatoes, remaining wine, and the vegetable stock. Add the remaining bay leaf, 2 sprigs of the rosemary, and the remaining 2 sprigs thyme. Season lightly with salt and pepper and keep at a low simmer.

13. To create the vegetarian "marrow" custard: Combine the remaining 2 teaspoons flour, the egg yolks, cream, and nutmeg in a glass bowl over a gently simmering pot of water. With an instant-read thermometer handy, stir constantly until the mixture reaches 115°F and thickens slightly. Remove from the heat immediately, and stop the cooking by resting the bowl in a larger bowl filled with ice water and stirring the mixture.

14. Remove the casserole dish containing the veal shanks from the oven and remove the lid. Place the dish on the stovetop, without removing the shanks, and begin to reduce the remaining sauce over low heat.

CONTINUES ON P. 156

15. In the meantime, remove **the Field Roast "shanks"** from the oven, and spoon some "marrow" custard into the **wells of the Field Roast "shanks"** until the wells are three-quarters full. Place back in the **oven, uncovered, for 15 minutes.**

16. When ready to serve, **remove the kitchen twine from the veal shanks** and the bay leaves and herb sprigs from the **sauces. The veal might fall away from the bone** slightly when the twine is removed—this is **how you know you have done a fine, fine job.** The sauces should be nicely reduced so that **there is only a little liquid left in them** but they are not completely dry. The "marrow" custard **in the Field Roast "shanks"** should be firm.

17. Spoon some Risotto **Milanese, if you are using it,** into four shallow bowls. Arrange 2 shanks per person in each **bowl, according to dietary preference, and dress** with the appropriate sauce. Drizzle the **truffle oil over the vegetarian shanks.**

18. Toss together the lemon **zest, parsley, and garlic in a bowl to create** the classic osso buco garnish, gremolata. **Garnish each plate with a nice sprinkling** of gremolata and a sprig of rosemary in the buco **of each shank (both meaty and vegetarian).** Serve immediately to very grateful guests.

Note: Risotto Milanese (page 184) is the classic accompaniment for osso buco, but there's already a lot going on in this recipe, so don't feel you have to make the risotto, too. Plain white or brown rice or some simple, well-seasoned pearl barley is a lovely base to absorb all the wonderful sauce in this dish.

 MAKE IT ALL VEGETARIAN: Omit the veal shanks and chicken stock, and use two 12-ounce Field Roasts.

 MAKE IT ALL MEAT: Omit the Field Roast, vegetable stock, egg yolks, cream, nutmeg, and truffle oil. Use 8 pieces of veal shank.

Tournedos Ninon à la Flint Hills

Serves 2 vegetarians and 2 meat-eaters

2 tablespoons unsalted butter

2 large portobello mushrooms, stemmed and dark gills removed

1½ teaspoons salt and ½ teaspoon freshly ground black pepper, mixed together

Two 5-ounce filets mignons, about 2 inches thick

1 recipe Potatoes Anna (page 202), cut into 4 equal portions

1 recipe Creamed Spinach (page 193)

1 recipe Béarnaise Sauce (page 169)

12 asparagus tips, about 3 inches long, blanched briefly, then shocked in ice water and drained

1 ounce black truffle, cut into matchsticks (optional)

We're both from Kansas, and we love Kansas. The Flint Hills in east-central Kansas represent some of the best of Kansas's scenery and prove that Kansas, despite rumors, is not completely flat. The stacked presentation in this dish, a twist on the French beef classic *Tournedos Ninon*, is our homage to our old home on the range.

1. In a heavy-bottomed pan over medium-high heat, add 1 tablespoon of the butter and melt until the foaming subsides. Add the portobello caps and cook for 2 minutes, cap side down. Season each cap with ½ teaspoon of the salt and pepper mixture, and cover the pan with a lid.

2. While the mushroom caps are cooking, place another pan on the stovetop over medium-high heat, and add the remaining 1 tablespoon butter. When the foaming subsides, add the steaks to the pan. Season each steak with the remaining ½ teaspoon of the salt and pepper mixture. Cook the filets for about 3 minutes.

3. Flip the steaks and mushrooms and cook for another 3 minutes, then remove from the heat.

4. To assemble the finished dish, start by adding a portion of the Potatoes Anna to each of four serving plates. Top each with a dollop of creamed spinach, smoothing the spinach over the potatoes. Place a steak or portobello mushroom atop the spinach. Spoon a nice ribbon of béarnaise across the steaks and mushrooms, and arrange 3 asparagus tips on each plate as garnish. For the final pièce de résistance, sprinkle some of the black truffle atop the béarnaise. Serve immediately.

 MAKE IT ALL VEGETARIAN: Omit the filets mignons, and use 4 portobello caps.

 MAKE IT ALL MEAT: Omit the portobello mushrooms, and use 4 filets mignons.

Sunday Roast

Serves 6 to 7
vegetarians and
6 to 7 meat-eaters

One 3-pound "7-bone"
chuck roast, bone-in,
trimmed of fat

Salt and freshly ground
black pepper

1 cup plus 3 tablespoons
all-purpose flour

¼ cup olive oil, plus
more as needed

12 medium-size carrots,
peeled and chopped
into 2-inch pieces

1 pound fresh pearl
onions

2 pounds new potatoes,
about 2 inches in
diameter

4 cups chicken stock
or broth, homemade
(page 100) or store-
bought

Who would have thought that such a cornerstone family meal could become such a head-scratcher? We created the Sunday Roast to solve the problem of how to prepare that traditional entrée in such a way that meat-eaters and vegetarians could gather after church or sleeping late and both enjoy the family meal in harmony. This dish requires some time and effort, but the end result is well worth it.

1. Preheat the oven to 325°F. Season the chuck roast liberally with salt and pepper. Place ½ cup of the flour in a shallow bowl, and dredge the roast in the flour.

2. In a large, heavy pot (enameled cast iron is ideal), heat 2 tablespoons of the olive oil over medium heat. Gently place the pot roast in the pot, and sear the roast on each side until a nice deep brown crust has formed (approximately 10 minutes per side), but do not let it burn. Transfer the roast to a large plate, reserving any rendered fat.

3. Add half of the carrots, onions, and potatoes to the pot, adding another tablespoon of olive oil if needed. Stirring with some frequency, cook the vegetables until lightly browned, 5 to 10 minutes.

4. Add 1 tablespoon of the flour to the pot and continue cooking and stirring for 1 minute. Raise the heat to high, and add the chicken stock, 1 cup of the wine, and 1 tablespoon of the tomato paste. Stir, scraping any browned bits from the bottom of the pan, until the contents return to a simmer and thicken ever so slightly. Then simmer for 1 minute only.

5. Return the chuck roast and any accumulated juices to the pot, making sure the roast is at least halfway submerged in the liquid. Cover tightly and bake in the oven for 3 hours.

6. After the roast has been cooking for about 2 hours and 15 minutes, heat 2 tablespoons of the olive oil over medium-high heat in another large pot or roasting pan. Place ½ cup of the flour in another shallow bowl, dredge

2 cups hearty red wine, such as Cabernet Sauvignon

2 tablespoons tomato paste

2 pounds seitan, drained well and sliced into slabs

3 tablespoons unsalted butter

1 teaspoon sugar

4 cups vegetable stock or broth, homemade (page 100) or store-bought

the seitan slabs liberally in the flour, and add them to the pot, browning them for 3 to 5 minutes on each side. (Seitan tends to be preseasoned, so add salt and pepper with extreme caution.) Transfer the seitan to a plate.

7. Reduce the heat under the pot to medium-low and add the butter, sugar, and the remaining carrots, onions, and potatoes. If there are a lot of browned bits stuck to the bottom of the pan from cooking the seitan, add a few table-spoons of vegetable stock to unstick them. Stirring the vegetables occasion-ally, cook until they reach a nice golden brown color, 10 to 12 minutes.

8. Raise the heat to medium, add the remaining 2 tablespoons flour to the pot, and cook, stirring, for 2 to 3 minutes.

9. Add the remaining 1 cup wine, the vegetable stock, and the remaining 1 tablespoon tomato paste to the pot, raise the heat to medium-high, and bring to a slow simmer, whisking continuously. This is the gravy for your seitan.

10. Remove the chuck roast from the oven, and check the consistency of the gravy and the internal temperature of the roast, which should be between 180° and 200°F. The gravy should be just thick enough to coat the back of a spoon, or just slightly thinner. If it is too thin for your liking, place the pot over medium-high heat without the lid and reduce the sauce, which should take 3 to 5 minutes.

11. Season both gravies with salt and pepper to taste, and return the seitan to the pot with the vegetarian gravy to reheat.

12. When the seitan is warm and the gravies are at the desired consistency, slice the chuck roast, arrange the beef and seitan slices on separate serving trays, and head to the table. And don't forget the gravy.

CONTINUES ON P. 160

Note: If the Sunday funnies were too engrossing and you lost track of either pot during the browning process, you can attempt a save by quickly adding the wine, stock, or water. This will, unfortunately, halt any further browning of the vegetables, but a few teaspoons of *glace* (page 88) added to the sauce at the end will go a long way. A great way to further enrich and thicken this wonderful gravy is to collect a few of the cooked vegetables and a bit of the sauce, and puree these together in a blender or food processor, then add them back to the sauce and return to a simmer.

 MAKE IT ALL VEGETARIAN: Omit the chuck roast and the chicken stock, and use 4 pounds seitan and 8 cups vegetable stock.

 MAKE IT ALL MEAT: Omit the seitan and the vegetable stock, and use two 3-pound chuck roasts and 8 cups chicken stock. (You could use one 5- to 6-pound chuck roast, but this will add 1 to 2 hours to the cooking time in step 5.)

Using Pre-Mades Isn't a Crime

In a perfect world, we'd all have that extra bit of time that every day seems to demand. We'd be able to make multi-course meals for all of our friends, using only ingredients that we'd grown ourselves (or picked at a place close to our home), and we'd be able to make our own pasta and stocks, and each afternoon we'd sit and paint and write poems about the merits of tofu. Of course, in most normal days we don't have this kind of time, as there are a million little things snapping up our time like snapping turtles—things like work, family, sleep, and dogs that need to be walked. Let me be clear: I think (as does Jeremy) that using as many homemade and homegrown ingredients as possible is best. And we've tried to suggest easy recipes for some basics throughout the book to help in this journey. But, darn it, once in a while you may just be in a situation that forces you into using a little store-bought stock, situations where it's either get a little pre-pared help or skip the meal and serve a bag of stale potato chips. I understand how it goes, and won't walk away from the table where some pre-mades make up the ingredient list. Just let me suggest a few tips to help out when shopping. First, find pre-mades that you like and stick with them. There are so many varieties out there, if you find something you can trust, there's no need to vacillate (and there are some actually tasty pre-made products out there). Second, don't be afraid to look deeply into the ingredient lists of the products. You'll want to be doubly careful, with items such as canned stocks, of salt amounts. Try to find low- or reduced-sodium products, and maybe cut back on extra seasoning. So, even though you're busy, take at least two extra seconds to read labels, and you'll save some time at the end (because you won't have to make anything twice).

Stroganoff and Spaetzle

Serves 3
vegetarians and
3 meat-eaters

Spaetzle:

5 teaspoons salt

3 cups all-purpose flour, sifted

3 large eggs, beaten

1 cup whole milk

Stroganoff:

½ cup (1 stick) unsalted butter

1 pound beef sirloin, lightly pounded and cut into 1 x 2 x ¼-inch strips

1 pound seitan, cut into 1 x 2 x ¼-inch strips

Salt and freshly ground black pepper

2 large shallots, finely chopped

As globalization marches forward, it's time, we think, to pair that German favorite, spaetzle, with a Russian stroganoff. For the vegetarian portion, this recipe uses seitan, which isn't devilish at all—instead, it's made from wheat gluten, and it is used in many Asian countries as a meat substitute due to its hearty texture and ability to pick up the flavors of whatever it is cooked with. While you can make your own seitan, it's much easier to go to your local grocery, gourmet, or health food store and pick some up.

1. To make the spaetzle: Bring 1 gallon of water to a simmer with 4 teaspoons of the salt.

2. Sift the flour and remaining 1 teaspoon salt together into a large bowl. Add the eggs and beat together by hand or with a mixer. When well blended, gradually add in the milk and beat for 3 to 4 minutes.

3. To form the spaetzle: Put the dough into a zipper-top plastic bag, snip off a corner, and squeeze out little pieces, or place the dough in a colander and squeeze the spaetzle out through the holes directly into the water. Add about 4 ounces of the spaetzle to the simmering water (enough to form a single layer on top of the water) and cook for 4 to 5 minutes. Transfer the spaetzle with a slotted spoon to a bowl. Repeat until all the spaetzle are cooked. Reserve 1 cup of the spaetzle cooking water in case the spaetzle need "loosening up" later.

4. To make the stroganoff: Heat two large skillets over medium-high heat. Melt 2 tablespoons of the butter in each pan until the foaming subsides. Raise the heat to high, and add the sirloin to one skillet and the seitan to the other skillet. Season both lightly with salt and pepper. Cook the sirloin and seitan strips for about 2 minutes on each side, then remove the skillets from the heat and transfer the sirloin and seitan to separate plates.

5. Using the same skillets, heat 2 of the remaining tablespoons of butter in each skillet over medium-low heat. (If there is some stuff stuck to the pan from the previous step, that's all good. That stuff is called *fond* and equals flavor.) Add half of the shallots to each pan and cook until translucent, 4 to

1½ pounds mushrooms of your choice, sliced

6 ounces Cognac

2 cups light cream

2 cups sour cream

5 minutes. Do not brown. Add half of the mushrooms to each pan and raise the heat to medium-high. Sauté, stirring, until the mushrooms release their liquid and the liquid mostly evaporates.

6. Remove the pans from the heat and add 3 ounces of the Cognac to each. If using a stove with an open flame, beware of possible flare-ups here. Add 1 cup of the light cream to each pan, and reduce for a minute or so over medium-high heat, then add the sirloin and seitan back to their appropriate pans and heat through for another minute or two.

7. Remove the pans from the heat, and add 1 cup sour cream to each. If there is not enough residual heat in the pans to heat the sour cream, place the pans back on the stovetop over low heat. Do not allow the mixture to boil at this point, for there's a good chance the sour cream will curdle, especially if using a low-fat variety.

8. Adjust the seasoning with salt and pepper as desired. Divide the spaetzle among six bowls, top with either the beef or the vegetarian stroganoff, and serve immediately.

 MAKE IT ALL VEGETARIAN: Omit the sirloin, and use 2 pounds seitan. Cook everything in one large skillet.

 MAKE IT ALL MEAT: Omit the seitan, and use 2 pounds sirloin. Cook everything in one large skillet.

Tagliatelle Bolognese

Serves 3 to 4 vegetarians and 3 to 4 meat-eaters

4 ounces dried black beluga lentils (see Note)

1 quart water

4 tablespoons olive oil, plus more as needed

1 medium-size carrot, chopped

1 medium-size onion, chopped

1 celery stalk, chopped

2 garlic cloves, minced

8 ounces ground pork

8 ounces lean ground beef or veal

2 ounces pancetta or unsmoked bacon, finely chopped

1 pound mushrooms, stems included, chopped (we recommend portobello for their size and ease of use)

Jeremy's favorite memory associated with pasta Bolognese: It was my great-aunt and great-uncle's 50th wedding anniversary, and my cousins threw a huge party at a resort outside of Phoenix to celebrate. It was the first time that both sides of the family—one side being Kansan, the other Icelandic-Canadian—had been together since the wedding of the guests of honor. The night before the shindig, my cousin Mark, Mark's childhood friend Louise, and I made a ridiculous amount of pasta Bolognese to feed 40 or so family members and close friends. Always the lord of the manor, Mark dispatched Louise to do the grinding of the meat for the sauce, and I jumped in later to handle the browning of the meat. We fiddled with the sauce for the better part of the day, and it culminated in the best possible pasta in the best possible company. Although we had many great meals during that trip, this is the one that will remain indelibly imprinted on my mind.

1. Place the lentils and water in a medium-size saucepan. Bring to a boil, then reduce the heat to a simmer and cook until the lentils are just tender, 10 to 12 minutes.

2. Heat 2 tablespoons of the olive oil in each of two heavy-bottomed saucepans over medium heat. Add half of the carrot, onion, celery, and garlic to each pan. Cook until the vegetables are soft, 10 to 15 minutes.

3. Increase the heat to medium-high and add the pork, beef, and pancetta to one pan; add the mushrooms and parboiled lentils to the other. Cook for another 10 to 15 minutes to brown the meat and mushrooms, stirring occasionally. The vegetarian sauce may get a little dry, so don't be afraid to toss in another tablespoon or two of olive oil if necessary.

4. Add half of the tomatoes and 1/2 cup of the wine to each pan. Scrape up any browned bits from the bottom of the pans, and stir them into the sauce with a wooden utensil. Add the vegetable *glace* to the vegetarian pan and cook for another 5 minutes or so to reduce the wine and tomatoes, stirring occasionally.

5. Reduce the heat to low and add 1/4 cup of the milk and 1/4 cup of the cream to each pan. (From here on, it is very important to prevent the sauce from bubbling too rapidly, as doing so will curdle the milk and cream rather

One 14.5-ounce can crushed tomatoes

1 cup white wine

1 tablespoon vegetable *glace* **(page 88), Marmite, or Vegemite**

½ cup whole milk

½ cup heavy cream

2 bay leaves

1 recipe fresh pasta sheets (page 172), well floured, rolled up, then cut into long tagliatelle noodles, or 1 pound dried tagliatelle or fettuccine

½ cup grated Parmigiano-Reggiano cheese (2 ounces), for garnish

unattractively. A little curdling is natural in this recipe, but you want to avoid a "cottage cheese" appearance.) Add 1 bay leaf to each pot and simmer the sauces for 45 to 60 minutes, stirring occasionally.

6. When the sauces are about done, cook the pasta in well-salted boiling water. If using fresh pasta, it will only need 2 to 3 minutes of cooking. If using dried pasta, cook according to the package instructions until al dente. Reserve a cup or so of the pasta cooking water to loosen the sauce as needed.

7. Divide the cooked pasta between two large serving bowls. Ladle about 1 cup of the vegetarian sauce into one bowl and 1 cup of the meaty sauce into the other bowl, and toss. The pasta should be lightly dressed, not buried under a mound of sauce. If the pasta and sauce mixture is too thick and difficult to toss, thin it out by adding some of the reserved pasta cooking water, 1 tablespoon at a time, until the desired consistency is achieved.

8. Garnish both bowls of pasta with Parmigiano-Reggiano, and serve.

Note: Look for dried black beluga lentils at Trader Joe's or in the bulk section of many natural foods stores. Any dark green or brown dried lentil can be substituted.

 MAKE IT ALL VEGETARIAN: Omit the ground pork, ground beef, and pancetta, and use 2 pounds mushrooms, 8 ounces lentils, and 2 tablespoons vegetable *glace*.

 MAKE IT ALL MEAT: Omit the mushrooms, lentils, and vegetable *glace*, and use 1 pound each of the ground pork and ground beef and 4 ounces of pancetta.

Lasagna

Serves 4
vegetarians and
4 meat-eaters

1 bunch kale, escarole,
or Swiss chard

2 tablespoons olive oil

1 pound hot or sweet
Italian sausage, loose
or removed from
casings

1 recipe tomato sauce
(page 186) or 2 cups
store-bought marinara
sauce

1 recipe fresh pasta
(page 172), rolled into
thin 3- to 4-inch-wide
sheets; 1 pound store-
bought fresh pasta
sheets; or one 8-ounce
box dried "no-boil"
lasagna noodles

1 recipe Béchamel Sauce
(page 168)

1 cup grated Parmigiano-
Reggiano cheese
(4 ounces)

A layered pasta dish revered by many the world over (with good reason, as it's easy to make, hearty as all get-out, and scrumptious), lasagna traces its history to Roman times—the name comes from the Latin word *lasanum*, which means "cooking pot." If you have time, consider making the lasagna noodles, too, because homemade noodles are so tasty, and because the recipe is simple. Although the ingredients are straightforward, any Italian will tell you that mastery of pasta making takes a while, so practice often. But if you're in a hurry and decide to go the pre-made noodle route, we won't laugh at you—as long as you save us a corner piece, that is.

1. Adjust an oven rack to the middle of the oven and preheat the oven to 400°F.

2. Remove the large fibrous ribs from the kale and coarsely chop the leaves.

3. Heat two skillets over medium-high heat, then add 1 tablespoon of the olive oil to each pan and heat for 15 to 30 seconds. Add the sausage to one pan and the chopped kale to the other. Cook the sausage, breaking it up into small pieces, until no longer pink, and set aside. Cook the kale until nicely wilted, 5 to 8 minutes, and set aside. Drain or blot away some of the sausage fat if it seems excessive.

4. For the vegetarian lasagna, spread a thin layer of tomato sauce on the bottom of a 9-inch square casserole dish. Top with a layer of the pasta, another layer of tomato sauce, a layer of the béchamel, and some of the wilted kale. Continue layering the components in this way until the casserole is filled to about 3/4 inch from the top, using all of the kale for the vegetarian lasagna. (Each lasagna should have about 3 layers.) Add one final layer of béchamel, and sprinkle 1/2 cup of the Parmigiano-Reggiano over the top.

5. For the meaty lasagna, repeat the process in step 4 in a second 9-inch square casserole dish, subbing in layers of sausage for the kale.

6. Bake for 30 to 40 minutes, until the lasagnas are bubbly and the cheese is nicely browned. Remove from the oven and allow to rest for 15 minutes before cutting and serving.

Note: Have no time or inclination to make fresh pasta but love its addictive taste and texture? Find a nice Italian restaurant in your neighborhood specializing in fresh pastas and see if they will sell you some. Since Italians tend to be superlative hosts and hospitable to a fault, especially when someone shows an interest in Italian food, there's a good chance that some fresh pasta can be had with little effort on your part. Of course, it certainly helps if you also frequent the restaurant for an occasional meal.

 MAKE IT ALL VEGETARIAN: Omit the sausage, and use 2 bunches of kale.

 MAKE IT ALL MEAT: Omit the kale, and use 2 pounds sausage.

Make Béchamel and Hollandaise Sauces

Learning to make your own sauces is simple, tasty fun. Béchamel sauce is called for in the recipes for Sformato (page 65) and Lasagna (page 166) and is often used as a base in sauces and gravies. Hollandaise sauce makes its silky self apparent in Eggs Benedict (page 54) and Vegetables Hollandaise (page 196).

Béchamel Sauce

MAKES ABOUT 2 CUPS

¼ cup (½ stick) unsalted butter

1 small onion, minced

1 teaspoon salt

¼ teaspoon freshly ground black or white pepper

¼ cup all-purpose flour

2 cups whole milk

Pinch of freshly grated nutmeg

1. Melt the butter over medium heat in a medium-size saucepan. Add the onion, salt, and pepper, and cook for 5 minutes or so, stirring occasionally, until the onion is translucent. Don't brown the onion.

2. Add the flour and stir it up. The mass will probably get a little lumpy, but it will be fine. Continue cooking over medium heat, stirring rather frequently, for 2 to 3 minutes. Again, try to avoid any browning during this step.

3. Add the milk and increase the heat to high. Whisk briskly for a minute or two to be sure the oniony roux will be evenly distributed and the sauce will be lump-free. Bring the sauce to a low simmer and add the nutmeg.

4. Decrease the heat to medium-low, and cook for 10 to 15 minutes, stirring occasionally but frequently enough to avoid scalding the sauce on the bottom of the pan. Serve immediately or keep warm in a double boiler. If not serving immediately, drop a pat of butter on the surface of the sauce to prevent "skin" formation. You can also refrigerate béchamel for future use—just whisk in a few table-spoons of milk or cream for every cup of sauce and reheat over low heat, stirring frequently.

Hollandaise Sauce

My favorite method of making hollandaise sauce (because it's the easiest and most foolproof) is based on the technique from the 1955 edition of the *Esquire Cook-Book*.

MAKES 1 SCANT CUP

1/2 cup (1 stick) unsalted butter, at room temperature, cut into cubes

Juice of 1/2 lemon

3 large egg yolks

1/4 teaspoon salt

Pinch of cayenne pepper

1. Bring a small pot of water to a low simmer.

2. In a medium-size glass or stainless steel bowl, melt the butter over the simmering water, whisking as you go.

3. Remove from the heat and add the lemon juice. Let cool to around body temperature. Test this by dipping a spoon in the butter and touching it to your lips—if it feels neither hot nor cold, you're good to go.

4. Add the egg yolks and return the bowl to the heat over the simmering water and whisk, whisk, whisk—but be careful not to curdle the eggs. Continue whisking until the sauce is fully emulsified and a pale yellow color. Thin with a few drops of water at a time, as needed.

5. Season with the salt and cayenne and serve immediately. Although a little delicate, hollandaise may be kept with relative assuredness for a few hours over a double boiler filled with water heated to 140° to 150°F. If you need to keep your hollandaise in this manner, I highly recommend using the splash of cream mentioned below.

Note: A small splash of heavy cream added with the egg yolks is a good insurance policy that promotes emulsion and prevents curdling. Also, as this sauce uses raw eggs, it shouldn't be served to the elderly or those with compromised immune systems. Using pasteurized eggs eliminates most, if not all, of the health risk associated with consuming raw eggs.

Variations: Now that you can make hollandaise sauce, known in the sauce world as a "mother sauce," you can easily make the following sauces by simple additions to 1 recipe of hollandaise:

Béarnaise: In a small saucepan over medium-high heat, combine 1 small chopped shallot, 1 tablespoon chopped fresh tarragon, some crushed peppercorns, and a good splash of white wine, then reduce until the contents are about 1 tablespoon. Add this reduction to one recipe of hollandaise and mix.

Choron: Add 1 tablespoon tomato paste or ketchup to béarnaise sauce and mix.

Maltaise: In a small saucepan over medium-high heat, reduce the zest and juice of 1 blood orange to 1 tablespoon. Add this reduction to one recipe of hollandaise and mix.

Dijon: Add 1 tablespoon Dijon mustard to one recipe of hollandaise and mix.

Mousseline or Chantilly: Mix equal parts hollandaise sauce and freshly whipped cream.

Potato Ravioli
with Baccalà or Cheese

Serves 2 to 3
vegetarians and
2 to 3 meat-eaters

4 ounces salt cod

1 large starchy potato
(about 12 ounces)

2 tablespoons olive oil,
plus more for serving

2 garlic cloves, minced

1 tablespoon fresh
oregano leaves

½ teaspoon freshly
grated nutmeg

¾ cup grated
Parmigiano-Reggiano
or other similar hard
cheese (3 ounces), plus
more for garnish

2 teaspoons salt

½ teaspoon freshly
ground black pepper

We've all purchased frozen ravioli from time to time. While there is no sin in this act, there is great satisfaction to be found in making your own ravioli. As compared to frozen ravioli, the only added cost is a little bit of your time (especially if you make a lot), but it will be worth it. Don't be afraid to get the kids involved in sealing up the ravioli. Although some may consider the flavor of *baccalà* (salt cod) to be a bit challenging for the tykes, we say what kid wouldn't eat mashed potato— and fish stick–flavored pasta, especially if they helped make it? This ravioli will satisfy like no store-bought version ever could.

1. Soak the salt cod for 4 to 6 hours in cold water. Drain and replace with fresh water, soaking for another 4 to 6 hours. This can be done a day before you begin making the ravioli.

2. While the cod is soaking, peel the potato and boil it in lightly salted water until a knife inserted into the potato slides in and out easily, 10 to 15 minutes. Drain and refrigerate until needed.

3. Cut the potato into manageable chunks and press through a ricer for best texture. If you don't have a ricer, try pressing the potato through a metal colander. If you don't have a metal colander, just get the darn potato mashed already.

4. After the salt cod has been soaked, remove it from the water and pat dry with a clean towel. Break the cod up into smaller pieces, place it in a food processor, and pulse until the fish is in somewhat small flakes.

5. Add half of the mashed potato, 1 tablespoon of the olive oil, half of the minced garlic, 1½ teaspoons of the oregano, and ¼ teaspoon of the nutmeg to each of two mixing bowls. Add the salt cod to one bowl and the Parmigiano-Reggiano to the other. Add 1 teaspoon of the salt and ¼ teaspoon of the pepper to each bowl and mix to combine.

6. You can shape the ravioli however you like, but we usually take the path of least resistance, meaning roughly square. Lay out 2 sheets of the pasta dough on a clean, lightly floured work surface. Drop 2 to 3 teaspoons

1 recipe fresh pasta (page 172), rolled into thin sheets, or 1 pound store-bought fresh pasta sheets

All-purpose flour for dusting

1 large egg, beaten

1 recipe tomato sauce (page 186) or 1½ cups store-bought marinara sauce

of filling (fish on one pasta sheet, cheese on the other) every 2 to 3 inches to cover the entire sheet.

7. Brush in between the mounds of filling with some of the beaten egg and place another pasta sheet on top of the filling. Compressing the filling slightly, seal the two layers of pasta together, being sure to press as much air out of the ravioli as possible while preventing any filling from escaping. Don't worry—it takes a little practice to get them all sealed, but it helps to use a slightly larger top sheet of pasta.

8. Use a pizza cutter or fancy ravioli cutter or press to cut the ravioli into individual pieces, then inspect the ravioli and reseal as needed. The ravioli can be used immediately, refrigerated for up to 1 week, or frozen for up to 2 months.

9. Bring a large pot of well-salted water to a boil.

10. Add 6 to 8 cheese ravioli per person to the boiling water. If using fresh ravioli, they should take only 2 to 4 minutes to cook; add another 30 to 60 seconds if they have been refrigerated or another minute if they are frozen. (The ravioli will cook for another minute or so in the sauce, so err on the less-cooked side.) Place the cheese ravioli in a warm bowl with a little hot pasta water while you cook the salt cod ravioli.

11. Repeat step 10 with the salt cod ravioli, and remember to reserve a cup or so of pasta water to thin the sauce later as needed.

12. Heat ¾ cup of the tomato sauce in each of two saucepans over high heat. Add the cheese ravioli to one pan, and the salt cod ravioli to the other. Toss the ravioli in the sauce for about 1 minute, thinning the sauce with a dash of pasta water as needed.

13. Serve immediately in warmed bowls. Garnish the cheese ravioli with a sprinkle of Parmigiano-Reggiano; garnish the salt cod ravioli with a kiss of high-quality olive oil.

CONTINUES ON P. 172

Notes: If you don't have the time to make fresh pasta or can't find it in your local store, try substituting wonton wrappers for the pasta squares. Also, if you have any leftover salt cod filling, mix it with 1 tablespoon of extra-virgin olive oil and 1 tablespoon of heavy cream for every 1/4 cup filling and you have the classic French appetizer *brandade*. Spoon the filling into a small ovenproof ramekin, bake at 400°F for about 15 minutes, and *voilà*, instant party. Serve with some crusty bread and an apéritif. By all means do the same to create a vegetarian version if you have some of the cheese filling left over.

JEREMY SAYS:

Make Your Own Pasta

Homemade noodles are so tasty, and the ingredients are certainly simple—just remember the Italian phrase *un uovo per etto*, or "1 egg for every 100 grams" (about 3 1/2 ounces) of flour. Although the ingredients are straightforward, any Italian will tell you that mastery of pasta making takes a while, perhaps even a lifetime, so practice often and enjoy the results.

MAKES ABOUT 1 POUND, ENOUGH TO SERVE 4 TO 8 PEOPLE

2 1/2 cups all-purpose or semolina flour (10 1/2 ounces),
    plus extra for kneading and rolling
3 large eggs

1. Mound the 2½ cups flour on a clean work surface. Make a well in the middle of the mound and crack the eggs into the well. Lightly beat the eggs within the well and gradually begin incorporating the flour into the eggs with a fork or your fingers.

2. When all the flour is incorporated, knead the dough for about 10 minutes. If the dough seems too dry, add a little water. If too soft, add a bit more flour. After kneading, allow the dough to rest for 15 minutes, then roll it into thin sheets with a rolling pin and cut into thin strips, or make it easy on yourself and get a pasta roller (the Atlas brand is highly recommended)—a very handy utensil if you plan on making fresh pasta often.

Variation: As much as we love ravioli adorned with red sauce, ravioli in a simple sage–brown butter sauce couldn't be more delicious or classic. When the ravioli are about 60 seconds away from coming out of the hot water, heat 2 tablespoons butter and 1 tablespoon olive oil in a large sauté pan over medium-high heat. Add 8 to 12 fresh sage leaves, and sauté until the butter turns the slightest brown color and the sage leaves are lightly crisped. Throw the ravioli in the pan directly after straining, season lightly with salt and pepper, give them a toss to coat, and serve the ravioli with the crispy sage leaves and browned butter on top.

 MAKE IT ALL VEGETARIAN: Omit the salt cod, and use 8 ounces Parmigiano-Reggiano. Combine everything in one bowl in step 5, and toss all the ravioli together with the sauce in one pan in step 12.

 MAKE IT ALL MEAT: Omit the Parmigiano-Reggiano, and use 8 ounces salt cod. Combine everything in one bowl in step 5, and toss all the ravioli together with the sauce in one pan in step 12.

Roulades

¼ cup olive oil

2 medium-size onions,
finely chopped

1 large celery stalk,
finely chopped

1 large carrot, finely
chopped

Salt and freshly ground
black pepper

8 ounces chopped
mushrooms of your
choice (a more meaty
variety like chanterelle
or lobster mushroom
would be especially
good, but any kind
will work)

4 ounces vegetarian
sausage crumbles or
vegetarian sausage

1 large egg, beaten

We're rollin', rollin', rollin', keepin' roulades rollin'. This recipe is guaranteed to garner oohs and ahhs from everyone at the table. To up the fancy factor, be sure to slice your roulades on the bias, exposing the internal swirl of stuffing. Serve with a simple pan sauce and your favorite starch and vegetable side dishes.

1. Heat 1 tablespoon of the olive oil in a sauté pan over medium heat and toss in the onions, celery, and carrot. Season the pan lightly with salt and pepper. Cook for 5 to 10 minutes (you want to soften the vegetables without really browning them, so stir occasionally).

2. Transfer one-half of the mixture to a bowl, and place the bowl in the refrigerator to cool a bit.

3. Add another 1 tablespoon olive oil to the pan with the remaining vegetables, and add the mushrooms and vegetarian sausage crumbles. Increase the heat to medium/medium-high, and cook until the mushrooms have released most of their liquid. This should take 7 to 10 more minutes. Taste the mixture and add salt and pepper to taste. The flavor should be a little on the assertive side, as this mixture will be rolled in the mostly flavor-neutral tofu skins. Transfer the contents of the pan to a bowl to cool to room temperature.

4. Add the beaten egg to the bowl with the mushroom mixture, and stir to combine.

5. On a clean work surface, roll out 8 inches of plastic wrap and place one of the tofu skins on top. Spread one-quarter of the mushroom stuffing in a little row along the edge of the tofu skin nearest you. Rolling the roulade away from you, roll the tofu skin and stuffing up tightly. Bring the roulade back to the edge of the plastic wrap nearest you and roll the roulade up tightly in the plastic wrap. Twist the ends of the plastic wrap tightly to compress the roulade into a nice tight package. Secure the ends with kitchen twine, and repeat with the remaining mushroom stuffing and tofu skins. Set the roulades aside until ready to poach.

6. Take the bowl of cooled sautéed vegetables out of the refrigerator. Add the loose sausage to the bowl, and stir to combine.

4 sheets tofu skin (also called yuba), each about 4 x 4 inches

6 ounces loose sausage of your choice

4 boneless, skin-on chicken thighs

7. On a clean work surface, roll out 8 inches of plastic wrap, and place one of the chicken thighs on the wrap, skin side down. Sprinkle a few drops of water on the chicken thigh, cover with another sheet of plastic wrap, and use a meat pounder to pound out the thigh until it is 1/8 to 1/4 inch thick. The thinner it is, the easier it will be to roll around your stuffing, but try your best not to create any tears or holes in the skin or flesh.

8. Following the instructions in step 5, create 4 roulades using the pounded chicken thighs and meaty stuffing, placing the thighs skin side down so that the skin will be on the outside of the roll.

9. Fill 2 pots sufficiently large enough to hold 4 roulades each with 3 inches of water, cover, and bring to a simmer over high heat.

10. Place the chicken roulades (still wrapped in plastic) in one of the pots of simmering water, and poach for 12 to 15 minutes, making sure the water does not go above a simmer. After the chicken roulades have cooked for about 6 minutes, add the veggie roulades to the other pot of water, and poach for 7 to 8 minutes. Using separate utensils for each kind of roulade, transfer the roulades from the cooking water to a plate.

11. Heat 2 sauté pans over medium-high heat, adding 1 tablespoon of olive oil to each. Remove the plastic wrap from the roulades, place the vegetarian roulades in one pan and the meaty roulades in the other, and brown, turning often, for 8 to 10 minutes. Remove from the pans and slice on the bias. Serve immediately.

 MAKE IT ALL VEGETARIAN: Omit the chicken and loose sausage, and use 1 pound mushrooms, 8 ounces vegetarian sausage crumbles, 2 eggs, and 8 tofu skins. Skip steps 2, 6, 7, and 8.

 MAKE IT ALL MEAT: Omit the vegetarian sausage crumbles, egg, and tofu skins, and use 8 chicken thighs. Keep the amounts of mushrooms and loose sausage the same, but use the sausage in step 3 to make a sausage-mushroom stuffing for half of the chicken roulades. Skip steps 5 and 6.

Piccata

2 boneless, skinless
chicken breasts, about
4 ounces each

2 vegetarian chicken
breasts

¼ cup olive oil

1 cup all-purpose flour,
for dredging

1 teaspoon salt, plus more
as needed

1 teaspoon freshly
ground pepper, plus
more as needed

2 garlic cloves, minced

½ cup dry white wine

1 cup chicken stock or
broth, homemade
(page 100) or store-
bought

Whether in Spanish as *picar* ("to poke"), in French as *piquer* ("to prick"), or in Italian as *piccare* ("to sting"), *piccata* has as its probable root the Latin word *picus*, meaning "woodpecker." Although that may not sound so good when talking about cooking, the only assault here is a savory attack on the taste buds. As delightfully bracing as running through the sprinkler on a hot day, this mouthwatering piccata first enlivens the palate with lemon and capers, then soothes with parsley and butter. Try serving this with Ratatouille (page 197).

1. Preheat the oven to 200°F and place two large heatproof plates on the oven rack.

2. Slice the chicken and vegetarian chicken breasts in half lengthwise. On a clean work surface, roll out about 8 inches of plastic wrap, and place one of the breasts on the wrap. Sprinkle with a few drops of water to decrease friction, cover with another sheet of plastic wrap, and use a meat pounder to pound the breast to about a ⅛-inch thickness. Repeat with the remaining 3 breasts (using new plastic wrap for each one). You should now have 8 cutlets—4 chicken and 4 vegetarian chicken.

3. In two large nonstick sauté pans, heat 2 tablespoons of the olive oil in each pan over medium-high heat. While the pans are heating, combine the flour, salt, and pepper. Dredge the vegetarian chicken cutlets through the flour mixture on both sides to coat; repeat with the chicken cutlets. (Be sure to do it in this order to avoid any unhappy looks from your vegetarian friends.)

4. Add the flour-coated chicken cutlets to one pan and the flour-coated vegetarian chicken cutlets to the other. Cook the cutlets until nicely browned, 3 to 4 minutes on the first side and 2 to 3 minutes on the second. Transfer the cutlets to the preheated plates in the oven. Placing a layer of paper towel on the plate under the cutlets will help preserve your lovely brown coating and keep it from getting soggy.

1 cup vegetable stock
or broth, homemade
(page 100) or store-
bought

3 tablespoons freshly
squeezed lemon juice

2 tablespoons capers

½ bunch fresh flat-leaf
parsley, chopped

¼ cup (½ stick) cold
unsalted butter

5. Using the same two sauté pans, add half of the garlic to each pan. Cook for about 30 seconds, stirring constantly, then add ¼ cup of the wine to each pan and increase the heat to high. Using a separate wooden spoon for each pan, scrape up any browned bits from the bottoms of the pans as the wine reduces. Add the chicken stock to the pan in which the chicken cutlets were cooked and the vegetable stock to the pan in which the vegetarian chicken cutlets were cooked. Continue to cook until the liquid in each pan reduces to about ¼ cup.

6. Add half of the lemon juice, capers, and parsley to each pan, and cook for 30 to 60 seconds. Adjust the seasoning with salt and pepper as needed. Turn the heat off under the pans. Adding 1 tablespoon at a time, whisk 2 table-spoons of the butter into each pan to enrich the sauces.

7. Arrange the cutlets on new serving plates and dress with their respective sauces. Garnish with a little extra parsley if desired. Serve immediately.

 MAKE IT ALL VEGETARIAN: Omit the chicken and the chicken broth, and use 4 vegetarian chicken breasts and 2 cups vegetable stock.

 MAKE IT ALL MEAT: Omit the vegetarian chicken breasts and the vegetable broth, and use 4 chicken breasts and 2 cups chicken stock.

Grilled Stuffed Radicchio

Serves 2
vegetarians and
2 meat-eaters

2 cups water or 2 cups
vegetable stock or
broth, homemade
(page 100) or store-
bought

⅓ cup dried lentils of
your choice

¼ cup plus 2 teaspoons
olive oil

8 ounces Italian sausage,
loose or removed from
casings

1 medium-size onion,
chopped

1 teaspoon red pepper
flakes (optional)

4 slices good-quality
white bread, crusts
removed, pulsed in
a food processor to
coarse crumbs

One of our favorite rock anthems from our college days is "Bitter Boy," penned by Truck Stop Love, one of the greatest bands to ever come from Kansas (Manhattan, Kansas—the Little Apple—to be specific). Though the song isn't a paean to bitter foods and drink (but someone should write that song), it does point to the fact that we tend to be pretty darn crazy about bitter things—although we are not (and were not, even when that song came out) particularly bitter about anything. We just happen to really dig the mild bite of pleasantly bitter consumables like Fernet Branca, the Italian *digestivo*, or the star of this recipe, a nice bunch of grilled radicchio. Here and there referred to as "Italian chicory," radicchio is a red-leafed veggie that's often used to add a little kick to salads, but it's also dandy in risotto or pasta and, naturally, grilled.

1. Place the water and lentils in a stockpot and bring to a boil. Reduce the heat to a simmer, and cook until the lentils are tender, 10 to 15 minutes. Drain.

2. Preheat the oven to 475°F. Preheat your outdoor grill to very hot. This part is going to smoke, so we can't really recommend an indoor preparation unless you have an amazing hood vent in your kitchen.

3. While the grill is heating, heat 1 tablespoon of the olive oil in a sauté pan over medium-high heat, and add the sausage. Cook, breaking up the sausage as much as you can with a wooden spoon, until the sausage is browned. When the sausage is nearly browned, heat 1 tablespoon of the olive oil in another pan over medium-high heat. Add half of the onion and ½ teaspoon of the red pepper flakes to each pan, and cook until the onions are soft, 5 to 8 minutes.

4. Add the lentils to the pan without the sausage, and heat for 1 to 2 minutes. Add half of the bread crumbs to each pan, stir, then season each pan with ½ teaspoon of the salt and ½ teaspoon of the pepper. Set aside.

5. Slice the radicchio in half lengthwise, leaving the roots intact to hold everything together. Drizzle each head liberally with 1 tablespoon olive oil and season each head well with ½ teaspoon of the salt and ½ teaspoon of the pepper.

1 teaspoon salt

1 teaspoon freshly ground black pepper

2 medium-size heads radicchio (see Note)

4 teaspoons balsamic vinegar

6. When the grill is hot, hot, hot, place the radicchio, cut side down, on the grill. You'll probably get a few flare-ups from the olive oil, but don't worry as long as they aren't excessive. Be wary, though—we are looking for a well-grilled, not burned, result.

7. After 1 minute, turn the radicchio 90 degrees, still cut side down, to get those professional-looking grill marks. Cook for 1 minute more, then flip the radicchio over like a turtle on its back and cook for an additional minute. Transfer the radicchio to a sheet pan and bring inside for stuffing.

8. When the radicchio and stuffings are just cool enough to be handled, stuff 2 radicchio halves with vegetable stuffing and 2 with sausage stuffing. Stuff everything loosely between the leaves of the radicchio, or create a little well by removing a few of the innermost leaves. Another option is to simply mound the stuffing atop the radicchio.

9. Place the stuffed radicchio, cut side up, in the oven and cook for 7 to 10 minutes, until tender. Test tenderness by inserting a knife or wooden skewer; the radicchio should give some, but minimal, resistance to such intrusion.

10. Remove from the oven and drizzle each radicchio half lightly with 1 teaspoon olive oil and 1 teaspoon balsamic vinegar. Season lightly with salt and pepper, and serve.

Note: Use the Treviso variety of radicchio if you can find it; it resembles endive in shape and gives a nice visual presentation. The more common Chioggia variety is a round head. Because radicchio is naturally on the bitter side, a low-acidity, "sweet" vinegar like balsamic is a natural counterpoint. If you're looking for a somewhat brighter taste, experiment with different citrus juices for the dressing instead of the balsamic vinegar.

 MAKE IT ALL VEGETARIAN: Omit the sausage, and use 2/3 cup dried lentils.

 MAKE IT ALL MEAT: Omit the lentils, and use 1 pound sausage.

Saltimbocca alla Romana

**Serves 2
vegetarians and
2 meat-eaters**

Four 3 x 5-inch pieces
yuba

1 tablespoon vegetable
glace (page 88), mixed
with 1 tablespoon red
wine

Four 3-ounce pieces
boneless veal, pork,
or chicken, lightly
pounded

2 vegetarian chicken
breasts, sliced in half
(yielding 4 portions
total) and lightly
pounded

Freshly ground black
pepper

4 slices prosciutto

8 large fresh sage leaves

2 tablespoons unsalted
butter

2 tablespoons olive oil

½ cup Marsala

Salt

Sing this song while hopscotching, or perhaps double-dutch jump-roping: "Saltimbocca, Saltimbocca / means 'jump in the mouth' / then it heads south / to the tummy, where it is yummy / Saltimbocca, Saltimbocca / Where you from? Where you from? / I'm from Rome / that's my home / Saltimbocca, Saltimbocca / Whatcha like? Whatcha like? / I like ham, I like butter / I like sage, now cook this page." For the vegetarian part of this recipe, we create a "vegetarian prosciutto" using yuba, also known as tofu skin. Yuba is available dried or in the freezer section of many Asian food stores.

1. Thaw or reconstitute the yuba according to the package instructions. Blot dry with paper towels. Brush both sides of each piece of yuba with the vegetable *glace* mixture, and set aside on a tray. This will serve as your "vegetarian prosciutto."

2. Season the veal and the vegetarian chicken breast with some pepper and wrap 1 slice of prosciutto around each piece of veal and 1 piece of vegetarian prosciutto around each vegetarian chicken. Cover the juncture where the ends of each piece of prosciutto meets with a sage leaf and secure the package with a toothpick.

3. Heat two sauté pans over medium-high heat. Add 1 tablespoon of the butter and 1 tablespoon of the olive oil to each pan. When the butter is melted and any foaming has subsided, add the veal, sage side down, to one of the pans and the vegetarian chicken, sage side down, to the other pan. Cook for 3 to 4 minutes, until nicely browned. Flip the veal and vegetarian chicken, and cook on the other side for another 2 to 3 minutes. During the last minute of cooking, add ¼ cup of the Marsala to each pan, and cook until the liquid in each pan is reduced by half.

4. Season to taste with salt and pepper. Serve immediately on warmed plates with the Marsala pan sauce.

Note: If all the toothpicking seems like too much work, by all means skip that step. Just slice the prosciutto and vegetarian prosciutto into thin strips, and add it to the pans with the sage when you flip the veal and vegetarian chicken. Then pour all the contents of the pans over their respective dishes at serving time. As long as we're not being saltimbocca purists, we might as well mention that adding a little squeeze of lemon to the pan at the end of the cooking time is pretty nice, too.

 MAKE IT ALL VEGETARIAN: Omit the veal and prosciutto, and use 4 vegetarian chicken breasts and 8 slices vegetarian prosciutto.

 MAKE IT ALL MEAT: Omit the vegetarian chicken breasts and vegetarian prosciutto. Use 8 pieces of veal and 8 slices of prosciutto.

Fricassee Acadienne

**Serves 4 to 5
vegetarians and
4 to 5 meat-eaters**

1 tablespoon olive oil

1½ pounds tofu, drained
(page 44) and cut into
8 pieces

6 tablespoons all-
purpose flour

9 tablespoons (1 stick
plus 1 tablespoon)
unsalted butter

4 cups vegetable stock
or broth, homemade
(page 100) or store-
bought

1½ teaspoons salt

¼ teaspoon freshly
ground black pepper

½ teaspoon cayenne
pepper

This recipe is our hybrid homage to the classic French and Cajun styles of fricassee, much like the word *fricasee* itself is most likely a hybrid of the French verbs *frire*, meaning "to fry," and *casser*, meaning "to break or crack." The use of cream, butter, and the carrot-onion-mushroom mixture comes from the French, but the use of roux and cayenne is all Cajun. Serve over fluffy rice or creamy grits.

1. Preheat the oven to 350°F. Grease a baking sheet with the olive oil. Place the tofu pieces on the oiled sheet and place them in the oven to dry for 30 minutes. Remove from the oven and set aside.

2. To make the roux, combine the flour and 6 tablespoons of the butter over medium-low heat in a medium-size saucepan. Cook, stirring occasionally, for 10 to 15 minutes. For this recipe, we like a medium-dark roux—not as light as peanut butter, or as dark as chocolate, but somewhere in between. Keep a constant eye on the pan and a spoon handy for when the roux is about to go too dark—it happens fast.

3. When the roux has reached the correct color, increase the heat to high, immediately add the vegetable stock, and whisk, whisk, whisk for a minute or two. When the sauce (called a velouté, if you want to impress your friends) has simmered and come together nicely, remove the pan from the heat. Add 1 teaspoon of the salt, the pepper, and the cayenne. Whisk together and set aside.

4. In a heavy skillet just large enough to hold the chicken in a single layer, melt 2 tablespoons of the butter over medium-high heat, and add the chicken pieces. Lightly brown the chicken on all sides, turning occasionally.

5. Add about 2 cups of the roux-thickened sauce to the skillet and reduce the heat to medium-low. This is the step that defines the dish as a fricassee—simmering the protein in a sauce. Cover the skillet with a lid or aluminum foil, and cook until the internal temperature of the thighs and drumsticks is 160°F at their thickest parts.

One 2½-pound chicken,
cut into 10 pieces
(2 legs, 2 thighs, and
2 drumsticks, with
breasts split into
2 pieces each)

12 ounces baby carrots

One 10-ounce bag frozen
pearl onions, thawed
and drained

8 ounces small cremini
or button mushrooms

½ cup crème fraîche or
heavy cream

6. While the chicken is having its steamy gravy bath, heat the remaining 1 tablespoon butter over medium-high heat in a skillet large enough to hold the carrots, onions, and mushrooms. Add the carrots to the skillet along with the remaining ½ teaspoon salt. Add water until the carrots are just barely covered. Cook for 3 minutes. Add the onions, and cook for 3 more minutes. Add the mushrooms, and cook for 4 more minutes, stirring occasionally. Raise the heat to high to evaporate any remaining liquid, reducing it until it's just a glaze over the vegetables. Set the veggies aside, loosely covered.

7. Reheat the remaining roux-thickened sauce over medium-high heat, stirring occasionally. Transfer the chicken from its skillet to a plate. Reduce all heats to medium-low. Add ¼ cup of the crème fraîche to the meaty sauce and ¼ cup of the crème fraîche to the vegetarian sauce, and simmer (do not let it boil) for 1 minute, stirring or whisking frequently.

8. Add the prepared tofu to the pot with the vegetarian sauce, and heat through for a minute or two.

9. Add half of the cooked carrots, onions, and mushrooms to each sauce, and stir to incorporate.

10. Add the chicken back to the pan with the meaty sauce and stir through for a minute or two to reheat the chicken. Serve immediately.

 MAKE IT ALL VEGETARIAN: Omit the chicken, and use 3 pounds tofu.

 MAKE IT ALL MEAT: Omit the tofu, and use 2 chickens, cut up as described. Use chicken stock instead of vegetable stock.

Risotto Milanese

**Serves 2
vegetarians and
2 meat-eaters**

2 tablespoons olive oil

3 tablespoons unsalted
butter

1 ounce bone marrow,
finely chopped (see
Note)

1 medium-size onion,
finely chopped

1 teaspoon crumbled
saffron

2 cups Arborio rice

½ cup dry white wine

3 cups chicken stock
or broth, homemade
(page 100) or store-
bought, or beef broth,
heated

3 cups vegetable stock
or broth, homemade
(page 100) or store-
bought, heated

2 cups grated
Parmigiano-Reggiano
cheese (8 ounces)

Risotto Milanese often gets paired with Osso Buco (page 154), but it is a wonderful treat all on its own. And, like many Italian dishes, it has a history. The story reaches back to 1574, when Milan's glorious *duomo*, or cathedral, was being built. Supposedly one of the younger apprentices working on it, whose name was Valerius, was being made fun of because the glass he was staining for the windows was so bright yellow that everyone thought he had added saffron to the paint. To get back at those teasing him, he added saffron to the rice at his master's wedding. It turned into a very tasty joke, as everyone loved the rice—so much so that it's still a favorite today.

1. Heat 1 tablespoon of the olive oil and 1 tablespoon of the butter over medium heat in a medium-size saucepan. Heat 1 tablespoon of the olive oil and the marrow over medium heat in another medium-size saucepan.

2. Add half of the onion to each pot, and cook over medium heat for 8 to 10 minutes, until the onion is soft and opaque. Add ½ teaspoon of the saffron to each pan, and cook, stirring, for 1 minute. Add 1 cup of the rice to each pan, and cook for 2 minutes, stirring frequently.

3. Add ¼ cup of the wine to each pan, and cook for 1 more minute, still stirring (there is a lot of stirring here, so it's best to get used to the motion). Add ½ cup of the meat broth to the pan with the marrow, and add ½ cup of the vegetable stock to the other pan; stirring constantly, cook for 5 to 7 minutes.

4. Once the stock has been almost fully absorbed, add the remaining stock, ½ cup at a time, to each pan and cook, stirring, until it is nearly absorbed. This should take 20 to 25 minutes. If at 25 minutes you still have extra broth, try tasting the rice. If it's still a little firm on the inside, but creamy and tender, then it's done. If not, keep cooking for a few more minutes.

5. Turn off the heat, and stir 1 tablespoon of the butter and 3/4 cup of the Parmigiano-Reggiano cheese into each pan. You want everything well mixed, but you don't want to be whipping it into a frenzy. Serve the risotto in shallow bowls or on plates, topping each serving with some of the remaining cheese.

Note: Bone marrow by itself may be hard to come by, but marrow bones certainly are not. Consult your friendly local butcher for a few marrow bones, then scoop the marrow out yourself. You can skip the marrow if you wish and use butter instead, but you'll be missing out.

MAKE IT ALL VEGETARIAN: Omit the bone marrow and meat broth. Increase the amount of butter to 4 tablespoons, using 1 tablespoon in step 1 instead of the bone marrow. Increase the amount of vegetable stock to 6 cups, and cook everything in one large pan.

MAKE IT ALL MEAT: Omit the vegetable stock. Increase the amount of bone marrow to 2 ounces, using 1 ounce of the marrow in place of the butter in step 1. Increase the amount of meat broth to 6 cups, and cook everything in one large pan.

For a Simple Tomato Sauce

This is a very versatile tomato sauce. It is relatively straightforward to make and can be prepared in minutes. For its myriad uses in Italian cuisine, a basic red sauce is a must-have in your culinary repertoire.

MAKES ABOUT 2 CUPS

1 tablespoon olive oil

2 garlic cloves, minced

1 small onion, minced

One 28-ounce can whole plum tomatoes

2 teaspoons dried oregano or leaves from 5 fresh oregano stems

Salt and freshly ground black pepper

1. Heat the olive oil in a large saucepan over medium heat.

2. Add the garlic and onion and sweat until translucent, 5 to 10 minutes. Do not allow the mixture to become so hot that the onions get too brown and take on a bitter taste. Add the tomatoes with their juice to the pan and crush into the other components with a potato masher, large fork, or hands if you're a tough guy. Cook for 5 to 10 minutes, stirring occasionally.

3. Add the oregano, cook for 2 minutes more, and season to taste with salt and pepper. (This is the quick version, but don't be afraid to simmer this sauce for an hour or two.)

satisfying sides

what would Pancho have done without Lefty?

Or Tom without Jerry? Why are there Oscars, Golden Globes, BAFTAs, and numerous other awards for best supporting actors and actresses? One of the great truisms of the world is that no man really stands alone, so why should the food world be any different? There is a somewhat unscientific agreement that the human palate dulls to and tires of the same flavor after three or four bites if uninterrupted by a different flavor. Other than its socially lubricating properties, this is a significant reason for serving wine with food. The same applies for side dishes. Would each bite of that expensive dry-aged steak be as enjoyable were it not for the occasional bite of creamed spinach, forkful of golden shoestring hash browns, or sip of a heady Bordeaux-style wine? We think not.

Side dishes by common practice, if not by specific definition, tend to be largely vegetarian fare. Although the overall aim of this book is to elucidate sensible ways that many dishes can be made in vegetarian and carnivorous fashion simultaneously, our recipes for these sides are largely vegetarian by design (Celery Amandine; Coleslaw, East and West; Ratatouille) or by technique, like our favorite potato-based sides. Bearing that in mind, Jeremy would kindly proffer that there is almost no side dish lily that could not be gilded with the addition of a little cured pork or imitation pork product, particularly Vinegar Greens, Mushroom Stuffing, and Delish Drop Biscuits.

From Creamed Spinach and Vegetables Hollandaise to Corny Corn Pudding and Herbed Home Fries, these sides are just what the doctor ordered to avoid the dreaded palate fatigue.

Celery Amandine

Serves 5 to 6

1½ pounds celery, cut
  into 4-inch pieces

¼ cup (½ stick) unsalted
  butter

1 cup slivered almonds,
  toasted (see Note)

½ teaspoon salt

½ teaspoon freshly
  ground black pepper

A French term that basically means "garnished with almonds," *amandine* is misspelled as "almondine" on a regular basis to match up more closely with its most recognized ingredient (almonds, that is). It may sound a little standoffish and reserved, but it's actually easy to make and cuddles up well with a variety of dishes, including most of those in Entertaining Entrées, but also those like Meat-and-Not-Meat Loaf (page 138). You will often see green beans prepared in this style, but using celery instead adds a distinctive touch to your meal.

1. Fit a steamer rack or basket into a large stockpot, and add water to just below the bottom of the steamer. Heat the water to boiling, add the celery to the steamer, and steam until the celery is tender, 5 to 7 minutes. Remove from the heat.

2. Melt the butter in a large skillet over medium heat. Add the almonds, and cook until the butter is bubbly hot. Add the salt and pepper, stir, remove from the heat, and add the steamed celery. Stir well to combine. Serve immediately.

Note: Toasting almonds (and other nuts) is easy and fun. Just place a smallish skillet on the stove over medium heat. Let the pan warm up a bit, and add the almonds. Cook for 3 to 5 minutes, stirring or tossing regularly, until the nuts have lightly browned.

Variation: As mentioned, you can sub in green beans here easily for celery, as well as other veggies, including broccoli and Brussels sprouts.

Coleslaw, East and West

Serves 4
vinegar-coleslaw
fans and 4 creamy-
coleslaw fans

1 medium-size head
 cabbage, cored and
 thinly sliced

3 large carrots, cut
 into matchsticks or
 shredded

2 teaspoons salt

1 cup mayonnaise

3 tablespoons rice wine
 vinegar

¾ cup sugar

1 teaspoon freshly
 ground black pepper

2 tablespoons cider
 vinegar

1 teaspoon celery seed

1 teaspoon mustard
 seed

Though the title for this recipe makes it sound as if we're going to have some sort of back-alley cabbage brawl, it's really just to show that there are multiple coleslaw varieties, and many have merit. We may disagree on which style is tops (Jeremy says more vinegar, and A.J. goes creamy more often than not), but we sure don't get into arguments about it—that'd take the fun away from the buffet. With this recipe you can offer guests both styles, which will make everyone happy. Just be sure to salt out your cabbage first, a trick A.J. learned from Jack Bishop's great book, *Vegetables Every Day* (William Morrow, 2001).

1. Combine the cabbage, carrots, and salt in a colander, stir well, and set in the sink or over a large bowl. Let sit for 1 to 1½ hours, then rinse with cold water and dry thoroughly, in a salad spinner if you have one.

2. Combine the mayonnaise, 2 tablespoons of the rice wine vinegar, ½ cup of the sugar, and ½ teaspoon of the pepper in a bowl, whisking until the dressing is smooth and not grainy.

3. In a separate bowl, combine the remaining 1 tablespoon rice wine vinegar, the remaining ¼ cup sugar, the remaining ½ teaspoon pepper, the cider vinegar, celery seed, and mustard seed. Whisk well, until the sugar has dissolved.

4. Divide the cabbage and carrot mixture between two large bowls. Pour the creamy dressing over one bowl, and the more vinegary dressing over the second bowl. Stir well and serve.

Note: The coleslaws can be refrigerated (and might just be better that way) for up to 5 hours before serving.

 MAKE IT ALL CREAMY: Want to go wholly cream-style? Just add another 1 cup mayonnaise, 2 more tablespoons rice wine vinegar, $1/2$ cup more sugar, and $1/2$ teaspoon more pepper in step 2, and omit the cider vinegar, celery seed, and mustard seed.

 MAKE IT ALL VINEGARY: Want to skip the creaminess altogether? Omit the mayonnaise. In step 3, use 2 tablespoons rice wine vinegar, $1/2$ cup sugar, 1 teaspoon pepper, $1/4$ cup cider vinegar, 2 teaspoons celery seed, and 2 teaspoons mustard seed.

Corny Corn Pudding

Serves 8

One 1-pound bag frozen
corn, thawed

¼ cup milk

5 large eggs

½ cup sugar

¼ cup (½ stick) unsalted
butter, at room
temperature, plus
more for greasing
the casserole dish

3 tablespoons cornstarch

½ teaspoon freshly
ground black pepper

½ teaspoon salt

¼ teaspoon cayenne
pepper

One 15-ounce can
cream-style corn

1 cup shredded cheddar
cheese (4 ounces)

Sure, this dish sits in the corner of the room cracking jokes along the lines of, "Why should you never make important arrangements with a piece of corn? Because corn flakes." But you'll find folks will put up with a whole lot of corniness—and will eagerly spoon up heaping helpings of this corn pudding—because it has such a good, down-homey taste (while still being acceptable alongside more refined main dishes).

1. Preheat the oven to 350°F.

2. Add half of the thawed frozen corn to a food processor fitted with a metal blade. Process for a few seconds until the corn is in small pieces. Add the milk, and process until combined. Add the eggs, one at a time, processing to combine after each one. Add the sugar and process until everything is cuddly and the sugar has dissolved. Add the butter and process a bit more.

3. In a large bowl, whisk together the cornstarch, pepper, salt, and cayenne. Transfer the corn mixture from the food processor to the bowl, along with the remaining thawed corn and the creamed corn. Stir well to completely combine, then add the cheese, stirring briefly.

4. Butter the inside of a casserole dish. Pour the corn mixture into the dish, and bake for 30 minutes. Stir briefly, and bake for 30 more minutes. It should be a golden color with just a hint of brown. Serve hot.

Creamed Spinach

Serves 6 to 8

2¼ pounds fresh baby
spinach

1 tablespoon unsalted
butter

½ cup chopped shallots

1½ cups heavy cream

1 cup grated Parmesan
cheese (4 ounces)

¼ teaspoon freshly
grated nutmeg

¼ teaspoon salt

¼ teaspoon freshly
ground black pepper

A wonderfully classless dish (not because it has no class, but because it works beautifully both in meals that wear tuxes and tails and meals that are comfortable in the backyard wearing cutoff overalls), creamed spinach is also a side you see made in a number of ways, from the more simple to the complex. Our version boasts a bit of cheese, to add a touch more flavor and because, well, we think cheese is almost always a good addition.

1. Fill a large stockpot three-quarters full with water, and bring it to a boil. Once boiling, add the spinach, reduce the heat, and simmer for 1 to 2 minutes, until the spinach turns a deep and vibrant shade of green. Strain the spinach, squeezing out as much liquid as you can, then chop it coarsely and set aside.

2. Melt the butter in a skillet or saucepan over medium heat. Add the shallots and sauté, stirring regularly, for 2 to 3 minutes.

3. Add the cream to the skillet and let the mixture cook for 10 minutes, stirring regularly.

4. Wipe out the stockpot and return it to the stovetop over medium heat. Add the spinach, the cream mixture, the cheese, nutmeg, salt, and pepper. Stir well, and let everything become acquainted for a couple of minutes. Serve hot.

Green Beans and Bacon

Serves 3 vegetarians and 3 meat-eaters

1½ pounds green beans, ends trimmed

1½ teaspoons unsalted butter

1 small onion, chopped

½ teaspoon freshly ground black pepper

¼ teaspoon salt

3 vegetarian bacon slices, cooked according to package directions

3 bacon slices, cooked until crisp (opposite page)

Green beans love bacon—it's one of those proven facts. This mystic commingling of veggies and meat brings two sort-of basics into a beautiful new realm, one where minstrels sing of side dishes while playing mandolins and wearing pouffy trousers. It used to be that only meat-eaters were able to reach this nirvana of the side-dish world, but thanks to those intrepid vegetarian-meat makers, now everyone can take the trip.

1. Fill a large stockpot or saucepan halfway with water. Bring the water to a rolling boil, then add the green beans. Cook for 2 to 3 minutes, until the beans are just tender and have turned a deep, vibrant shade of green, then drain and set aside.

2. Melt ¾ teaspoon of the butter in each of two sauté pans or skillets over medium-high heat. When the butter starts to bubble, add half the onion to each pan. Sauté the onion, stirring, until golden brown, 4 to 5 minutes.

3. Add half of the green beans to each pan, and cook for a minute or two while stirring. Add ¼ teaspoon of the pepper and ⅛ teaspoon of the salt to each pan and cook for 1 more minute. Crumble the vegetarian bacon over one pan and stir. Crumble the bacon over the second pan and stir. Serve hot.

 MAKE IT ALL VEGETARIAN: Omit the bacon, and use 6 vegetarian bacon slices. Cook everything in one pan beginning in step 2.

 MAKE IT ALL MEAT: Omit the vegetarian bacon, and use 6 bacon slices. Cook everything in one pan beginning in step 2.

Best Bacon Cooking

First a quick word about buying bacon: Buy the good stuff and buy it thick-cut. Otherwise you're paying for strips of mostly pork fat of inferior quality that will be thin and pale reminders of what bacon should be. As with cooking steaks, the degree of bacon doneness depends on personal preference and how you're using the bacon in a recipe. If the bacon is going to be crumbled, it should be on the crispier side. For BLTs, I like it less crisp. There are three methods you can use—pan-frying, baking, and microwaving. Overall, I try to avoid the microwave, so we'll focus on the first two.

For pan-frying, a heavy pan (like cast-iron) produces the best product. I go for a slow burn over medium heat on the stovetop. A lower cooking temp will render out much more of the fat, and also lovingly auto-baste the meaty part with that selfsame delicious hog-butter.

The same theory applies to oven-baking. I use a low-ish temperature (say, 350°F) on a baking sheet just large enough to hold the amount of bacon you are going to cook. Cook at this temp until the desired degree of doneness is achieved. The main advantage of oven-baking is odor and splatter reduction.

With either method, I would suggest blotting the excess fat from the bacon strips if saving them for future applications like Cobb Salad (page 102) or *Omelettes du Matin* (page 56).

Vegetables Hollandaise

Serves 4 to 6

1 pound mixed fresh
vegetables (such as
asparagus, green
beans, Brussels
sprouts, broccoli,
baby carrots)

1 cup Hollandaise
Sauce (page 169)

Everyone likes hollandaise sauce. Everyone. In fact, in the summer of 1972, all-American rockers the Beach Boys packed up their gear and headed to the Netherlands, presumably to record an album, but inside sources reveal that the original impetus for the trip was actually their own quest for liquid gold—hollandaise sauce. Any Beach Boys memoir will point out that the band's time amongst the Dutch was often clouded by the specter of Dennis Wilson's and Ricky Fataar's hollandaise abuse. However, record store clerks and *sauciers* all over the world agree that the end product, the album *Holland*, is one of their best (despite any perceived turmoil and the album's relative lack of critical acclaim). Much like mixing hollandaise sauce with vegetables is one of the best side dishes.

1. Fill a large stockpot three-quarters full with water and bring it to a boil. While you're waiting for the water to boil, trim and cut your vegetables into similar-size pieces.

2. Blanch the vegetables in the water (in shifts if needed) until they are tender—just a few minutes—then make sure they're drained well.

3. Place the vegetables in a warmed casserole or serving dish, and top them with the hollandaise sauce. Serve immediately.

Ratatouille

Serves 4 to 6

2 zucchini, chopped into a 2-inch dice

2 yellow squash, chopped into a 2-inch dice

1 large eggplant, peeled and chopped into a 2-inch dice

1 green bell pepper, seeded and chopped into a 2-inch dice

1 red bell pepper, seeded and chopped into a 2-inch dice

3 tablespoons olive oil

1 teaspoon salt

1 teaspoon freshly ground black pepper

1 large onion, sliced into rings

4 garlic cloves, minced

One 14.5-ounce can diced tomatoes

3 sprigs fresh thyme

1 sprig fresh rosemary

1 bay leaf

Extra-virgin olive oil for drizzling

Contrary to the sound of the name or the suggestions of a popular animated movie, ratatouille has nothing to do with rodents. Instead, the name is a Franco-smashup of the verbs *ratouiller* and *tatouiller*, both implying "to stir or toss up." Jeremy was first introduced to ratatouille Niçoise (a dish most closely associated with southeast France) at the age of 19 while working at the University of Kansas Alumni Center under his second chef, the mad Frenchman Etienne Jehl. Jeremy remembers him well for many things, among those two things specifically attached to this dish: how Etienne always pronounced it "ra-ta-too-ee," enunciating every syllable in staccato fashion, and the constant mantra of *"Assaisonnez! Assaisonnez!"* or "Season it! Season it!"—really, some of the best advice a novice can receive. Thanks, Chef Etienne.

1. Preheat the broiler.

2. In a large bowl, toss the zucchini, squash, eggplant, and bell peppers with 2 tablespoons of the olive oil and 1/2 teaspoon each of the salt and pepper. Spread the vegetables out on a large baking sheet. Broil for 20 minutes, checking and turning the vegetables every 5 minutes for even browning. Keep a close eye on them, to avoid burning.

3. On the stovetop, heat a large, heavy casserole dish over medium-low heat. Add the remaining 1 tablespoon olive oil, the onion, garlic, and the remaining 1/2 teaspoon each of salt and pepper. Cook, stirring occasionally, for 5 to 7 minutes, aiming for a light golden hue.

4. Remove the vegetables from the oven and transfer them to the casserole dish with the onion and garlic. Add the tomatoes, thyme, rosemary, and bay leaf. Taste for seasoning and add more salt and pepper as needed, and add a splash of water if the mixture seems too dry. Cook on the stovetop over medium heat for 20 to 30 minutes.

5. Remove the herb sprigs and bay leaf, and serve warm with a little drizzle of extra-virgin olive oil.

Vinegar Greens

Serves 2 to 3 vegetarians and 2 to 3 meat-eaters

3 thick-cut bacon slices, finely chopped

4½ teaspoons olive oil

2 medium-size onions, finely chopped

2 bunches greens of your choice (mustard, collard, beet, or kale), spines removed and chopped (7 to 8 cups)

¼ cup red wine vinegar

1 cup chicken stock or broth, homemade (page 100) or store-bought

1 cup vegetable stock or broth, homemade (page 100) or store-bought

½ teaspoon kosher salt

½ teaspoon freshly ground black pepper

4 vegetarian bacon slices, cooked according to package directions and crumbled

There are two schools of thought on the cooking of these greens—cook them a little, or cook them a lot. On one hand, the light-handed approach retains most of the vibrant color and toothsome texture of the greens. On the other, the long, loving approach renders a soul-satisfying side dish that promenades beautifully with almost every incarnation of Southern food. We like both methods and employ either depending mostly on time constraints and general whimsy. Regardless of which you choose, there can be no doubt that onions, vinegar, and some smoky goodness must come along for the ride. A little dash of hot sauce never hurt a green, either.

1. Place the bacon in a large pot over medium heat to begin rendering the fat.

2. When the bacon fat has rendered and the bacon bits are nicely browned, place a second pot on the stove over medium heat and add the olive oil.

3. Add half of the onions to each pot, and increase the heat to medium-high. Cook until the onions achieve a light-brownish hue, 7 to 8 minutes.

4. Add half the greens and 2 tablespoons of the vinegar to each pot; then add the chicken stock to the pot with the bacon and the vegetable stock to the other pot. Add ¼ teaspoon of the salt and ¼ teaspoon of the pepper to each pot.

5. Cover the pots and decide if the greens are in for a short steam or a long schvitz. If going the quicker route, cook for about 5 minutes. If going for the longer cook time, cook for 20 to 25 minutes.

6. The greens with the bacon are now ready to serve. Serve the vegetarian greens with the crumbled vegetarian bacon on top.

 MAKE IT ALL VEGETARIAN: Omit the chicken stock and bacon, and use 2 cups vegetable stock, 8 vegetarian bacon slices, and 3 tablespoons olive oil. Cook everything in one large pot.

 MAKE IT ALL MEAT: Omit the olive oil, vegetable stock, and vegetarian bacon, and use 6 bacon slices and 2 cups chicken stock. Cook everything in one large pot.

Mushroom Stuffing

Serves 6

¼ cup (½ stick) unsalted butter

1 medium-size yellow onion, finely chopped

1 celery stalk, finely chopped

2 pounds cremini mushrooms, stemmed and chopped

2 garlic cloves, minced

¼ cup chopped fresh flat-leaf parsley

½ teaspoon freshly ground black pepper

½ teaspoon salt

8 slices hearty wheat bread, coarsely chopped (about 6 cups)

3 cups vegetable stock or broth, homemade (page 100) or store-bought

Stuffing gets short shrift for the most part, only trotted out for the third Thursday in November. A sad state of affairs for our old friend stuffing, because there are many ways to make this dish your own and have it taste delicious. We're presenting a mushroom version here, because it's tasty, easy to make, and a family favorite.

1. Preheat the oven to 450°F.

2. Melt the butter in a large skillet over medium heat. When the butter is hot, add the onion and cook for about 4 minutes. Add the celery and cook for 2 more minutes.

3. Add the mushrooms to the pan and stir well. Continue to cook, stirring occasionally, until the mushrooms have released their liquid—6 to 8 minutes should do it. Add the garlic, parsley, pepper, and salt, and cook for 3 to 4 more minutes. Most of the mushroom liquid should have evaporated by this time.

4. Remove the pan from the heat, and transfer the mixture to a large bowl. Add the bread to the bowl, and pour in the stock. Stir well.

5. Pour the stuffing into a large casserole dish. Bake for 35 minutes. Check to make sure it has cooked through by inserting a knife or toothpick until it comes out clean. Cook in additional 10-minute increments as needed.

Note: If your stuffing seems to have dried out a bit near the end of the baking in step 5, you can always add a little more stock to moisten it.

Variations: As mentioned, there are many things you can do to personalize your stuffing. You can prepare a meat and meat-free version by dividing the stuffing between two bowls in step 4 and adding 1 cup cooked sausage to one bowl and 1 cup cooked vegetarian sausage to the other. You could also use different spices to create interesting new versions. Want a little nutmeg? Give it a shot. How about some cayenne to create some heat? Play around, adding a little at a time, and you'll discover a world of stuffing possibilities.

Mashers with Multiple Gravies

Serves 3 to 4 vegetarians and 3 to 4 meat-eaters

6 large potatoes, peeled and cut into chunks (about 8 cups)

6 tablespoons (¾ stick) unsalted butter, at room temperature

½ cup all-purpose flour

1½ cups vegetable stock or broth, homemade (page 100) or store-bought

1½ cups chicken stock or broth, homemade (page 100) or store-bought, or beef broth

¼ cup soy sauce

½ cup minced fresh flat-leaf parsley

½ teaspoon freshly ground black pepper

¾ cup milk

Maybe mashed potatoes aren't the king of side dishes, but they do occupy a special position among side-dish royalty, as they are traditionally paired with the holiday most associated with eating (don't get stuck into thinking they're only for Thanksgiving, though). And this exalted position means they're a perfect standard bearer for the *Double Take* philosophy of meat-eaters and vegetarians at the same table. The fact that making a big batch of mashed potatoes with both meat-based and veggie-based gravies is fairly easy is a bonus.

1. Place the potatoes in a large stockpot and fill it with water, until the water covers the potatoes by a couple of inches. Place the pot on the stove over high heat. Bring the water to a boil, stirring occasionally, and let the potatoes cook until they easily slide off a fork, about 15 minutes.

2. While the potatoes are boiling, melt 4½ teaspoons of the butter in each of two saucepans over medium heat. Add ¼ cup of the flour to each pan. Whisk briskly (you may need to bring in a pal here, or stagger adding the flour to the pans), and cook for 30 seconds.

3. Add the vegetable stock slowly to one pan while whisking, until it is smoothly combined, then add the meat broth to the other pan, using a different whisk.

4. Let both pans cook for 2 to 3 minutes, then add 2 tablespoons of the soy sauce, ¼ cup of the parsley, and ¼ teaspoon of the pepper to each pan. Continue to cook, stirring or whisking continuously, until the gravy thickens. Reduce the heat to low, and cook for 10 to 12 minutes, stirring occasionally. Your gravy should be nearly done when your potatoes are tender.

5. When the potatoes are done, drain them thoroughly. Either run them through a potato ricer (A.J.'s favorite method) into a large bowl, or transfer them to a bowl and use a potato masher to mash them up. Once fairly well mashed or riced, add the remaining 3 tablespoons butter to the bowl, along with the milk. Stir well with a spoon, then serve while they're still steaming, with the gravies alongside in separate bowls.

Note: Russets make great mashed potatoes, so use them if possible.

 MAKE IT ALL VEGETARIAN: Omit the meat broth, and use 3 cups vegetable stock. Cook the gravy all in one pot.

 MAKE IT ALL MEAT: Omit the vegetable stock, and use 3 cups meat broth. Cook the gravy all in one pot.

Potatoes Anna

Serves 4 to 6

2 pounds waxy potatoes, such as Yukon gold

¾ cup (1½ sticks) unsalted butter

Salt and freshly ground black pepper

Everyone loves potatoes, one of the many reasons low-carb diets are doomed to certain failure. When a special occasion arises, one of Jeremy's absolute favorite tater dishes is *pommes* Anna (and A.J.'s pretty fond of it as well). Traditionally served with meat and poultry, this classic French side will certainly appeal to anyone who's into potatoes, not to mention butter.

1. Peel the potatoes and slice them thinly, ⅛ inch thick or less (a mandoline is the perfect tool for this job if you have one). Submerge the potatoes in a bowl full of water.

2. Melt the butter in a microwave or saucepan. (Purists would say the butter should be clarified—a simple process where the milk solids are separated from the fat component of butter—but we actually prefer the taste when "whole" butter is used.)

3. Preheat the oven to 400°F. Drain the potatoes and pat them dry with paper towels. Generously grease a heavy, 8- to 10-inch ovenproof omelet pan, skillet, or unperforated pie tin with some of the melted butter. (For fancy individual portions, use small ramekins.) Begin to arrange the potato slices in the pan in a clockwise spiral pattern from the center outward. After the first layer is complete, sprinkle with some of the melted butter and season lightly with salt and pepper. For the second layer, repeat the spiral pattern in a counterclockwise fashion. When the second layer is complete, again sprinkle with butter and season with salt and pepper. Repeat this process, alternating clockwise and counterclockwise layers, until the potato cake is about 1½ inches thick. Press the cake firmly with a spatula to compress.

4. Place the pan on the stovetop over medium-high heat, and cook for 3 to 5 minutes. Cover the pan, slide it into the preheated oven, and bake for 25 to 30 minutes. Test the doneness with a toothpick—it should slide through the cake easily but the potatoes should not feel mushy. While still hot, place a plate over the pan and drain off any excess butter. Slice into wedges and serve immediately.

Potatoes Lyonnaise

Serves 4 to 6

1 teaspoon salt

2 pounds medium-size russet potatoes, peeled

3 tablespoons unsalted butter

3 tablespoons olive oil

2 medium-size onions, sliced into rings

½ teaspoon freshly ground black pepper

1 bunch fresh flat-leaf parsley, chopped

Let us be counted among those to lionize potatoes Lyonnaise. So simple and yet so delicious, they are a perfect side for any meal. Pay close attention to the browning of the ingredients—this is where the magic will happen.

1. Fill a large stockpot halfway with water. Add ½ teaspoon of the salt and bring the water to a boil. Add the potatoes and cook for 3 minutes. Let cool, then slice the potatoes thinly, ⅛ inch thick or less.

2. In a large nonstick skillet over medium heat, heat 1 tablespoon of the butter and 1 tablespoon of the olive oil. In another large nonstick skillet over medium-high heat, heat the remaining 2 tablespoons butter and 2 tablespoons olive oil.

3. Add the onions to the first pan and the potatoes to the second pan, and add ¼ teaspoon of the salt and ¼ teaspoon of the pepper to each pan. Stirring and turning occasionally, cook for 5 to 7 minutes. The onions should be slightly caramelized and the potatoes should be taking on a bit of brown themselves.

4. Combine the ingredients into one skillet, and cook for another 3 to 5 minutes, until things are a lovely golden color. Add in the parsley, stir, and serve.

Note: For larger gatherings, this recipe can be scaled up easily by doubling the amounts of potatoes and onions. Caramelize your onions as instructed and use thin slices of raw potato arranged in layers in a large casserole or baking dish, season with salt and pepper, adding onions, parsley, and melted butter within the layers willy-nilly. Splash with a few tablespoons of the stock or broth of your choice, cover with aluminum foil, and cook in a 450°F oven for 20 minutes. Remove the foil and cook for another 10 minutes and *voilà*, potatoes Lyonnaise for a party! Now who's being lionized?

Herbed Home Fries

Serves 2 to 3
vegetarians and
2 to 3 meat-eaters

2 tablespoons olive oil

1 tablespoon unsalted
butter

1 tablespoon duck fat
(see Note)

2 pounds potatoes of your
choice, cut into 1-inch
cubes and placed in
cold water

2 sprigs fresh rosemary,
leaves removed and
chopped

1 small bunch thyme,
leaves only

½ teaspoon coarse salt

½ teaspoon freshly
ground black pepper

½ cup chopped fresh
flat-leaf parsley

There's no reason this recipe couldn't be anything but vegetarian, vegan even, if you really wanted. Making it *Double Take*–style, though, gives meat-eaters what Jeremy considers the best potatoes they'll ever have in their lives (and that might make the meat-eaters wake up a little quicker). These are great anytime, at any meal, but we definitely have our eye toward breakfast where home fries are concerned.

1. Preheat the oven to 375°F.

2. Add 1 tablespoon of the olive oil to each of two large, ovenproof shallow pans over medium-high heat. Add the butter to one pan and the duck fat to the other.

3. When the foaming in the pan with the butter has subsided, add half of the potatoes to each pan and toss to coat the potatoes. Reduce the heat to medium and allow the spuds to cook undisturbed for about 3 minutes so they begin to develop a nice crust. Give them a toss and cook undisturbed for another 3 minutes. Give them another toss and another undisturbed 3 minutes of cooking.

4. Add half of the rosemary, half of the thyme, ¼ teaspoon of the salt, and ¼ teaspoon of the pepper to each pan, give everything in each a quick toss, then place the pans in the oven.

5. Cook for 8 to 12 minutes, until the potatoes are crispy on the outside and tender on the inside.

6. Remove the potatoes from the oven, add 2 tablespoons of the parsley to each pan, and stir briefly. Adjust the seasoning with more salt and pepper if desired. Serve immediately.

Note: Rendering duck fat is a relatively easy proposition. After purchasing a duck from your local butcher or grocery, remove any excess skin from around the neck and gather the two fatty lumps from behind the thighs at the rear cavity, reserving the duck for another time. Chop these skin and fat pieces coarsely. Place these pieces in a smallish, sturdy pot over medium-low heat, and add 1/4 cup water. Do not boil; simmer lightly and avoid browning. At first the liquid will be cloudy as the fat and water are mixing. Eventually (after about 2 hours), the water will have evaporated and the remaining fat should be a beautiful golden color. Drain the fat into a clean glass jar; it will keep in the refrigerator up to 1 month. (While your significant other is out of the house and not around to give you an earful about "health," microwave the remaining duck skin between multiple layers of paper towel until crispy. Lightly season with salt and pepper, and devour this delightful treat before said significant other returns home.) When cooled, the duck fat should be as white as fallen snow. Alternatively, type "purchase duck fat" into any Internet search engine to locate a nearby source for the pre-made version.

 MAKE IT ALL VEGETARIAN: Omit the duck fat, use 2 tablespoons butter, and use it in both pans in step 2.

 MAKE IT ALL MEAT: Omit the butter, use 2 tablespoons duck fat, and use it in both pans in step 2.

Rice Pilaf

Serves 4 to 6

2 cups long-grain white
rice, such as basmati
or Texmati (do not use
converted rice or you
will have mush)

2 tablespoons olive oil

2 tablespoons unsalted
butter

1 medium-size onion,
finely chopped

½ cup slivered almonds,
toasted (see Note
page 189)

½ cup dried currants

3 cups vegetable stock
or broth, homemade
(page 100) or store-
bought

1 bay leaf

2 sprigs fresh thyme

½ cup chopped fresh
flat-leaf parsley

Rice pilaf is a dish that's really as much about technique as it is about ingredients. The technique is not difficult, but it should be followed as closely as possible to create the fluffiest possible end product. Once you have the technique down, the variety of pilafs to be made is limited only by your imagination and your pocketbook. This is a very straightforward and tasty version that would feel right at home next to any fish, poultry, or vegetable dish.

1. Soak the rice in cold water, agitating occasionally, for 15 minutes. Drain and soak again, in fresh water, for another 15 minutes. Doing so removes the surface starch that would otherwise lead to a sticky pilaf. Drain the rice.

2. Place a large heavy pot over medium heat. Add the olive oil, butter, and onion to the pot. Cook the onion until translucent, about 10 minutes, then add the drained rice to the pot.

3. Cook the rice, stirring frequently, until it is mostly translucent. A little pale browning of the rice won't hurt and will impart a nice nutty flavor. Add the almonds and currants to the pot and give a quick stir or two.

4. Increase the heat to medium-high, and add the vegetable stock to the pot. Bring to a simmer and toss in the bay leaf, thyme, and parsley. Cook, uncovered, at a steady simmer for about 10 minutes, adjusting the heat as necessary, until most of the liquid has evaporated.

5. Decrease the heat to low, cover the pot, and cook for 10 minutes. If you want to go the extra mile, first cover the pot with a clean kitchen towel, then cover with the lid. Just be careful that your heat is sufficiently low so the ends of the towel do not burn. The towel will prevent water from dripping back into the pilaf—another insurance policy against gumminess.

6. After 10 minutes, remove the lid and turn off the heat. The rice should look fluffy and dry, with individual grains of rice easily identifiable. Give a quick "fluff 'n' stir" with a fork to evenly distribute all the goodies, and serve. If there's a little crusty brown part at the bottom, don't worry—that's the best part. The Persians call this *tah dig*, meaning "bottom of the pot," and it is served to the special guests at a party. After serving the pilaf, use a wooden spatula to remove this brown goodness and distribute to the most deserving of your guests.

Note: We love wild rice in a pilaf. If you do, too, be sure to boil the wild rice separately for about 20 minutes (maybe while the long-grain rice is soaking) to soften it. Wild rice is actually a grass, not truly rice per se, so it cooks in a different fashion. After the wild rice has cooked for 20 minutes, drain and give it a quick rinse. Then toss it in at the same time you add the vegetable stock.

Delish Drop Biscuits

**Makes 10 to
12 biscuits**

1 ¾ cups all-purpose
flour

1 ½ teaspoons baking
powder

¼ teaspoon salt

½ teaspoon freshly
ground black pepper

3 tablespoons plus 1 ½
teaspoons vegetable
shortening

¾ cup milk

Though the word *biscuit* comes from the French *bis cuit*, or "twice cooked," this recipe calls for cooking them only once, as you probably won't be taking them on a long sea voyage where they'd need to be hard morsels able to stay edible (in a fairly loose definition of that term) for months. But biscuit recipes do have a long history, passed from generation to generation and served to sop up gravy, to eat with butter, or just to have alongside a main dish that needs a hearty sidekick.

1. Preheat the oven to 450°F.

2. In a bowl, mix together the flour, baking powder, salt, and pepper with a fork or whisk, making sure everything gets thoroughly combined.

3. Cut the shortening into the dry ingredients, then add the milk. Using your hands or a spoon you trust implicitly, stir until the mixture has combined into a soft dough. Knead lightly on a clean counter or baking board (use just a touch of flour to keep it from sticking) until the mixture just comes together in a cohesive mass.

4. Lightly grease one or two baking sheets (depending on the size of your sheets). Using a spoon, portion out tablespoon-size balls of dough onto the baking sheets in an orderly fashion, at least 1/2 inch apart. Once all of the dough has been spooned out, place the sheet(s) in the oven and bake for 10 to 12 minutes, until lightly browned.

Variations: Want cheesy biscuits? Add 3/4 to 1 cup shredded cheddar cheese to the dough before kneading in step 3. Feeling like a ham? Add 1 cup chopped cooked ham to the dough before kneading in step 3, or, to please both vegetarians and meat-eaters, separate the dough into equal halves before kneading and add 1/2 cup cooked ham to one half.

Spicy Cornbread

Serves 6 to 8

1 cup all-purpose flour

2 cups stone-ground
cornmeal

1 tablespoon double-
acting baking powder

1 tablespoon salt

1 tablespoon sugar

1½ cups buttermilk

3 large eggs

1 jalapeño chile, sliced
in half, seeds and ribs
removed, and finely
chopped

1 chipotle chile in adobo,
finely chopped

2 tablespoons unsalted
butter

Man, oh man, do we love us some cornbread. Whether sweet or savory, we can't say that we've ever been introduced to a cornbread we didn't like, or at the very least one that couldn't become a friend with a generous application of butter. A spicy complement to Chili con/non Carne (page 120), this recipe hits the spot every time. Certainly cornbread can be made in any vessel appropriate for baking, but the amity between cornbread and a cast-iron skillet is a thing of transcendent beauty. Serve this with plenty of butter and even some honey—the spicy/savory/sweet combination is outta this world.

1. Preheat the oven to 375°F.

2. Mix the flour, cornmeal, baking powder, salt, and sugar in a large bowl and combine the buttermilk, eggs, and chiles in a medium-size bowl.

3. Slowly fold the wet ingredients into the dry ingredients and mix evenly.

4. Melt the butter in a 12-inch cast-iron skillet over medium heat, being careful that the butter does not become too brown. Coat the sides of the skillet with the butter using a pastry brush or the like.

5. Pour the cornbread batter into the skillet and cook undisturbed on the stovetop for 5 minutes. This will create an awesome crust on the bottom of the cornbread. Slide the cornbread into the oven, and bake for 20 to 30 minutes, depending on your oven and the thickness of the cornbread. The cornbread is done when an inserted toothpick comes out clean.

6. Remove from the oven, cool for 5 minutes, and cut into wedges while still in the skillet. Serve warm.

measurement equivalents

liquid conversions

U.S.	METRIC
1 tsp	5 ml
1 tbs	15 ml
2 tbs	30 ml
3 tbs	45 ml
¼ cup	60 ml
⅓ cup	75 ml
⅓ cup + 1 tbs	90 ml
⅓ cup + 2 tbs	100 ml
½ cup	120 ml
⅔ cup	150 ml
¾ cup	180 ml
¾ cup + 2 tbs	200 ml
1 cup	240 ml
1 cup + 2 tbs	275 ml
1 ¼ cups	300 ml
1 ⅓ cups	325 ml
1 ½ cups	350 ml
1 ⅔ cups	375 ml
1 ¾ cups	400 ml
1 ¾ cups + 2 tbs	450 ml
2 cups (1 pint)	475 ml
2 ½ cups	600 ml
3 cups	720 ml
4 cups (1 quart)	945 ml

(1,000 ml is 1 liter)

weight conversions

U.S./U.K.	METRIC
½ oz	14 g
1 oz	28 g
1 ½ oz	43 g
2 oz	57 g
2 ½ oz	71 g
3 oz	85 g
3 ½ oz	100 g
4 oz	113 g
5 oz	142 g
6 oz	170 g
7 oz	200 g
8 oz	227 g
9 oz	255 g
10 oz	284 g
11 oz	312 g
12 oz	340 g
13 oz	368 g
14 oz	400 g
15 oz	425 g
1 lb	454 g

oven temperature conversions

°F	GAS MARK	°C
250	½	120
275	1	140
300	2	150
325	3	165
350	4	180
375	5	190
400	6	200
425	7	220
450	8	230
475	9	240
500	10	260
550	Broil	290

Please note that all conversions are approximate.

index